Teaching and Learning History 11–18

Teaching and Learning History 11–18

UNDERSTANDING THE PAST

Alison Kitson and Chris Husbands
with Susan Steward

McGraw Hill

Open University Press

Open University Press
McGraw-Hill Education
McGraw-Hill House
Shoppenhangers Road
Maidenhead
Berkshire
England
SL6 2QL

email: enquiries@openup.co.uk
world wide web: www.openup.co.uk

and Two Penn Plaza, New York, NY 10121-2289, USA

First published 2011

A catalogue record of this book is available from the British Library

ISBN-13: 978 0 335 23820 0 (pb)   978 0 335 23821 7 (hb)
ISBN-10: 0 335 23820 3 (pb)   0 335 23821 1 (hb)
eISBN: 978 0 335 23822 4

Library of Congress Cataloging-in-Publication Data
CIP data applied for

Typesetting and e-book compilation by
RefineCatch Limited, Bungay, Suffolk
Printed in the UK at CPI Antony Rowe, Chippenham

The **McGraw·Hill** Companies

Contents

List of text boxes

Acknowledgements

This book has been influenced by many people and there is insufficient space to acknowledge them all here. However, some deserve a particular mention. Our former colleague Arthur Chapman was exceptionally generous in allowing us to draw heavily on his work in parts of Chapter 7, especially around causation and interpretations, and his general support and good cheer have always been greatly appreciated. The frequent references to the work of Peter Lee, Ros Ashby and Denis Shemilt in Chapters 5, 6 and 9 are testament to their enormous contribution to history education in general and to their work on children's understanding of history in classrooms in particular. Specifically, the opening of Chapter 7 was inspired by Peter's work (e.g. 2005) and discussions with Ros were especially influential on our thinking about evidence and we are deeply grateful for her time and generosity. We are very fortunate to work with many wonderful colleagues at the Institute and we thank all those who have influenced and supported the writing of this book, especially Katharine Burn, Paul Salmons, Robin Whitburn, Stuart Foster, Jonathan Howson, Gunther Kress and Carey Jewitt. Katharine's influence can be felt throughout the book, especially in Chapter 10, where her determination not to label pupils and to provide engaging and challenging learning opportunities for all finds strongest expression. Paul has helped us to think more carefully about why we teach history through his exemplary work on the Holocaust Education Development Programme, and conversations with Gunther Kress and Carey Jewitt were enormously helpful in shaping parts of Chapter 8. Of the many outstanding history educators in the United States, Keith Barton and Linda Levstik have had the greatest influence on our thinking, not least because of the way they bring a welcome sense of perspective to the teaching of history in schools which is rooted in the reality of classrooms and the reality of the world outside. Keith's work with Alan McCully in Northern Ireland helped us to understand the way in which pupils make sense of a controversial past and reconcile it (or not) with versions of the past encountered elsewhere. Christine Counsell has influenced the book in many ways, through her own work – including her work on literacy, diversity and history for all – and through her role as editor of *Teaching History*. This would have been a very different book without Christine's tireless work on – and transformation of – that journal. Michael Riley's work on historical enquiry provides the foundation for Chapter 6 while Jamie

Byrom was the inspiration for our argument about 'resonance' in Chapter 12: both are brilliantly attuned to what motivates, engages and inspires children to learn about the past and they have, in turn, inspired us too. We lean heavily on Ian Dawson's work in Chapter 10 and are grateful to him for discussions about his work. The support he has given to teachers through his excellent website (http://www.thinkinghistory.co.uk), through his textbooks and through his thinking about thematic stories is unparalleled. Martin Roberts was, as ever, stimulating and rigorous in helping our thinking about content. Throughout the book, we draw on examples of work from schools, lesson observations and interviews with pupils in schools in London, south eastern and eastern England. We are grateful to those teachers who so generously allowed us access to their classrooms and discussed their work with us so openly: Ruth Oji and Paul Cornish at Pimlico Academy, London; Ian Startup and colleagues in the history department in King Edward VI Upper School, Bury St Edmunds; Victoria Payne, history colleagues and pupils at Highams Park School, Waltham Forest; Jo Philpott and colleagues in Dereham Neatherd High School; Rebecca Bealey and her department in Norwich High School for Girls; Karen Reynolds, history colleagues and pupils in North Walsham High School, who shared their oral history work with us; David Leece and sixth form historians in Notre Dame High School, Norwich and Carol McWilliams at Mossbourne Academy, Hackney. Finally, our thanks to history PGCE students at the Institute past and present for continually asking questions and for being hungry to learn: they have inspired us to write this book. In spite of all this help and guidance, we have undoubtedly got things wrong: the interpretations, arguments and, of course, the errors are ours alone.

No book is ever written easily, and this one has taken us too often and too long away from our families; Darren, Nicky and Harry have, for each of us, been forbearing and supportive throughout, and we are very grateful to them.

INTRODUCTION
Reading and using this book

This book has been written for history teachers, both novice and experienced. We hope that it provides several important resources to support successful classroom practices. First, we hope it provides information, insights and ideas which help to make sense of the contexts in which history teachers work. Secondly, we hope that by offering descriptions and accounts of practice it provides understandings of the nature of practice in real classrooms. Thirdly, and as a result of the first two, we hope that it provides a basis for developing the practice of history teaching in the complex world of the twenty-first century classroom. The book draws on a wide range of research and perspectives on the teaching and learning of history from around the world, but more importantly on insights gained from teachers and their pupils in schools we are privileged to have worked with and visited.

As we explain throughout the book, history is a deceptive subject to teach and to learn. Beneath the seductive simplicity of a strong narrative thread of the human past are profound questions about the nature of knowledge, the nature of learning and the complexities of modern society. Underpinning the book are four themes, and it is worth setting these out here. We did not start with these themes as organizing principles for the book; rather, they emerged from our engagement with the practice and issues we explored in classrooms and schools. The themes, crystallized during the writing of the book, encapsulate our vision for teaching and learning history in schools. By setting out the themes explicitly, we hope to provide readers with a framework for their understanding of history teaching.

The first theme relates to history in the **contemporary school curriculum**. The school curriculum is changing rapidly and, in some schools, profoundly. History is under considerable threat in schools as a result of diminishing curriculum time, pressures from competing disciplines and a genuine sense of doubt about what the curriculum needs to be if it is to prepare young people for life in the twenty-first century. Although we do not necessarily take a position on issues of curriculum structure or the way timetables are organized, central to our approach is the conviction that learning about the past forms part of the irreducible entitlement for *all* learners in contemporary schools, and that the realities of a changing world make this more, not less, pressing.

The second theme relates to **inclusion**. One of the dimensions of curriculum change in schools is the development of increasingly differentiated curricula for different groups of children and young people. In many schools, history is seen as part of an 'academic' curriculum, available to higher achieving or academically 'elite' pupils rather than as an essential component in every pupil's learning. This is mistaken. The task of the history teacher – and the curriculum he or she works with – is to help all children to think historically. One of the underlying issues we address is the question about who, in our society and our schools, is allowed to be a historian; given the complex issues facing us, ensuring that all learners have the opportunity to think historically – to be historians – is a critical aspect of the curriculum.

The third theme relates to **pedagogy**, and the question of what constitutes good history teaching. 'Pedagogy' is a challenging concept, either wholly misunderstood or often conceived as being concerned simply with teaching techniques. Our view is broader. Our conviction is that it is history's job to enable thinking and history teachers' job to teach it in ways which expand learners' conceptions of what is possible. In the pursuit of this, we develop arguments about the distinctiveness of history pedagogy, which is concerned with language, narrative, chronology and sequencing, and fundamentally with ambiguity in understanding complex human situations.

The fourth theme relates to issues of **professionalism and innovation**. In the course of our work, we have seen exciting examples of curriculum innovation in history which engage and enthuse learners, but we have also seen powerful cultural and institutional constraints on innovation. We have seen examples in which history teachers deploy creativity, independence of thought and imagination, and in which they accept responsibility and accountability for the use of their professional expertise. We have also seen instances in which the powerful 'performance culture' in schools, affecting the limits to teacher agency, acts as a constraint on the deployment of these attributes. Our conviction is that the professionalism of history teachers is intimately bound up with their ability to exercise their professionalism in the development of the subject.

These themes are developed throughout the book. In the first part of the book, our focus is on what history is, and means in the classroom; we explore this by considering how the past is presented in different places and then how it is mediated into schools through formal curricula – notably the national curriculum. We consider the resources history teachers have at their disposal – material, intellectual and digital. In the second section, our focus moves to pupils. Drawing extensively on our work with learners, we consider what pupils want from their encounter with history, why history is difficult for many pupils and whether there is a distinctive history pedagogy which shapes their learning. The third part of the book takes the insights we have developed in Parts 1 and 2 and explores the ways in which teachers plan learning in classrooms through the concepts, themes and preoccupations of history teaching. In the final section, the lens broadens and we explore what history teaching in schools could be for learners, exploring the content of history and the nature of 'relevance', of 'heritage' and of diversity. In our final chapter we consider history teaching in the context of the moral and political challenges of the world into which pupils are growing in the twenty-first century.

At the core of the book, and central to our purpose, is the learning of young people in real classrooms in contemporary schools. Taken as a whole, the book offers a radical way of thinking about history teaching, which is nonetheless grounded in what we have seen and found in schools. We hope that it will, in equal measure, challenge and inspire history teachers, providing them with some tools to develop the quality of what they do and to articulate a rationale for the subject in a rapidly transforming curriculum. Throughout the book we use 'text boxes' scattered through the chapters to provide examples or evidence to crystallize our thinking.

This book explores the decision-making history teachers engage in as a result of the underlying problems which arise from the choices with which they are presented or which they create. It sets out to analyse the issues which impinge on these choices, to clarify the ways teachers address them, and to understand ways in which they interact with learners as a result. Of course, all teachers, whatever their subject discipline, are required to make decisions about the way they choose, organize, present and assess subject matter. We draw on work in relation to teachers' decision-making and on teaching and learning more generally, but our primary concern is to illuminate the issues in the context of teaching and learning about the past, and to do so in ways which support teachers in developing their own decision-making and the quality of their pupils' learning experiences. Our starting points for this are classrooms, and the ways in which teachers and pupils develop understandings of the past in classrooms, and we do this in the context of the choices which teachers make in developing history teaching.

Part 1

History in schools

'History' is a widely used and misleadingly simple word which conceals complexity: 'history' refers to 'the past' (things happened 'in history') as well as the process by which we understand the past (we 'do history'). 'History' is an academic discipline, produced by scholars working in archives, and yet 'history' is all around us in the buildings we pass every day, the institutions which govern us and the languages we use. 'History' is communicated in extensively researched books and popularized for television and film. 'History' is the result of years of study, and something which we all carry in our everyday assumptions.

The first section of this book explores the processes by which history 'inside schools' relates to history 'outside schools' – the academic discipline of history and its popular manifestations. In the first chapter we consider the choices which underpin the history curriculum in schools. In the second chapter we look in more detail at the nature of the school history curriculum, at its aims, its content and some of the pressures on the history curriculum and history teachers. In the third chapter we move from the curriculum and the school into the places where history is taught and learned – mostly into classrooms, but also to historic sites and other out-of-school learning environments.

1

What is school history?

In this opening chapter, we explore some of the central challenges facing school history through three lenses. The first is the lens of curriculum content and the choices which underpin the selection and presentation of content for the school history curriculum. The second is the lens of learning history, exploring some of the ingredients which combine to make up the process of learning about the past. Finally, we relate the challenges of content and learning to ideas about the nature of history as an academic and intellectual discipline.

Introduction: the question of choice

The central problem is that there is just too much history to teach. Any history curriculum explores only a tiny selection of the history that could be taught. This would be true even if the time available for teaching history in schools were unlimited, but given the demands on teaching and learning time, and the competing priorities for schools, the pressures are acute. Decisions to teach some topics are decisions not to teach others. Decisions about what to teach and how to teach it, or what not to teach and how not to teach it, reflect assumptions about the sorts of knowledge which matter, the values and beliefs of the curriculum developer, understandings about children's needs, futures and learning, and the very purpose and nature of history itself. These decisions are never value-free: by selecting some content, value is attributed to the ideas and the meanings it carries for teachers and for children. Selection might privilege the recent past over the distant past, or national history over international history or local history over national history. Some topics might be selected to throw light on others, to illustrate general themes, or to develop particular concepts and ideas. Selection may be made deliberately to represent the experiences of the cultural and political elites of the past, or to recover the experiences of the marginalized and excluded. Selection may reflect the cultural and demographic makeup of the school population. Selection will be made across local, national, regional and world history and will imply some patterns of connection between them. Over time, the selection will change, reflecting changing assumptions about the ideas which relatively powerful groups in society have about the past and its implications for the present (MacMillan 2009).

The content of the school history curriculum has always been disputed (Ferro 1984). In many countries in the nineteenth and twentieth centuries, school history was seen as way of promoting ideas about the development of the nation state. Priority was given to content related to the formation of the nation and national institutions – government, monarchy, parliament, and struggles for independence, or to events and individuals which crystallized ideas about national myths. Curricula and text-books rarely gave prominence to the experiences of marginalized or oppressed groups (Chancellor 1970). In the later twentieth century, as interest grew in social and economic history and as school populations became more diverse, the experiences of these groups were often explored in greater detail in schools. In the early twenty-first century all over the world, greater attention is often given to international history, to histories of migration and interdependence, to the emergence of a global world, to the legacies of imperialism, diaspora and post-colonialism (e.g. Lo 2000). Increasingly, schools have come to be seen as more or less autonomous in matters of curriculum, so that the national and governmental-level debates about the history curriculum have also been played out in schools themselves. There, concern is often expressed less in terms of particular periods or topics but rather in terms of the underlying concepts on which understanding history depends – ideas about causation, significance, change, continuity – or the perceived 'needs' of particular groups of learners. Each approach reflects assumptions about how to allocate the limited time available for learning about the past, and each perspective carries implications for pupils' understanding of the past and its relationship to the present (Chapman and Facey 2004). The underlying challenge of teaching history in schools arises from decisions about what to teach, how to structure the content which is to be taught, what methods to adopt, and how to assess and evaluate the effectiveness of what is taught.

Making history in schools: the challenge of content

Although this book explores pedagogy, progression, inclusion and the communication of history, questions about the processes by which the raw material of 'the past' becomes 'history' in classrooms are fundamental. Obviously, this involves questions of power and its distribution between governments, academics, assessment authorities, teachers and others, who will have often conflicting views about what should be taught and why. Debate between them is often intemperate (Phillips 1998); debates about national curricula are frequently debates about power and authority (Ferro 1984). Even when formal curricula are defined, selecting content is only one step in translating 'the past' into programmes of study for the classroom. History teachers are concerned with content, but they are also concerned with presenting it to often diverse pupil populations in ways which enthuse, stimulate and engage. They do this to develop understandings of historical ideas and processes and to open up a dialogue between what has passed – the historical record – and pupils' lives as they are lived in a rapidly changing present. Critical in making a history curriculum is clarity about the historical ideas and concepts which it is intended to develop. Historians explore the past through debate about concepts such as historical change and continuity, causation and consequence, significance, turning points and trends, and about the evidential basis for what we know, which itself involves concerns about reliability, bias, utility and interpretation. The core relationships in history curriculum development are between the substantive content of history, the second order or key concepts of history teaching and the interests and concerns of stakeholders – parents, learners and so on. The decision-making implied here is the process of curriculum development in schools, sometimes under tight external constraints such as examination syllabi or curriculum specifications, and sometimes under relatively loose constraints.

The processes by which some historical topics become features of the school curriculum are not straightforward. For every topic taught to pupils, a decision has been made to include it in a programme of study. In most countries, some topics have an iconic significance – the French Revolution in France, the American Civil War and the Civil Rights movement in America, the Battle of Britain and the Home Front of World War II in England – and are required elements of the curriculum in all schools. Some other topics transcend borders; the Holocaust and the consequences of the slave trade are themes in history curricula all over the world. Other topics – and the way they might be taught – are more contentious, and yet others are left to local decision-making. In the lesson sequence for 14-year-olds on Charles Darwin (Box 1.1), a local decision has been made to deal with the history of scientific ideas. At the core of this lesson sequence is the historical idea of significance: the importance of Darwin's ideas and their impact on the way people thought – and think – about their world. There are several simultaneous ways in which claims of significance underpin and run through this lesson sequence. The first, and perhaps most profound, is the nature of scientific achievement and, within that, the notion that ideas and ways of thinking about the world can exercise a powerful influence on the course of history. There is not really any debate about whether Darwin should be considered historically significant or not. A question such as 'is he significant?' or even 'how significant is he?' would not challenge pupils: they would merely have to describe what Darwin did. The outcome of the sequence therefore focuses more on *what* is worth knowing about Darwin. This involves turning the raw material of historical knowledge – Darwin's ideas and achievements – into a set of propositions which can be explored in the classroom and used to engage pupils' own thinking about the significance of what they are exploring. By the end of the lesson sequence, this means that the pupils themselves have begun to think hard about what it means to claim that something is significant, as well as having built up understandings about a historical figure of considerable importance, albeit one often neglected in lower secondary school history. This idea of what it means for a person or an event to be significant will be developed through later stages in the pupils' learning, so that they will learn themselves about how 'significance' is attributed.

Box 1.1 What is worth knowing about Charles Darwin? A six-lesson enquiry for Year 9

By the end of the sequence it is hoped that Year 9 pupils will know who Darwin was, what he was like as a man and what he achieved, setting this in the broader context of the nineteenth century and the industrial and scientific revolutions. Pupils will understand why many people found his ideas threatening at the time and hopefully realize that it is possible to change the world by having ideas. Ultimately, the enquiry focuses on significance, not in terms of whether Darwin **is** significant, but rather in terms of what it is about Darwin that is 'worth knowing'. The enquiry question assumes that the answer is not straightforward and that individuals make choices about what is worth knowing that are highly influenced by their cultural and social contexts. In this sense, the enquiry is quite a sophisticated attempt to explore the ways in which significance is closely linked to interpretation. However, the primary aim behind the question is to persuade pupils, quite overtly, that Darwin is worth knowing about and to have them explain why. The sequence starts with a lesson which explores who Darwin was. This is followed by a brief explanation about Darwin's theory of evolution, drawing on work already done in science lessons. The third lesson examines what people at the time thought about Darwin's theory while the fourth lesson brings it up to date by asking whether Darwin's big idea has changed the world. The final two lessons pull the enquiry together as pupils decide for themselves what is worth knowing about Darwin and write a one-minute introduction to Darwin's home, persuading people to visit.

Sometimes content is more obviously problematic. The 'Indian Mutiny' of 1857–58 (see Box 1.2) crystallizes important issues in the selection of content for the history curriculum. It was rarely taught in English secondary schools until the 1990s, when the national curriculum obliged teachers to teach about the British Empire, and remains controversial. The controversy begins with how the events should be described. The 'Indian Mutiny' was the label given soon after the events of 1857 by the British; they are rarely referred to in this way by Indians, who prefer the name 'First War of Independence', 'Great Rebellion' or 'Uprising of 1857'. Beyond this – and to some extent conditioned by it – there are questions about how to present these events in the classroom. 1857 was, and remains, a critical event in the later development of the British Empire, with huge implications for colonialism and post-colonialism, for the creation of an Indian middle class and for models of government throughout south Asia and Africa: it is therefore highly significant. However, it depends on the development of some other core historical concepts, notably causation and consequence. The causes of the events were complex, which makes it simultaneously a productive and challenging topic to teach. It is generally argued that the events of 1857 were *triggered* by the introduction of the new Enfield rifles to the Indian army, but that the *causes* were longer standing factors including attempts to Christianize India and to extend British control through taxation and law. The topic presents some tough teaching challenges: how much weight to give to immediate causes, how to convey understandings of the background, how to convey the issues at stake in twenty-first-century culturally diverse classrooms. Equally, the events of 1857 had short-term and longer term consequences. The reimposition of British authority afterwards was savage, but there was an equally dark legacy shaping western representations of the sub-continent around an imperialist rationale of domination (Nagy-Zekmi 2006), which shaped both British attitudes to India and the experiences of south Asian migrants to Britain, and which persists. In 2005, the *Daily Telegraph* reported that the UK Film Council had invested '£150,000 of lottery funds in a Bollywood film that savages British rule in India' (*Daily Telegraph*, 13 August 2005). Teaching about the 'Indian Mutiny' requires teachers to make choices about how to describe it, what concepts to develop and how to represent the issues in the classroom – in a limited amount of time.

Box 1.2 Which History? India, 1857

At the fortress town of Meerut, forty miles north-west of Delhi, 85 skirmishers of the 3rd Light Cavalry were court-martialled on 9 May 1857 for refusing to accept the cartridges of new Enfield rifles, which were greased with a combination of pig fat and grease. Assembled on a dusty parade ground in stifling heat, the cavalrymen were ceremonially stripped of their uniforms, chained and marched off to begin a ten-year sentence. At sunset next day, wrote Elisa Greathed, resident in Meerut, 'disturbance commenced on the Native Parade ground. Shots and volumes of smoke told of what was going on': in the course of the evening, about 50 officers and other British residents were killed by the soldiers, who burned and plundered the residency buildings before marching on Delhi. The rising in Meerut triggered a wider rebellion and focused a series of long-running grievances against the East India Company: the increasing drive to Christianize the country by western missionaries, who had first been admitted in 1813, a concerted British attack on Indian customs and religious practices, the annexation of independent princely states, and reform of traditional revenue systems. Over the next six weeks, what was in England called the 'Indian Mutiny' spread across northern and central India, threatening British control of large parts of the sub-continent. The rebellion saw atrocities on both sides. At Kanpur, besieged Europeans who had apparently been offered a safe passage after surrendering were massacred as they climbed into boats. At Fatehpur, nearby, the British commanding officer ordered all villages beside the Grand Trunk Road to be burned and their inhabitants to be hanged. It was not until June 1858 that the British were in control of India once more and they embarked on a savage policy of repression, including large numbers of executions and a crackdown: taxes on salt, for example – an essential for daily life – were increased and vigorously enforced. To ensure that the mutiny could never happen again, the army was reorganized and Indian soldiers were issued with rifles inferior to those used by their British counterparts. But it has also been argued that the events of 1857–58 marked a long term turning point in the development of policy towards India. Attempts at Christianization were abandoned. Universities were established, and a local white-collar Indian professional class began to develop.

Sources: Chakravarty (2005); Brendon (2008)

History teachers try to use techniques and resources which interest, engage and stimulate learners, and which also introduce them to the provisional nature of historical knowledge. But most of the resources available to them present difficulties of one sort or another: the textbook summarizes too quickly, the monograph is too dense. Making the past accessible is difficult. The difficulties are nowhere more apparent than in video or film clips, often used to communicate some aspects of history teaching. Filmic portrayals are not 'history', but entertainment (see Box 1.3) borrowing from some history, but easing in and out of the documented past at will and, perhaps, telling us more about ideas of the past than the past itself. Portrayals of Robin Hood are a good example, presenting anachronisms and distortions, mixing fictional stories with a backdrop which is partly historical – deploying 'real' historical characters, treating the past as backdrop – but more imagined, and playing fast and loose with historical setting. The psychologist Andrew Butler has argued that inaccuracies in screen presentations of historical events are so likely to confuse young people that they should be used with caution (Butler *et al.* 2009) or not at all. And yet more young people will have seen one or more of these movies, if only on a wet afternoon of old TV repeats or on http://www.youtube.com, than will ever read a textbook on medieval history. Popular portrayals of the past are hugely influential; often historical, anachronistic and plain wrong, but with some skill deploying ideas about place, time and motivation. The question these portrayals pose of teachers is real: how to present history in ways which are likely to engage pupils but which do not distort history to the point of make believe. Moreover, for all their faults, the screen versions tell us something. Errol Flynn's version was a Robin for the 1930s, Richard Greene's for the 1960s and Kevin Costner's for the 1990s. In this sense, they provide access to the dialogues with the past of which classrooms are part. The choice history teachers have to make is how to turn the way the past is represented into something which serves a purpose in the classroom. Imaginative teachers have used clips from films precisely to open up questions about representations of the past and history.

Box 1.3 Story, myth and history: filmic portrayals of Robin Hood

Robin Hood *appears* to have been a historical figure – probably an outlaw in Barnsdale, south Yorkshire, sometime in the early fourteenth century (Holt 1989). He was first portrayed on the screen in 1938 in a swashbuckling Hollywood film starring Errol Flynn – a Robin Hood by turns fearless, dashing and jaunty. Flynn's men of Sherwood fight to defend the liberties of the Saxon population against Prince John and the Norman lords. Most film critics have seen the 1938 portrayal of Robin Hood in terms of contemporary issues – the power of a small, committed band of well-motivated heroes to resist wicked regimes, the need to stand up to fascism. In the early 1960s Robin reappeared on the screen, now a teatime TV series with Richard Greene as 'Robin Hood, Robin Hood, riding through the glen, Robin Hood, Robin Hood, with his band of men, feared by the bad, loved by the good, Robin Hood, Robin Hood'. Over four series, Robin and his men outwitted, outfought and overcame John and the Sheriff of Nottingham. Greene's Robin Hood is different from Errol Flynn's. The medievalist Stephen Knight dubbed him 'squadron leader Robin Hood...He's an officer class type, and the outlaws are very much lower deck or non-commissioned officers or working class' (Knight 1999). The film historian Jeffrey Richards has called him 'everyone's favourite uncle' (Richards 1977), with a steely determination and a friendly glint in this eye; a 'Robin Hood for the welfare state' righting social wrongs in an imagined, but largely contented England. Robin reappeared on the big screen in 1991 in Kevin Costner's *Robin Hood – Prince of Thieves*. The film begins not in Sherwood but in Jerusalem where Robin of Locksley is an imprisoned Crusader. Robin acquires a Muslim companion, Azeem, played by Morgan Freeman – Robin had saved Azeem's life, so Azeem the Moor promises to stay with Robin until the debt is repaid. Robin and Azeem return to England, where they find Robin's father has been murdered and his home destroyed by the Sheriff of Nottingham, who runs a gang of devil-worshippers intent on conquering England. After meeting up with Marian, the younger sister of a dead crusading comrade, Robin and Azeem flee to Sherwood Forest and join an outlaw band. Robin teaches them to fight back, and soon they embark on bold robberies and attempt to thwart the sheriff. Costner's Robin Hood is a comic book hero projected onto a multi-cultural canvas for the 1990s; through common (cross-cultural) endeavour, even the most intractable of (devil-worshipping) evil can be conquered.

http://www.youtube.com/watch?v=Y2NOX9U41Jc (Richard Greene, accessed November 15, 2010),

http://www.youtube.com/watch?v=Iu8WQwTAYTk (Errol Flynn, accessed November 15, 2010)

http://www.youtube.com/watch?v=KXTj5nd2oKQ (Kevin Costner, accessed November 15, 2010)

Three historical topics – Charles Darwin, the events of 1857 in India and the legends of Robin Hood – competing for a position in a crowded history curriculum; each providing a rich context for the exploration of challenging ideas about the past, whether issues of significance, cause and consequence or the nature of historical evidence and interpretation. Each topic, too, illustrates some of the potential and challenges of making a history curriculum from the enormous available range. In the rest of this chapter, we consider what it means for learners to access this range.

What history offers: the learning journey

Tom Stoppard's play *Rosencrantz and Guildenstern Are Dead* opens with the two minor courtiers centre stage. Guildenstern asks 'What's the first thing you remember?', and Rosencrantz replies 'It's no good. It was a long time ago.' Guildenstern presses the point 'What's the first thing you remember after all the things you've forgotten?' and Rosencrantz completes the joke with 'I've forgotten the question'. It is a question which early years teachers use: what is the first thing you remember, what do your parents remember, and your grandparents: it helps young learners encounter the past. The history learning journey begins with the familiar, establishing a connection to history through evidence (recollection) and key concepts (change). This is a common starting point for learning in history. The national curriculum for the Key Stage 1 programme of study begins by asking teachers to explore 'changes in [pupils'] own lives and the way of life of their family or others around them' (QCA 2007a). The 2009 Australian national curriculum requires that in the 'early years of schooling the curriculum should enable pupils to explore their own and their family's history. Through hearing the stories of other pupils' lives and examining artefacts such as photos and objects, pupils also recognize that people have different histories' (National Curriculum Board 2009). The Massachusetts standards for history and social science are similar: 'At preschool and kindergarten level, learning in history and social science is built on children's experiences in their families, school, community, state, and country'(Massachusetts Department of Education 2003: 5). These curriculum requirements reflect research and practice in early years: learning is grounded in the experienced and recalled. Experience provides the basis for language and thinking: 'Children between the ages of three and seven try to use the terminology of time measurement'. They learn to sequence, to arrange, to categorize, and to understand before and after, then and now. 'They also engage through the immediate with the key historical concepts of change and continuity. They know what has gone for good. They also know that other things still exist' (Hoodless 1996: 32). They explore the past through story and through environment and learn to understand and to use the language of time and change (Cooper 2005). Skilled early years practitioners deploy familiar tools – language, experience, imagination – to encounter unfamiliar settings: Magellan's voyages, the Ancient Egyptians, or emotive stories such as the story of Florence Nightingale or Guy Fawkes. Experience, encounters with the unfamiliar, underlying concepts and, above all, language remain tools throughout the learning journey.

Beyond the early years, 'learning history is something of a social equivalent to personal memory' (Bage 2000: 12), built from the interplay of five aspects: time and memory, historical knowledge and understanding, historical interpretations, historical enquiry, and organizing and communicating. Language and memory, suggests Bage, 'define humanity', so that history in schools 'entails asking questions about the past, making selections from memories or records and joining these selections together into an explanatory narrative' – what others have called a 'map of the past' (Rogers 1987). The idea of time – time on the short scale, such as the intensity of the moment by moment stand-off over the Cuban missile crisis in 1962, or on the long scale such as the long-term rise and then decline of the Roman Empire, the long-wave patterns of migration and human movement associated with the development of early agriculture – depends on pupils building up understandings over different contexts and over time. We expect pupils to 'remember' implicitly – the history they have encountered last week, last month, last year, in their primary school – but this is a tall order without systematic teaching and support.

There is a deeply entrenched assumption in education that the idea of time is developed simply through an over-arching chronological structure, so that younger children study more historically remote periods and older children more recent historical periods. In a spat between academic historians at the 2010 Hay Festival, Niall Ferguson suggested that ancient history should be taught in the primary school curriculum as it was 'simpler and thus easier to understand than later societies', provoking a response from Richard Miles, a Cambridge historian of the ancient world, that 'You could only think the ancient world was simple if you knew bugger all about ancient history' (*Guardian*, 5 June 2010). The evidence for a chronologically structured history curriculum is weak. Extensive empirical research (e.g. Lee *et al*. 1993; Dickinson *et al*. 2001) suggests that historical understanding is built through the interplay of contexts and concepts. Put differently, a sense of chronology does not flow from the chronological sequencing of the historical curriculum: it needs to be taught, and built up, through careful visiting and revisiting.

The third aspect described by Bage, historical interpretation, involves building and comparing accounts, including stories, and versions in order to develop an understanding that histories are always provisional. This is not simply about examining accounts provided by different historians but of developing pupils' ideas about the ways accounts are built up. Bage's fourth aspect, historical enquiry, is a reminder that using historical evidence in schools is not an end in itself: historians use evidence *only* in response to an enquiry question. Finally, argues Bage, the organization and communication of knowledge is critical to history teaching. It is often through organizing knowledge that pupils realize what they know, and it is through communicating for a purpose that facility in communication develops.

History in schools: choices and professional autonomy

'History' is a taken for granted term: we 'understand' history, we 'study' history, and we 'know' history. History is not 'the past'; there was a past, which is unrecoverable and unknowable, and there is the study of that past. We use the term to describe both the object of study – French history, English history, the history of thought – and the process by which historians work – 'doing history', 'reading history'. Sheila Rowbotham captured a critical idea when she wrote about the experience of women in the past as being 'hidden from history' (Rowbotham 1975): part of the past, but excluded from it, because of their exclusion from historical documents and the structures of power and domination which constructed the records on which accounts depend.

The first historian, Herodotus, writing in the early fifth century before the Common Era, used the term 'historia' (ίστορία), which was literally an 'enquiry' (Burrow 2007). Herodotus had a specific question for his enquiry: why was the Persian Empire unable to conquer the Greek city states, or, put differently, as Herodotus did, why were the city states able to resist the Persians? The principle of constructing an account of the past in response to a specific question is one which we will return to repeatedly, as historians have. But Herodotus illustrates another point. For him, the failure of the Persian assault was explained culturally and socially: the forces of Persian slavery were defeated by Athenian freedom and Greek unity. He was writing about the past in terms of his own present: ironically, at the time that Herodotus was writing, Athens had become imperialist itself. All historical enquiries illuminate two times – the past they explore and the present in which they are formulated.

Alongside ίστορία there are other ideas in the word 'history'. The French term *l'histoire* translates as both history and story, the narrative threads of actions, consequences and reactions. John Burrow traced the development of history from Herodotus through early Christian scholars to sixteenth-century humanists and on to those nineteenth-century historians who had enormous confidence about the possibility of producing a definitive account of human experience. He identified common themes: the relationship between enquiry and story, the remoteness and oddness of the past and radically different ideas about the relationship between the past and the present. Sometimes historians' ideas were of decline and loss, sometimes of steady if uneven progress, sometimes of a working out of destiny, whether Christian, liberal or Marxist. Burrow concludes that 'almost all historians except the very dullest have some characteristic weakness: some complicity, idealization, identification; some impulse to indignation, to right wrongs, *to deliver a message*. It is often the source of their most interesting writing' (Burrow 2009: 51, emphasis added). What we call history rests on our relationship with the past. If this is true of what historians do, it is no less true of history teachers in schools: the school history curriculum and the individual lessons that make up pupils' experiences are driven by choices about content, what purposes content serves, and ideas we have about our relationships with it.

Keith Jenkins draws a distinction between what he calls 'upper case History' and 'lower case history'. Lower case history refers to the way historians – and others – believe they are explaining or describing the past 'as it was' – to 'reconstruct' the past. Upper case, or 'constructionist' History is different: it refers to the past retold, reinterpreted through the lens of a particular perspective – such as Economic History, the Marxist Interpretation of History – or the lens of the analytical tools and procedures of the Historian (Jenkins 1997; Evans 1997). Often, however, the two are confused. The confusion comes from the interchangeability of the language: pupils, and often parents and politicians, frequently believe they are learning lower case history by accessing knowledge 'about' the past. History teachers, and academic historians, are more likely to believe that they are teaching upper case History – a set of tools, procedures, concepts and techniques to develop not just an understanding of the past but a cast of mind, a way of thinking, an approach. The confusion runs through presentations of much of the debates over teaching history: the events of 1857 have a narrative (a lower case history) but acquire meaning when seen through the lens of an upper case History through processes such as the intensification of racism in the later nineteenth century, the decline of the British Empire, and so on. They acquire meaning for learners only as part of a learning journey through those aspects of history which make up their historical learning. Media portrayals of the Robin Hood myth are in no serious sense lower case history; the twelfth century was not 'like that', but they tell us a great deal about the time they were made and the audience they were made for (upper case History), and their interrogation in the classroom may, through the exploration of evidence and interpretation, help to constitute young people's exploration of history.

This distinction between history and History is complicated by the distinction between academic and popular histories. This is not simply a different way of representing the distinction between lower case history and upper case History. A television documentary about the myth of Robin Hood is a form of popular upper case History, concerned with evidence and its provenance, impact, influence and importance. School history often falls between the demands of academic and popular history. Young people often bring into school conceptions and misconceptions about the past and these ideas can influence their attitudes to the subject, and their ability to learn it. History teachers need to move between young people's prior understandings, educational objectives and priorities, and the nature of history as an academic discipline.

Conclusion

We have begun to explore the complexity of the content of the history curriculum and of the conceptual basis of 'learning' about the past, and we have considered some of the ways in which History in schools relates to history outside schools. Each of these issues will be explored in different ways throughout the book, recognizing the central importance of, first, understanding pupils' starting points and second, the challenge that teachers face in addressing these complex issues in classroom contexts. There are, however, two further underlying issues. The debate in this chapter has explored some dimensions of history as a subject in schools, but we also need to indicate how the issues we have explored are underscored by a sense of the fragility of the subject in schools, and – not unrelated – a sense of the power relationships which shape the school curriculum. Teaching about the past is often difficult and controversial. Politicians seeking to shape a sense of national identity – and those seeking to transform or undermine it – look to the way the past is taught in schools as a handy weapon. This makes history a dangerous subject in school, and one endlessly subject to external pressures. The temptation is to simplify, or ignore it: if there is no obvious agreement on what should be taught, or too many debates about what matters, perhaps curriculum planners might conclude that, after all, none of it is that important. If the concepts and ideas are complex and challenging, perhaps the discipline does not have a place in the education of all, but only in the education of a more literate minority. In the rest of this book, we will explore the challenges which arise from the precarious position of history in schools.

2

History and the curriculum

In this chapter we explore history in schools through the lens of the school curriculum and history's place in it. Although the place of history in schools is protected by a national curriculum in England and elsewhere, in practice it is under enormous pressure. We consider debates about what purposes history can serve in the school curriculum and set out an argument based on the entitlement of all learners to understanding the past in some form. We consider the evolution of the national curriculum and the implications for teaching in schools.

History in schools

History occupies an ambiguous place in the school curriculum. On the one hand, almost all governments expect schools to ensure that pupils gain an understanding of the past – normally incorporating a version of the national past which reflects current constitutional arrangements. On the other hand, few school systems provide adequate time for the realization of the often lofty aims for the history curriculum. In many, the subject is under pressure from other curriculum areas or other policy priorities; at a time when education reform globally is focused on the skills demands facing the twenty-first-century workforce, the study of the past in schools can feel marginal. Margaret MacMillan's analysis of the 'uses and abuses of history' observes that 'educating the next generation and instilling in them the right views and values are things most societies take very seriously' (MacMillan 2009: 113), but in practice, the curricular, physical and time resources made available to do this are limited. In their 2007 report on history in English schools, Ofsted conclude, starkly, that 'the biggest issue for school history is its limited place in the curriculum' (Ofsted 2007). The Historical Association (2010b) found that in a significant number of schools curriculum time for the subject has been reduced.

We saw in Chapter 1 how learning about the past involves five interlinked aspects which shape the history curriculum over the learning journey: time and memory, knowledge and understanding, interpretation, enquiry, and organization and communication. A nagging question is the extent to which they are distinctive features which justify history's place in the curriculum. There are a number of issues at stake here. The first is about what history contributes to pupils' overall curricular experience, and whether it is sufficiently distinctive to justify a place in a crowded curriculum; a second is whether its contribution – if distinctive – depends on history being taught as a single subject or whether it can be effectively taught through integrated, or interdisciplinary work.

Is history different? The purposes of history

There is no shortage of claims for the place of history in the curriculum. 'Through school history pupils develop knowledge and understanding of the past in order to appreciate themselves and others, to understand the present and to contribute to debate about planning for the future', declares the 2009 Australian national history curriculum document (National Curriculum Board 2009: 3.1). Following the end of apartheid, the South African government set about rewriting the history curriculum. Their expert report argued that school history 'helps to prevent amnesia, check[s] triumphalism, oppose[s] the manipulative or instrumental use of the past and provide[s] an educational buffer against a "dumbing down" of our citizens' (Chisholm 2004: 21). The argument in both Australia and South Africa is that history education provides a collective memory, impacting on young people's understandings of themselves and the society into which they are growing. The New York state standards for social studies – incorporating history and geography – in schools spell this out:

> A strong and effective Social Studies program helps pupils make sense of the world in which they live, it allows them to make connections between major ideas and their own lives, and it helps them see themselves as members of the world community. It offers pupils the knowledge and skills necessary to become active and informed participants on a local, national and global level.
>
> (New York City 2009: 3)

Such lofty aspirations provide a secure sociopolitical rationale for the teaching of history in schools, but this is not ideologically value-free. As the South African example makes plain, the content of history in the school curriculum is always influenced by the political history of the nation. This is encapsulated in the views of one recent English commentator, who argues that the teaching of history should 'serve the civic function of giving pupils the wherewithal for feeling justifiably proud of being British and for being attached to their country and its traditions' (Conway 2005: 21).

More recently, history's claim to a distinctive position in the school curriculum has been seen not simply in terms of the subject matter, but based on the extent to which it is a vehicle for the delivery of generic curriculum aims. The school curriculum is one of the means by which schools discharge their responsibilities for educating the next generation of adults, though society's demands on schools obviously change over time. For example, by the beginning of the twenty-first century it was assumed that schools would equip young people with ICT skills which simply did not exist twenty years earlier. In many countries, it has become increasingly important for schools to play a part in promoting social cohesion; and it may be that understanding of climate change becomes a central feature of the school curriculum over the next twenty years. From a whole-curriculum perspective, the question for any subject is how effective it is in promoting wider curriculum aims. It is here that the argument becomes more challenging for history teachers. On the one hand, there is a desire to defend the contribution of history to pupils' skills, for example in appraising and evaluating evidence or communicating the results of enquiries. Such claims make a strong case for history in a skills-led curriculum. On the other hand, history is not the only subject in which pupils learn to use evidence: they use evidence in science, in geography, in English. Although the nature of evidence may differ in each subject, what history teachers would need to claim is that the distinctive nature of historical thinking is sufficiently significant in young people's general education to merit claims to extensive curriculum time. While history may be a vehicle for organization and communication – especially in constructing and deploying an argument – many other subjects develop these areas: English, geography and modern languages.

The distinctive contribution of history to the school curriculum must therefore depend on one of two things: either its *intrinsic* value because of the knowledge base it provides – that is, that the knowledge acquired through learning *history* is sufficiently important to command curriculum time – or its *extrinsic* value to pupils' general education through its particular combination of knowledge, attributes and skills. Neither of these arguments depends on the importance of particular historical topics. It could be argued that history provides young people with knowledge which helps them understand the world into which they are growing. It could also be argued that history offers young people an understanding of their own identity, of the ways in which other individuals and groups differ, and that at different times people have organized their lives and societies in quite different ways. It is a component in what it means to become an educated person (Pring 2003). Nonetheless, this can be a difficult argument to sustain, and the introduction of citizenship as a compulsory subject since 2002 made it more so, since citizenship courses deal with issues of personal and social identity and the development of democratic institutions. At a time when skills-based approaches to curriculum planning are dominant, and vocationally oriented qualifications are being promoted, the role of history in a general education is a difficult case to make, but it is the case which needs to be made.

Curriculum reform and change is widespread in contemporary schools; there is a drive to develop new curriculum forms which will prepare young people for what is seen as being a rapidly changing world. In some versions of curriculum reform, subjects are seen as part of 'the problem': they create barriers to learning, rather than structures for learning, and reflect a largely nineteenth-century construction of the curriculum which does not adequately reflect changes in knowledge and its production. Schools in England are required to teach the content of the national curriculum, but can organize its delivery in a number of ways. In some secondary schools, history has been combined with geography, religious education and other subjects in humanities courses; these may be thematic or modular. In other secondary schools, part of the curriculum is taught through themes which draw together three, four or more subjects. In these arrangements, there may be benefits to pupils' learning – it makes little sense, for example, to teach the geography and history of India without reference to each other – but critics have argued that combining subjects dilutes their distinctiveness and makes it more difficult to establish links and progression within subjects. Obviously, it is desirable for learners to see links between subjects. Studying the poetry of Wilfred

Owen in literature lessons while learning about the First World War in history makes sense, just as learning about Darwin in history while studying evolution in science is helpful. The difficulties arise when subjects are 'merged' in integrated structures and the distinctiveness of each subject in terms of its conceptual structure is diluted and taught by non-specialists (Seixas 1994). It may be possible to design lesson sequences and outcomes which are faithful to the conceptual frameworks of more than one subject but this is challenging and needs time to plan and develop. Subjects offer learners and teachers a conceptual structure which sits behind content and syllabus requirements and, as a result, provide a basis for pupils to understand more than might otherwise be possible.

Making choices: the national curriculum

Until 1991, there was no national curriculum, so questions about selecting, presenting and accessing content were answered by teachers themselves. Examination requirements dictated the content of school history for older pupils but there was no prescription of content outside examination courses. In primary schools, whether history was taught or not depended on the enthusiasm and interest of the teacher; in secondary schools, while the subject curriculum was well established, content, organization and structure were left to teachers. In practice, dependence on textbooks reduced the variability of content: schools were dominated by a largely chronological and English curriculum, or, in John Slater's characterization, 'Celts looked in to starve or to rebel, northerners to invent machines and foreigners to surrender' (Slater 1989: 1). In principle, however, history teachers could, for most of their teaching, teach what they wanted in the way they wanted, and some did, not least at 11–14 after the liberating impact of the Schools Council History Project. In 1987, following the General Election, the re-elected Conservative government developed plans to introduce a national curriculum into English and Welsh schools. The 1988 Education Reform Act translated these plans into legislation, and detailed programmes of study for national curriculum subjects were produced. Critics at the time, and since, commented on this as a top-down, centralized and directive approach which produced a framework within which teachers had to make choices about their teaching.

General guidance was set out for the subject working groups which required them to work within a common framework of Attainment Targets and programmes of study, built around four key stages of learning (5–7, 7–11, 11–14 and 14–16). In guidance to the History Working Group, Kenneth Baker, the Secretary of State for Education, stipulated that 'the programmes of study should have at the core the history of Britain, the record of its past and, in particular, its political, constitutional and cultural heritage' (DES 1989: 43). In a neat comment, the History Working Group Interim Report declared that they had 'placed British history at the core of our proposals, but that does not mean it has to be the centre of gravity', and stressed the importance of a 'broad and eclectic view of British history' (DES 1989: 27, 17). The Working Group insisted on the importance of acquiring 'knowledge as understanding', and put this understanding in a framework which included an attainment target focused on interpretations of history – 'an understanding that history ha[s] been written, sung about, spoken about, painted, filmed and dramatized by all kinds of people for all kinds of reasons'. Such innovative elements meant that many of the Working Group's proposals commanded professional support, although in her own autobiography Margaret Thatcher expressed regret that the national curriculum for history had become more complex than she had ever envisaged (Thatcher 1995: 231). Even so, the structure of the history national curriculum turned out to be constraining: the final report set out prescribed and optional teaching units which were forbidding in detail, and removed substantial elements of decision-making from teachers, including – except in relation to some elements of local history – the ability to shape content to local circumstances and to structure the curriculum distinctively. At one stage, Kenneth Clarke, the then secretary of state, ordered that history teaching should stop short at 20 years before the present day, making it more difficult for teachers to help pupils understand the present in the light of the last. A 1991 political decision to remove history from the core curriculum 14–16 effectively decapitated the ornate content structure of the History Working Group.

In 1994 a major overhaul of the national curriculum took place to address what had become an unworkably crowded structure. In history, Attainment Targets and content were both slimmed, programmes of study were amended to fit a 5–14 rather than 5–16 structure, and 'key elements' – underpinning ideas, such as interpretation and communication – were introduced to provide a more coherent structure for school-based timetable planning, and to provide somewhat more space for individual approaches to teaching and learning.

Subsequent reviews in 1999–2000 and 2007 brought about further changes in three important respects. Following the 1997 General Election, citizenship was introduced into the school curriculum as a compulsory subject in 2002. The Crick Report on citizenship (QCA 1998) had argued that while History and citizenship shared some preoccupations, History itself was not an adequate vehicle for the development of political and participatory education in schools. Secondly, and especially in the 2007 review, innovation was permitted in the structure and organization of the school curriculum. Schools were encouraged to combine subjects, to develop thematic approaches, to organize their timetables in novel ways. These radical innovations – adopted in small but growing numbers of schools – raised questions about the nature, structure and organization of history in what was, in some schools, a radically different curriculum structure. The third change relates to the organization of the history curriculum. The overall structure of the 2007 curriculum was provided by key concepts, which define the planned outcomes, and key processes ('enquiry', 'using evidence' and 'communicating about the past'). Content prescription took a different form, declaring that 'the study of history should be taught through a combination of overview, thematic and depth studies' (QCA 2007a). Content requirements were set out in general terms and provided overarching structures for organizing content.

This liberalized structure for the history national curriculum was largely a response to critics from a variety of positions – some more well-informed than others. In 2007, Ofsted, drawing on evidence from the period 2003–07, argued that 'too great a focus on a relatively small number of issues means that pupils are not good at establishing a chronology, do not make connections between the areas they have studied and so do not gain an overview, and are not able to answer the "big questions"' (Ofsted 2007: 2). The academic historian and television pundit David Starkey railed that 'the way we teach history is fundamentally wrong…The skills-based approach to the teaching of history is a catastrophe…which prioritizes the historian over history and method over content' (Starkey 2005). In 2006, the Labour MP and former historian Gordon Marsden, who had chaired a review group on the subject, bemoaned what he called a topic-based 'yo-sushi experience of historical understanding', where teachers picked and mixed topics without situating them in any kind of broader context or narrative, and called for long-term narratives, emphasizing Britain's worldwide historical reach (Marsden 2006). These concerns about 'big picture' history and children's apparent lack of ability to discern bigger narratives and themes exerted a heavy influence on the 2007 revision. Criticisms continued after its introduction, however, and certainly sooner than the effects of the revised curriculum could be discerned. The influential historian Niall Ferguson, for example, claimed that a creeping concern with twentieth century history – often in the name of current 'relevance' – had displaced critical earlier turning points and individuals: as Ferguson put it on one occasion, Martin Luther King had entirely displaced Martin Luther (*Observer*, 21 March 2010).

In 2010, only two years after the revised national curriculum was introduced in schools, the incoming Conservative secretary of state for education ordered a review of the history curriculum, with the specific aim of restoring both an overarching narrative and the centrality of the British identity, asking the academic historian Simon Schama to advise on its content. In some respects, the national curriculum has come full circle, since it was precisely this concern with a central narrative of British history which underlay guidance to the History Working Group in 1988. In other respects, however, the context in 2010 was different from 1988. The national curriculum, over its many revisions and iterations, had provided history teachers with a coherent framework in which to explore the relationship of content to purpose, and the relationship between history in school, history as an academic discipline and the historical past.

History in schools: limitations and concerns

In this chapter, we have reviewed arguments about the purposes of history in school curricula across the world and focused in detail on the development of history in the national curriculum in England. In their 2007 report on school history, Ofsted described a range of pressures on the subject in schools:

> History, along with some other subjects, has been relatively neglected in primary schools in recent years as schools have focused on literacy and numeracy. History's limited role is also apparent in secondary schools. In Key Stage 4, only just over 30 per cent of pupils study history and fewer still post-16. In addition, there is evidence that the subject is becoming even more marginal with some schools' introduction of the two-year Key Stage 3 curriculum and the increased interest in vocational subjects.
>
> (Ofsted 2007: 28)

The Historical Association survey suggested that while 30 per cent of pupils study history beyond the age of 14, in some schools the figure was considerably less. Moreover, there was evidence that the figure tended to be smaller in more innovative schools such as academies which had enjoyed greater curriculum freedoms at Key Stage 3 than other maintained schools. Examining patterns in the take-up of history beyond 14, the Historical Association uncovered evidence that significant numbers of schools placed restrictions on pupils, choices beyond 14, and that these were largely based on academic achievement. The authors concluded that 'many teachers expressed deep regret about the fact that history was effectively out of bounds for lower attaining pupils' (Historical Association 2010b: 21). Marked disparities were found between and within schools: history was less likely to thrive in schools with less affluent intakes, while within schools it was higher attaining pupils who were more likely to be offered an academic curriculum including history.

This is the context for the teaching of history in the twenty-first century. The aims and objectives which surround national history curricula emphasize the importance of learning about the past, and of developing the understandings and competencies which history as an academic discipline makes possible. The reality in schools is somewhat different: a fragile subject, competing for a place in a curriculum struggling to adapt to the multiple demands placed on schools. There is some evidence that access to history is increasingly confined to higher attainers and more affluent pupils, while the majority of pupils abandon history before they have the maturity to address some of the more complex and challenging issues history introduces. England is one of just four European countries which do not require some study of history through to the end of compulsory schooling: the others are Wales, Northern Ireland and the Netherlands. This does not mean that all learners should be expected to take a single subject history course to examination level at 16. However, it is a reminder that the curriculum in schools can be constructed in ways which support rather than deny access for all, and that if history is to meet the lofty objectives which national and state curricula frequently set for it, imaginative curriculum structures may be necessary.

3

Teaching and learning in classrooms and beyond

In this chapter we begin to explore the raw materials for teaching history in the classroom – desks, walls, textbooks, but also the pupils and, most importantly, the teachers themselves. We consider the knowledge base needed to teach successfully, the way this is used by effective history teachers and some of the challenges posed by historical language.

Resources for teaching and learning: the classroom and beyond

Most history teaching takes place in classrooms. Many classrooms have changed considerably in appearance over the last thirty years, though not all have. Lift-top desks which dominated classrooms from the later nineteenth to the mid-twentieth century have gone, replaced by light, manoeuvrable laminate tables; in some classrooms, rectangular tables have been replaced by triangular, rhomboid or hexagonal worktops. Chalkboards have gone, replaced first by whiteboards, and now supplemented by interactive whiteboards. Televisions arrived, were supplemented by video players and both have now gone as digital technologies open access to web-based and stored resources. Classrooms sport power towers or laptop access points; wireless connectivity has replaced fixed internet connections. However, in the vast majority of classrooms, layout remains stubbornly traditional, with rows of desks facing the teacher and the teacher's resources at the front of the room.

In some classrooms, greater attention is now given to display – not simply to the display of pupil work or maps, but to charts which explain the language of time, sequencing and dating, of analysis, evaluation and synthesis, of historical concepts, ideas and understandings. In some classrooms, there are timelines, sequencing historical time on a grand scale or within particular periods and topics. The best history classrooms offer a rich environment in which to learn about the past, with ideas, language and images presented around the room as tools for teacher and pupils. However, in many schools, specialist teaching accommodation for history teaching does not exist; unlike science, or technology, the case for a specialist teaching space for history is not an obvious one to make, though its importance has been noted. Ofsted, in 2007, describing one inspected school, commented: 'This is a reflective and collegiate department that works together very well. It is delivering a very high quality learning experience for pupils *despite the difficulties presented by substandard accommodation'* (Ofsted 2007: para 67, emphasis added).

The physical setting for history teaching in schools varies considerably, then. One obvious question is how the physical environment is used. There is considerable evidence of increased thought among researchers and policy makers about the importance of the learning environment for the quality of pupils' experiences, but less evidence of impact on practice (Galton *et al.* 1980; Galton and Williamson 1992). Despite some radical thinking about classroom layout and pedagogy (e.g. Waterhouse 1983), there is evidence that classroom layouts have moved back towards a focus on the teacher. In itself, as we shall see, this is no bad thing, but it is worth digging a little deeper into three elements which shape the way classrooms are used as settings for children's learning: the technologies at the disposal of the teacher, the ideas about teaching and learning which are brought into the classroom and the work of history teachers themselves.

Extensive claims are often made for the transformative effects of technology on classrooms and on teaching and learning more generally. Where classrooms have changed in appearance substantially over the last thirty or forty years, this is often a result of technological change – laminate tables instead of wooden lift-lid desks, or interactive whiteboards instead of chalkboards. It is certainly the case that digital technologies put a much greater range of resources at the disposal of the history teacher than was the case with print technologies. The history teacher teaching about the Italian Renaissance can access the entire Uffizi collection online (http://www.uffizi.com/), examine the drawings of Leonardo da Vinci in detail (http://www.drawingsofleonardo.org/) or embark on a virtual tour of Florence (http://www.italyguides.it/us/florence/florence_italy.htm). These opportunities come at a price: ease of access to resources does not necessarily make for guarantees of quality. As Ben Walsh stresses, teachers must 'insist that proper historical method is used at all times' (Walsh 2008: 7). Sally Burnham has demonstrated how effectively pupils can use movie-making technology to demonstrate historical understanding – but also the importance of structuring their learning around significant historical questions and a sequenced plan of activity (Burnham 2008).

It would be foolish to underestimate the importance of technological innovation, but it is equally important not to overstate it. New technologies are frequently used to support existing pedagogies rather than to extend, challenge or replace them. The government-commissioned evaluation of the use of interactive whiteboards in London suggested that while teachers used the technologies extensively to present material to pupils, few thought in sufficient detail about the way pupils were to navigate their way through the classroom presentations thus created, and many taught lessons with *greater* emphasis on presenting material *to* pupils rather than on pupil understanding *of* the material (Moss *et al.* 2007): as Carey Jewitt puts it the 'worksheet, for example, migrates to the interactive whiteboard' (Jewitt 2008). Terry Haydn has suggested that interactive whiteboards in history classrooms have encouraged teachers to think more about their own performance, and the elegance of their presentation, rather than the interactivity which is made possible (Haydn 2004b). It proved easier to amend a chalkboard diagram or a marker pen diagram on a whiteboard in discussion with a class, for example. Technologies in classrooms are *permissive* at best: they make different sorts of learning and interaction possible. Whether the possibilities are realized depends on other things, and notably on the ability and willingness of teachers to use the technologies as tools for teaching in innovative ways.

The way classrooms and their physical resources are used depends fundamentally on the ideas teachers have about teaching and learning. As Robin Alexander suggested in his study of primary teaching in five countries, these ideas are often deeply embedded in cultural assumptions about what teaching involves (Alexander 2000). Ideas about teaching and learning can and do change. In the mid-twentieth century, research into children's learning and cognitive development was heavily influenced by the work of the Swiss psychologist Jean Piaget, which emphasized the way in which the child interacted with objects and experiences. Piaget's approach to child development emphasized three elements: the way a child explored her environment, the developmental stages through which children passed in making sense of the environment and the role of adults in assessing a child's 'readiness' to learn. In later twentieth-century research, Piagetian ideas were largely supplanted by constructivist theories of learning heavily influenced by the work of the Soviet psychologist Lev Vygotsky. In place of the 'lone' child interacting with her environment, Vygotsky stressed the centrality of language and dialogue. Learning, for Vygotsky, depended on social and cultural interaction and, importantly on the role of an adult who is able to 'scaffold' a child's understanding through structured learning:

> What the child can do in cooperation today he can do alone tomorrow. Therefore the only good kind of instruction is that which marches ahead of development and leads it...For a time, our schools favoured the 'complex' system of instruction, which was believed to be adapted to the *child's way of thinking*...In offering the child problems he was able to handle without help, this method failed to utilize the zone of proximal development and to lead the child to what he could not yet do.
>
> (Vygostsky 1962, quoted in Alexander 2000: 431, emphasis added; Alexander notes that the phrase 'zone of proximal development' is perhaps better translated as 'zone of potential development')

Piagetian ideas were dominant in pre-service teacher training in the 1960s and 1970s, when training was more theoretical in orientation than it is now. Such ideas emphasized the importance of the child's interaction with the world and the importance of teachers' ability to assess a child's readiness for learning. Now, constructivist theories tend to be dominant in research, with an emphasis on the importance of discussion, dialogue, the social context of learning and teachers' ability to scaffold pupils' learning beyond their current stage of understanding. However, few teachers are likely to have a close acquaintance with these ideas as a direct result of their training so the ideas have tended to spread in a relatively haphazard way. Although Vygotskyan ideas underpin many of the theoretical arguments in favour of deploying group work in classrooms, teachers who use group work need to be clear about their own practical rationale for asking pupils to work in this way, and skilled at structuring group work successfully (e.g. Woolnough 2006).

What this means is that the principal resource for learning – the resource on which all else depends – is the teacher. There is now compelling international evidence that it is teacher quality which is the single most important in-school factor in securing high-quality learning outcomes (Sanders and Rivers 1996; Barber and Mourshed 2007). Outstanding teachers inspire, motivate and cajole learners, extending their learning through imaginative lessons, sophisticated long-term planning and judicious interventions in classroom interactions. All this is clear. What is somewhat less clear is what determines teacher quality. Considerable recent attention has been focused on teachers' own cognitive ability (Hanushek and Welch 2006) and the importance of subject knowledge as a basis for effective pedagogic practice. Obviously, classroom teaching depends on much more than simply knowing a good deal about the subject, important though this is. In this context, Lee Shulman's 1986 paper on 'pedagogic content knowledge' ('PCK') has been hugely influential. Shulman developed the concept of 'pedagogic content knowledge' as a way of connecting distinct bodies of knowledge for teaching. 'It represent[s] the blending of content and pedagogy into an understanding of how particular topics, problems, or issues are organized, represented, and adapted to the diverse interests and abilities of learners, and presented for instruction' (Shulman 1986: 8). PCK requires teachers to be able to deploy analogies, illustrations, examples, explanations and demonstrations as conduits for their subject knowledge to engage and enthuse pupils, to make decisions, often 'on the hoof', about what to do, drawing on a range of understandings about subject and teaching. Studies since 1986 have suggested complex relationships between subject knowledge and pedagogic knowledge (Wilson and Wineburg 1988; Turner-Bisset 1999). More recently, it has been argued that history teachers routinely draw on different types of knowledge which work in relationship with each other. They are able to deploy knowledge and understanding of subject. They 'know' how the discipline works and can call on detailed contextual knowledge of the topics they are teaching. In addition they deploy knowledge and understanding of pupils, including understanding of how pupils make progress in learning history and of a range of pedagogic practices. It is the active relationship between these sorts of knowledge which underpins successful classroom teaching (Husbands 2010).

Most history teaching takes place in classrooms. But not all does. Some, perhaps the most productive, takes place outside classrooms, on historic sites, in museums or in galleries or simply in the environs of the school. Proponents of out-of-school learning argue that 'learning outside the classroom supports pupils' learning and development. It has the potential to enrich and enliven teaching' (House of Commons Children, Schools and Families Committee 2010: para. 11). Realizing this potential outside the classroom is no less challenging than securing high-quality learning inside the classroom; pupils are no more likely to learn successfully outside the classroom than they are inside it unless their learning is actively planned, managed and consolidated. Successful learning outside the classroom demands skilful planning; as with all learning, it demands attention to learning objectives, but also to how pupils will *learn* in different settings and the best settings to support different sorts of learning. Although some sites – castles, museums, abbeys – may form particularly strong foci for learning, almost every school has scope for supporting history learning outside the classroom on its doorstep. In the 1970s, the Schools History Project proclaimed its faith in 'History Around Us'. The local war memorial can offer rich opportunities to explore historical significance (Brown and Woodcock 2009), local oral history projects can motivate the most reluctant of learners (Johansen and Spafford 2009) and using the local town as a case study renders the Industrial Revolution more relevant and personal (McFahn *et al.* 2009). Museum-based learning offers rich possibilities for enriching children's understanding of evidence and the ways in which we build up ideas about the past. Out-of-school learning offers the opportunity to explore new surroundings. However, successful out-of-school learning involves going beyond the nature of the experience of being out of school itself to think about how it engages learners, and how the focus of the learning relates to what has gone before and comes later (Hooper-Greenhill 2007).

Organizing and presenting history: language and resources

The lesson in Box 3.1 was taught to a class of 12-year-olds. The lesson is interesting in a number of respects: it required high-level listening and speaking skills, drew on pre-lesson preparation by the pupils and led into a sophisticated piece of written work requiring extended argument and critical skills. The focus of the lesson was on the deployment of higher order reflective skills, and depended on the pupils' active engagement not simply with the context but with historical arguments about the context. Yet in other respects it was curious. While it rested on, and managed, high levels of pupil engagement, it deployed no resources: there was no use of the whiteboard, no textbooks, no worksheets, no technology. Instead, it rested on the use of discussion and active listening to develop understanding and argumentation. As in so many complex lessons, what was happening on the surface – a pupil debate about the causes of the Civil War, about which historians have disagreed extensively of course – involved a sophisticated set of processes brought together by the teacher. In this lesson, the girls' oral and listening skills were the centrepiece, without which nothing else would have been possible, but they themselves had been developed through other exercises and lessons earlier in the curriculum. The teacher used her own deep subject knowledge not just to structure the debate but to feed observations (or interpretations) into it. The lesson had been actively planned and positioned at a point in the scheme of work where pupils knew enough to engage with the issues but not too much to squeeze out their own understanding and observations – even where these were anachronistic. The relationship between teacher and pupils was rich in terms of extended dialogic teaching (Alexander 2000, 2006).

This is an extreme example in a number of respects: few lessons are so resource-free, and few depend so much on talk. As Grant Bage notes, the 'traditional way of mediating [history] curricula has been through talk; especially teacher talk'. Bage quotes his own research suggesting that 'listening to teacher' was the activity which pupils cited most frequently as helping them to learn, and observes that this is 'hard evidence of a commonsense assumption: teachers are the richest historical resource to which most children have access' (Bage 2000: 56). For over forty years, since the work of Douglas Barnes and James Britton, the inter-relationship between the focus of the curriculum and its communication between teachers and learners has been a central theme of research and understanding (Britton 1970; Barnes 1976). What Barnes showed was that forms of communication in the classroom shaped understandings as powerfully, if not more so, than the intended content of the curriculum. In the context

---

Box 3.1 Year 8 debate the execution of Charles I

Classroom – a very small room for 22 pupils but at least dedicated to history teaching. Tables arranged in a horseshoe with two tables parallel to the sides. Some girls had their backs to other girls and some were sitting at right angles to the board. There was no fussing or any issues around seating – there was no evidence of a seating plan.

0:00	T[eacher] registered the class electronically on the computer at side of the room by calling out names.
0:02	T discussed the aim of the lesson (which followed on from one previously) – '*How much have you understood the causes of the Civil War? At the end we will have a vote as to whether it was King or Parliament who were responsible.*'

T asked S[tudent]s to recap the events leading up to the war – Ss had their exercise books with a sheet of information but the onus seemed to be on remembering and sifting relevant facts as they did not really appear to use this sheet.

T: '*Why didn't the Protestant Parliamentarians like the French princess?*'

Ss discussed who was responsible in the various stages.

T recapped and pointed out that the three arguments were about 'money', 'religion' and 'power/politics'; she asked which was most important? T pointed out that all were present at one time so '*we could argue that this is why this particular crisis led to the Civil War*' (as previous crises had only involved one of these factors). '*It was a big smelly soup of economic, religious and political fights.*'

0:15	T: '*Shall we fight for the King or the Parliament?*'

She asked for two '*advocates*' – one for each side (homework had been to write a speech for either side).

S1 defended the King in the role of someone who was there at the time. T and Ss made notes of important points – S1 used arguments like '*God-given authority…*'. T summed up and congratulated S1 for being '*very convincing.*'

S2 defended Parliament: '*We have the right to choose our leaders. He has no God-given right.*' T also congratulated S2 and said her speech was '*pretty radical*'. She likened her to Oliver Cromwell and told the class they would be studying him after Easter. She also picked up on S2's use of language by saying she liked the phrase '*tossed around on the seas of religion*'.

S3 then was chosen to defend the King – she had prepared cue cards. T picked up the fact that S3 introduced herself as a woman and reminded them that although women had no political rights or representation at that time there were some women who had campaigned for both sides and of one woman who disguised herself as a man. She said she liked S3's '*emotional appeal*'.

S4 then read out her speech on behalf of Parliament – the T praised her for pointing out the '*economic side*'.

0:30	The vote! T told the girls to shut their eyes *'to make it more exciting.'* The vote took place twice as T had to clarify *'who is to blame'.* (The only writing all lesson) On board: King 12, Parliament 9, Abstentions 2 T: *'This group believes the King was to blame.'* T then asked class if they were interested in what she thought – they were so she told them she agreed it was the King and gave her reasons. Their homework was to make sure that they had written up their speeches in the front of their books over Easter (most had done so anyway).
0:34	Ss were asked to write in their books: 'The Civil War was the fault of … I think this because…'
0:36	There was some discussion around the issues that came out of this lesson. The news that morning (on BBC Radio 4) was that Gordon Brown was going to repeal the 300-year-old law that the monarch or heir to the throne could not marry a Catholic. Another girl had also listened to this radio report – T picked up on this and reminded the class of the Human Rights Act i.e. the freedom to marry who you want and of freedom of religion. She said it was *'about time'* and that these old laws were in conflict with the human rights of the monarch.
0:40	Bell goes – class dismissed. No (need for?) formal ending or summing up of what had been covered in the lesson.

of what were then – and in many ways still remain – transmission-based models of teaching, what Ian Luff in 2001 memorably captured as 'I talk, you listen' (Luff 2001), this closes down, rather than opens out the potential for teaching and learning history. This model of history teaching has been enormously dominant. David Sylvester called it the 'great tradition' in which the 'history teacher's role was didactically active; it was to give pupils the facts of historical knowledge, and to ensure through repeated short tests that they had learned them' (Sylvester 1994: 18); it was overlain by a powerful moral and interpretive mission.

The civil war example, although it demonstrates the extent to which access to the past in history lessons is powerfully mediated through language, and depends on language, was not dependent on teacher transmission talk but on extended speaking and listening skills on the part of the pupils. There is extensive research to demonstrate the power of structured speaking and listening in supporting pupils' historical thinking, and their learning more generally (Alexander 2000; Bage 2000; Coffin 2007).

Conventionally, history teachers have drawn extensively on paper and book resources to supplement or extend their own expertise. In the vast majority of history lessons, paper resources have been the artefacts through which the past is presented and through which pupils access it. Paper resources take many forms: textbooks, reproduced, and normally edited, extracts from primary historical documents, reproduced photographs, artworks, pictures of objects. For much of the period since education became compulsory in 1870, the textbook has dominated the teaching of history.

There is an extensive tradition of textbook analysis, much of it subtle and sophisticated, and textbooks have been used to illuminate the mediation of curriculum into the classroom (Chancellor 1970; Nicholls 2006). Even so, textbooks can be misleading, and teachers need to use them, not to be used by them (Foster and Crawford 2006). Eamonn McCann recalled an extreme example in his experience of learning history in Northern Ireland in the 1960s:

> History lessons did not always follow the curriculum laid down by the Northern Ireland Ministry of Education. One teacher, admittedly regarded as something of an eccentric, was at pains to discredit English propaganda…At the beginning of a new school year, he would lead the class through the set text books instructing them to tear out pages of fiction…That done, the lessons could begin.
>
> (McCann 1993)

The Schools Council History Project set out to provide pupils with the opportunity to understand the process as well as the product of history in the 1970s and to grapple with the challenges and fascination that the imperfect, incomplete traces of the past present to the historian (Schools Council 1973). Linked with the late 1970s reprographics revolution, SCHP encouraged history teachers to produce and reproduce evidence extracts which underpinned classroom work. Textbook publishers responded quickly too, and the standard history textbook ceased to be the analytical narrative text and became instead a collection of authorial text and edited evidential extracts. We will explore the practical implications of placing evidence and enquiry at the heart of the history classroom, but the key point to make here is about the nature of the resources at the disposal of the classroom teacher – his or her own voice, the work of textbook authors, and extracts from historical source material – and the extent to which they are all to some degree dependent on language. History is a school subject drenched in language – the teacher's language, the pupils' language in response, the written texts, and in a language with its own vocabulary, register and genres (Edwards and Furlong 1978; Husbands 1996). Partly for this reason, history has gained a reputation as one of the most difficult of school subjects: learning history involves mastering much of the language of historical times and ideas, and finding ways to express this in controlled and sustained argumentation in order to convey the complexity of understandings of the historical past (Andrews 1995; Counsell 1997).

Although history is predominantly explored through the written word, many of the most promising of materials are non-written, and the skill of the successful history teacher lies in combining text and non-textual resources to explore and develop the language and ideas of historical thinking – whether inside the classroom or outside it. Sixteenth-century conceptions of monarchy are perhaps best accessed through portraits of monarchs; the rise of Nazism through newsreel or extracts from newsreel, and the legacy of the Roman Empire through Roman remains, whether on site or on screen. Artefacts, whether encountered in handling sessions, in museums or remotely through digital images, are more than simply objects. Frances Sword, in yet another context – Egyptian mummies in a museum – puts it like this:

> The functions of many objects are multi-faceted and complex. An Egyptian coffin, for example, was made to hold not just a body but a belief system: the body was contained in the coffin, and the belief system is contained in its style. The

object contains many sorts of information but, as with so many artefacts, style is the thickest cable of communication...Whatever the object, if it communicates through its style, we are presented with ideas held in shape, form and colour which are often far more important than those held by any other aspect of the artefacts.

(Sword 1994: 9)

In the contemporary history classroom the concept of the 'thickest cable of communication' is the critical one. Language, knowledge and resources are the raw materials of the history teacher from which she fashions the 'thickest cable of communication'. The materials at the history teachers' disposal are richer and more complex than ever before. Box 3.2 provides one example of such a resource provided through the collaboration between the British Museum and BBC Radio 4 to trace the history of the world in a hundred objects, from any number of perspectives, challenging conventional perceptions of the past. However, rich though this resource is, it and others are useful only in so far as they are used effectively in classrooms, and the practices underlying their use are central to the craft of the history teacher.

Conclusion

History teachers themselves are pivotal to young people's experiences of learning about the past. Successful learning depends to a large extent on the ways in which teachers make active use of the tools and resources at their disposal – the ways in which they are able to use and navigate language, the ways they define historical problems and the ways they marshal the extensive resources at their disposal to support learning. The best history classrooms are rich settings for children's historical – and general – learning, places where language, text and objects are combined to support high levels of enquiry and thinking. In our work in classrooms for this book, we came across another significant dimension of this: pupils' own perceptions of the way their teachers worked. Effective teachers appeared open to pupils' ideas and interests – in effect pupils felt they and their teacher were learning together. In some classrooms there was a sense of a 'shared experience' where teachers also took part in the historical explorations of their pupils. In one classroom the teacher 'modelled' a presentation he had produced so the pupils could understand how to assess each others' presentations, 'because we can't ask you [pupils] to do something that we [teachers] are not prepared to do ourselves'.

Box 3.2 A History of the World in a Hundred Objects

The BBC 'History of the World in a Hundred Objects' is a hugely ambitious and accessible attempt to trace major themes in world history through objects. A partnership between the BBC and the British Museum, it uses radio programmes and a linked website – from which the programmes are downloadable – to explore objects. The series travels 'through two million years from the earliest object in the collection to retell the history of humanity through the objects we have made'. Sequences of objects are tied to a particular theme, such as 'after the ice age', 'pilgrims and traders' or 'the beginning of science and literature'.

The website provides rich resources for learning: http://www.bbc.co.uk/ ahistoryoftheworld/. Each object is available as a zoomable image, and a set of commentaries provide context, together with interpretations of the objects offered by academics. For example the Kilwa pot sherds are

> broken pieces of pots ... found on the shores of Kilwa Kiswani, an island off Tanzania, which was once home to a major medieval African port. The pale green porcelain pieces are from China, the dark green and blue pieces come from the Persian Gulf and the brown unglazed pieces were made in East Africa. This rubbish reveals a complex trade network that spread across the Indian Ocean, centuries before the European maritime empires of Spain, Portugal and Britain. From around AD 800 merchants from Africa, the Middle East, India, and later even China flocked to the East African ports of Kilwa and Mombasa, which quickly grew into wealthy cities. These merchants traded in pots, spices, ivory, gems, wood, metal and slaves. A new language, Swahili, developed in this multicultural environment, combining existing African languages with Arabic. Islam was adopted as the religion in these ports, perhaps to aid in trade relations with the Middle East and also to protect African merchants from being enslaved by other Muslims.

This one object – a pile of rubbish – is used quickly to highlight major themes of cultural exchange and migration on a global canvas – to move from an object to a wide canvas, on which a big picture can be sketched.

Part 2

Learning history in schools

In Part 1, our attention was focused on history as a subject and on the curriculum framework in which it is embedded. In this section, we turn our attention to learners. Too often, debates about school subjects and the ways in which they should be taught can ignore the interests, needs and, indeed, voices of the learners themselves. In this section we seek to remedy this, although of course it is not possible entirely to separate discussion of learning from discussion of teaching. Chapter 4 begins with a general review of the literature on 'pupil voice' before going on to explore what we know about what pupils want from the study of history. Chapter 5 takes a different tack; given that history is often seen as being one of the more difficult subjects for pupils to learn, we try to use pupils' own voices to explore what it is that they find difficult.

4

What do pupils want from learning history?

In this chapter we explore the perspectives of learners in the history classroom. We try to look at the history classroom from the point of view of what learners want as a way of inviting teachers to do the same. Like the previous section that considers the general issues of history and history teaching, this section too focuses on learners in schools generally and in the history classroom specifically. Throughout we have tried to include the voices of learners and their teachers that we have met in the schools we visited.

Why consult pupils about learning?

A good deal has been written about the aims of school history, about what should be included in the curriculum and how it should be taught. There is also a strong research tradition exploring young people's cognitive development in history which examines the difficulties that pupils face in understanding different aspects of the past and why this is the case. However, there is considerably less work on the views and voices of pupils themselves. There are pupil voices in research on historical understanding but fewer studies of what pupils think history is, how they perceive history's value and whether they enjoy studying it. As one commentator puts it, 'Somehow educators have forgotten the important connection between teachers and pupils. We listen to outside experts to inform us, and, consequently overlook the treasure in our very own backyards, the pupils' (Soo Hoo 1993: 389). In this chapter, we draw on existing evidence and our own experiences to explore pupils' perspectives because we believe it to be an essential resource for teachers in thinking about their own practice. We do so by drawing, first, on the general literature on 'pupil voice'; secondly on the fairly limited research carried out on pupils' attitudes and experiences of studying school history and finally on some of the voices of pupils that we have heard in our own work with schools. We cannot claim that the voices that we have chosen to include are necessarily representative or statistically sampled – in many ways these student contributions result through serendipity rather than design – but we present them here because they challenge thinking about what history teaching currently is and perhaps what it could be.

Consulting children, that is those under the age of 18, about things which affect them is an increasingly common feature of planning and delivering services for children. Children can be, and increasingly are, consulted in a variety of ways. The roots of current practice in consulting children lie in the UN Convention on the Rights of the Child (1989), in particular Article 12 which states that each country 'shall assure to the child who is capable of forming his or her own views the right to express those views freely in all matters affecting the child, the views of the child being given due weight in accordance with the age and maturity of the child'. For all of its expansiveness, the UN Convention had relatively little direct influence on practice in English education until the early years of the twenty-first century, when a wider interest in understanding, children's perspectives through the *Every Child Matters* initiative (DfES 2003) began to influence work in schools. Jean Rudduck, who developed much of the theoretical understanding and the realization of the potential of children's consultation in schools, explained that

> pupil voice is the consultative wing of pupil participation. Consultation is about talking with pupils about things that matter in school. It may involve: conversations about teaching and learning; seeking advice from pupils about new initiatives; inviting comment on ways of solving problems that are affecting the teacher's right to teach and the pupil's right to learn; inviting evaluative comment on recent developments in school or classroom policy and practice.
>
> (Rudduck 2005)

Rudduck and McIntyre define pupil consultation as 'talking with pupils about things that matter to them in the classroom and school and that affect their learning'. Ideally consultation is a conversation that builds a habit of easy discussion between pupil and teacher about learning. They add that real consultation occurs when pupils 'know that their views are being sought because it is expected that they will have something to contribute' (Rudduck and McIntyre 2007: 36).

There are practical and pragmatic reasons for 'consulting pupils'. While some teachers might be initially sceptical that not all young people would take the consultation process seriously or that they might suggest ridiculous ways of working, evidence from the Consulting Pupils project (Flutter 2002) suggests otherwise: pupils responded with insight and intelligence when consulted meaningfully. The evidence also suggested that being consulted directly about the classroom issues that most affect them actively generated greater pupil 'motivation' towards learning (McIntyre et al. 2005: 150). Drawing on pupil perspectives, the Consulting Pupils project team identified four dominant themes which pupils saw as key elements for effective teaching to generate learning (Box 4.1). In many ways these findings may appear self-evident but it is worth noting that they draw on the unprompted voices of pupils themselves, and help to frame directly thinking about teacher practices. It is also interesting that many of these correspond with other research findings from history classrooms coming from pupil surveys. Our own visits and discussions with pupils also elicited similar responses on which we draw throughout this chapter.

Box 4.1 Key elements of effective teaching for learning: dominant themes from the Consulting Pupils about Teaching and Learning project

---

Interactive teaching for understanding – teachers need to actively engage with what pupils bring to their own learning.

The need for teachers to contextualize the learning so that new ideas are connected with something pupils are already familiar with.

Learning tasks that foster a stronger sense of ownership and that recognize pupils' growing sense of independence and maturity.

Collaborative learning that promoted greater discussion and working together on shared tasks.

http://www.consultingpupils.co.uk/

Consulting pupils in history classrooms: what do we know about pupils' views?

The most recent survey of pupils' attitudes towards school history was carried out by Richard Harris and Terry Haydn for the Qualifications and Curriculum Authority in 2005 (Harris and Haydn 2006, 2008). This study was one response to a reported increase in pupil disaffection towards schooling in general and the researchers were keen to investigate the factors that led to greater or lesser pupil engagement and enjoyment in history. They were also influenced by the ideas emerging from the Consulting Pupils projects and cite the argument that an understanding of pupils' perspective is critical because of its potential to give teachers resources for strategies based on a deeper knowledge and firmer understanding of the complex processes of teaching and learning (Flutter and Rudduck 2004: 2).

Harris and Haydn based their work on 1740 questionnaire responses from Key Stage 3 pupils in 12 schools from the east of England, London and the south coast, followed up by more in-depth focus group discussion in each school. They did find that the majority of pupils said that they enjoyed history – overall it was the fourth most enjoyable school subject among boys after physical education, design and technology and ICT and the fourth among girls after art, physical education and design and technology, which, the authors remark, made it the most popular 'academic' subject at KS3 (Harris and Haydn 2008: 40). However, pupils' enjoyment varied greatly between schools and there was evidence that it is teachers and teaching style that have greatest impact on the attitudes of pupils in history rather than the nature of the subject itself. Harris and Haydn concluded that 'what they are taught, how they are taught and by whom they are taught are very important in determining their level of interest. Active and participatory teaching approaches are rated very highly' (Harris and Haydn 2006: 321).

Results from this study chime with the general results found in much larger studies focused on 'pupil voice' (e.g. McIntyre et al. 2005) across different subject areas. The teaching strategies, and therefore learning processes, that pupils identify as most 'enjoyable' in history were also found to be 'investigative work, group work, discussion and debate'. The types of activities that were popular were cited as 'interactive' activities, such as role-play, drama, presentations, discussion, debate, making things, and other creative activities. So much is clear, and our own work with schools has generated countless examples of individual activities which involve alternative forms of communication which do not depend on extended writing. Underlying this is a profound tension for pupils and for teachers: as we saw in Chapter 3, learning history depends fundamentally on the acquisition of the language and argumentation of history. Thus, while it is possible to devise classroom activities which enthuse, the challenge is to develop these and to connect them together in ways which allow pupils to engage with complex historical ideas.

Many of the negative comments that pupils made about history classrooms centred around 'written work' and most particularly related to writing tasks that did not offer a sense of 'ownership' – such as copying from the board – or tasks requiring higher level literacy skills such as extended writing, or argumentative writing in a particular style. However, the same pupils often said that they enjoyed tasks using creative writing, drama and historical texts that require the development of empathetic understanding. Empathy is often perceived, by history teachers, as either too difficult or too problematic not only because pupils are required to assume (often adult) roles from the past but also because, as one teacher remarked, 'the history can get lost and the English takes over'. Harris and Haydn note that while interactive teaching approaches were mostly popular, this was not always the case, especially if only used sporadically or if the teacher was not skilled in their use. The authors conclude that in history 'the teacher matters – a lot', not only in how skilled they are in their teaching approach but also in how they talk to pupils and relate to them. Again the finding that the relationship between pupils and their teacher is a key factor in pupil enjoyment of a subject resonates with findings from the 'pupil voice' project. In our own visits to schools we also found evidence of the importance of the relationship between history teachers and their pupils. Teachers and pupils in one successful history department appeared to be constantly developing, challenging and debating with each other to create their own learning community. In one outer London comprehensive school, the history department had established a history working group involving pupils to explore ways of teaching and learning with which pupils felt they could engage. The pupils suggested new units of work, such as examining the history of crime locally.

Harris and Haydn were also interested in pupils' perceptions of history as a subject and therefore probed their understandings of its 'usefulness' alongside their 'enjoyment' of it. An earlier survey of Year 9 pupils' perceptions of history and geography carried out by Adey and Biddulph (2001) revealed a large discrepancy between the numbers of pupils who enjoy geography and/or history at Key Stage 3 and the number who opt to study each subject at GCSE, arguing that 'for a large number of pupils, "enjoyment" of history or geography is not an adequate reason for opting to study it further' (2001: 449). Adey and Biddulph suggested that perceptions of 'usefulness' in relation to future careers were more important than 'liking' the subject in shaping option decisions and that most pupils saw 'usefulness' in terms of direct application to employment (2001: 449). Although Harris and Haydn found that a much higher proportion of pupils in their survey did think that history as a school subject was useful, on the whole, their pupils could also not say *why* it was useful. Again the authors comment that the results were also highly dependent on the school surveyed

---

Box 4.2 Pupils' understanding of the purposes of learning history

(a) History 'to help understand the present' type responses

School 6 (13- to 14-year-olds)	32.5% of comments
School 8 (13- to 14-year-olds)	4.5% of comments

(b) History for 'vocational' reasons
(e.g. to be a history teacher or archaeologist)

School 3 (11- to 12-year-olds)	22% of comments
School 10 (11- to 12-year-olds)	1.5% of comments

(c) History 'to avoid making the same mistakes' type responses

School 10 (13- to 14-year-olds)	28.5% of comments
School 12 (13- to 14-year-olds)	2% of comments

Source: Adapted from Harris and Haydn (2008: 47)

(Box 4.2), suggesting that some schools made the aims and therefore possible purposes of history much more explicit than others.

Making choices: history and the options maze

Pupils in English schools are required to make choices about the subjects or routes they wish to pursue beyond the age of 14 at some midpoint in what is normally their third year at secondary school. As we have seen, something like a third choose to continue their study of history to GCSE (Harris and Haydn 2008). This figure is highly variable; in some schools the figure is well over 60 per cent and in others it is below 10 per cent (Historical Association 2010). History teachers themselves differ in their view of the figure. Some argue that GCSE history is extremely difficult and that it is unfair to lower attaining pupils to put them through an examination course on which they are likely to struggle; one teacher in an outer London school said to us that 'we don't say "no" to any student at GCSE, but we think management guide some pupils to other courses, so we don't see them'. A teacher in the same school said 'We have not been given any E or F pupils since last year...some pupils are only offered integrated humanities or vocational courses.' A teacher in the 2010 Historical Association survey saw the development of vocational, diploma courses as a serious threat to the attractiveness of history to lower attaining pupils: 'History was very popular among the weaker pupils who are now not able to take it. They are increasingly encouraged into vocational streams' (Historical Association 2010b: 23). The overall educational logic for an options-based post-14 system is that it should allow pupils to build a curriculum around their long-term aspirations, strengths and interests. The danger is that the pressure on schools to secure high levels of performance in examination, coupled with increasing vocational pressures on the 14–19 curriculum, means that some subjects – including history – become inaccessible to lower attaining pupils, removing what ought to be their entitlement to learn about the past.

Late in 2010, the new coalition government made a potentially decisive intervention in the post-14 curriculum, by defining some GCSE subjects as an 'English

Baccalaureat'. The 'E-bacc' was to be awarded to pupils who secured GCSE grades at C or better in English, mathematics, science, a language and either history or geography. For history *teachers* the development of the E-bacc appeared to secure a position in the post-14 curriculum, defining the subject as a part of an academic core. For *pupils* the impact is more difficult to predict. It appears that one motivation underlying the E-bacc was to redefine expectations around the central academic purposes of the post-14 curriculum, but it is equally likely that the E-bacc will be used to distinguish between those pupils deemed able to cope with an intensively academic curriculum and those less able to do so.

In discussions with pupils in schools we detected a certain pragmatism among many pupils in discussing their future choices – particularly from those placed in lower attaining sets. Different forces are at play in their responses (see Box 4.3): there is an understandable, if in some cases naive and under-informed sense, that GCSE choices are connected to the demands of the employment market, coupled with a sense that the pupils should choose subjects they are good at for largely instrumental reasons – they are less likely to do badly – and, underpinning both, a reminder that they might also be influenced by their enjoyment of a particular subject. There is a complex relationship between liking and being good at a subject: in general most pupils are uncomfortable with subjects they find difficult but being good at something does not necessarily mean that the pupil likes it. It is difficult to generalize from the evidence

---

Box 4.3 12-year-old pupils discuss the subject choices they face in school

Interviewer: Next year in Year 9 you've got to make options. Do you know what you want to do?

Girl 1: PE, drama and music.

Interviewer: Would anyone choose history?

All: No.

Girl 2: …maybe.

Boy 1: If it helps you in the army – yes.

Interviewer: When it comes to the two options you've got to choose will you choose things you like or things you're good at or things that are useful for a job?

All: Useful for a job.

Interviewer: What about you [2]?

Boy 2: Good at – 'cos then I won't fail it.

(Another girl also said 'good at')

Interviewer: So none of you are saying that you would choose things you enjoy? Or are the things that you are good at the things that you enjoy?

All: Yes.

we have available, but there is some concern that the position of history in the post-14 curriculum is increasingly fragile as options choices, and pupils' own expectations, are geared to 'sorting' pupils into academic and non-academic choice routes.

History at Key Stage 3 may frequently be highly enjoyable, but for some pupils, the demands of GCSE are forbidding. In a school that used group work extensively and successfully in Year 9, a pupil's reaction to history in Year 10 was 'It's not like last year – we do more writing and less discussion'. Another girl said that she was 'not enjoying it as much as I thought' and others felt the same even though they recognized that the teacher had to adopt a more strategic approach because of the examination demands of the course. In this school, the head of history felt that there were constraints on the way he could teach the subject at GCSE, but the tension between the pressures he experienced and the perceptions of pupils was clear. Of course, there is ample counter-evidence; the evidence of Ofsted inspections and GCSE results is that history post-14 is successfully taught to those who opt for it, particularly to those who experience examination success. The point here is different: the gap between teachers' experiences of teaching the subject and pupils' experiences of learning it is critical, and can only be closed by listening hard to pupils about their experiences.

Learning from listening to pupils

McIntyre and his colleagues noted that 'pupils who have experienced most success in school learning tend to be the most articulate about what helps them to learn. Those from whom teachers most need to hear are those whom it will be most difficult to consult' (McIntyre *et al.* 2005:167). There is a powerful message here for history teachers about their relationship with pupils. The scattered and perhaps unrepresentative voices we have drawn on suggest that the messages from pupils become more comfortable and 'easier' to hear as we deal with pupils who are older and academically successful; the voices which are most difficult and challenging to listen to are those who find their engagement with school learning the most challenging and difficult. The 'uncomfortable' learning for history teachers may focus specifically on those pupils who need to be engaged and enthused with their Key Stage 3 history if they are to consider the subject beyond 14, and those for whom GCSE is a struggle. The challenge for history teachers if they want to realize the potential of pupil voice is to ensure that all pupils are consulted and all are heard. It is easy to focus on the higher attainers, yet at KS3 all pupils should have the entitlement of studying history in ways that enable them to enjoy and gain from it.

During our visits we did find examples of history teachers consulting pupils and acting on this consultation. In one school pupil consultation led to a rethink of how the school dealt with the local history of migration to the town as pupils said that the only images of black people in the history curriculum were those of slaves (Sheldrake and Banham 2007). History teachers worked with the local Afro-Caribbean community to produce a DVD detailing their early experiences of moving to and living in the town. These resources were used in the classroom and pupils saw local people talk about their experiences. These examples of pupils contributing to their own history curriculum to produce units of work that acknowledge local contexts and the people who live there suggest that 'pupil voice' is a route to exploring what pupils want and how it might be achieved.

5

What do we know about pupils' understanding of history?

In this chapter we explore challenges that learning history presents for pupils in some way or another. In doing so, we remain faithful to our belief that any child can learn 'good' history, based in part on our experiences of observing and meeting teachers who make history an engaging, challenging but also accessible and attainable subject in school, and on our own classroom experience. There is a perception that pupils find history difficult. To some extent, this is to be celebrated: without challenge, history would lack engagement and meaning and its role in the school curriculum would be less valuable, though we acknowledge that for some pupils history can seem prohibitively difficult. Clearly, the more teachers understand about what makes history difficult, the more they can plan to address this in the classroom. We suggest that pupils bring with them their own knowledge and interests that need to be explicitly recognized and built upon.

Understanding substantive knowledge

Box 5.1 16-year-old history pupils discuss the difficulty of history

---

Interviewer: People say that history is difficult – is history difficult?

Mary: I find it quite difficult. It's not just looking back over the facts, you have to interpret them and always provide evidence for your opinion – like why something happened or what the most important consequence of something was. So it's not just the pure history – you have to put your own spin on it. It can be quite difficult to look at sources and use them to come to a conclusion. It's quite a difficult skill I think.

Joanne: I think it's hard because history is ongoing. One of the topics we did was the Arab–Israeli conflict and our teacher would say 'Did you see this in the news?' We looked at the bombings in America and she covered the bit after that and you can see how that links on to where we are today. I think that was quite mind-blowing: we looked at the origins and you can see how it has developed and it is still going on

> today. And I think that what's hard to grasp about history is that it is so much bigger than you and it has formed how we are today and even looking back at, say, how parliament used to be, it is difficult to get your head round.

We are often told that 'kids don't know history' (Wineburg 2000: 307) and that many young people are leaving school not only with very little historical knowledge but with little understanding of how to apply what they do know to the world around them: in short, that they have very little 'substantive' or content knowledge of history. For example, a Conservative Party conference delegate complained that there is no specific reference to Winston Churchill in the history national curriculum (Gove 2009) and the American history education academic Sam Wineburg found that more than a third of Texan teenagers could not identify the year of the US Declaration of Independence (Wineburg 2000). What is less clear is what 'knowing history' means for learners – or, indeed, for adults. Although, as Chapter 1 explores, knowing and understanding history is about more than knowing the 'facts' or the 'story', for some commentators it means this alone, because this is their conception of what history is, because it suits their purpose to see history as a relatively unproblematic narrative or because they believe pupils in schools are too young to handle anything else. Mary, quoted above, believes in the existence of 'pure history', which is denied her in the classroom. Substantive knowledge is important, though the extent to which it can ever be 'pure' is highly doubtful for reasons explored in Section 1. Nevertheless, knowledge of the past is a central part of what it means to 'know history'. Here, we use the term substantive knowledge to refer to the 'substance' or content of history and to differentiate it from knowledge about the process or discipline of history. Some subjects – mathematics, physics – have a clearly hierarchic structure, in which more complex material depends on the acquisition of simpler concepts. It may be that some historical topics are *intrinsically* more challenging than others, though the underlying challenges of 'good history' remain the same. Nevertheless, it is likely that 13-year-olds will understand the complexities of the wars of the Spanish Succession less well than the causes and consequences of the Great Fire of London because of the differences of scale and complexity in the two. In addition to the intrinsic cognitive challenge of some topics, there are questions of emotional engagement: studying the Holocaust is challenging at any age, but the possibilities of developing understanding of the enormity of the issues must surely decrease the younger the pupils are. Joanne, above, puts this very well when she said that 'history is so much bigger than you' and that it is 'mind-blowing'. She understands that a crucial skill of the historian is to see temporal and spatial connections in the past, including links between the past and the present. To do this well, extraordinary breadth of knowledge of both the past and of current affairs is required, and at 18 this must seem beyond reach. Shemilt believes that this should not restrict our ambition, however:

> What has not been attempted in Britain is to teach pupils how to handle the past as a whole. In consequence, few 15-year-olds are able to map the past; even fewer can offer a coherent narrative; and virtually none can conceive of anything more subtle than a single 'best' narrative.
>
> (Shemilt 2000: 86)

Shemilt likens pupils in history classrooms to children who have never watched a cinematic film but are expected to understand a particular film from brief and disconnected trailer clips – that they can understand each clip but not the film's narrative and its purpose, or 'the bigger picture'. He goes on to argue that the problem is not so much failure to understand bits of content in isolation as failure to conceive of 'event space' in ways that allow them to 'construe each part in relation to the whole and the whole as more than the sum of the parts' (Shemilt 2000: 86).

There is evidence that some pupils do have a big picture understanding of the past. The Usable Historical Pasts project asked 15-year-old pupils to write an account of British history over the last 2000 years. The results suggested that

> a significant number of pupils seem to be limited to providing an account of British history in the form of a list of undifferentiated topics, events, famous people and colligations sometimes in chronological order and sometimes not. Among these pupils there is no evidence of a coherent narrative and the topics seem to reflect the discrete and unconnected history taught at Key Stage 3 and at GCSE, such as the Normans, Medieval Times, Tudors and Stuarts, Industrial Revolution, Black People of the Americas, World I, World War II, Cold war and the Nazis.
>
> (Howson 2007)

One tentative finding of the project was that the more pupils were able to stand back and consider the longer term changes and developments of British history, the more they were able to draw on this knowledge to inform current and future issues – for example when speculating on whether or not the USA would always be the most powerful country in the world (Foster *et al.* 2008). Shemilt insists that this is a teaching issue: pupils are unable to see the bigger picture if they are not helped to do so by the way the curriculum is structured and taught (Shemilt 2009). It is also a learning issue: the full scale of history is 'mind-blowing'. While it is desirable for pupils to gain some kind of overview or big picture of the past, this may pose enormous challenges to pupils struggling with fairly basic notions about what history is or failing to be engaged by it.

Wineburg argues that assessment of what pupils know often focuses on what we *want* them to know rather than what they actually do know and that, consequently, insufficient account is taken of what they bring into the classroom with them. There is a growing body of research to suggest that preconceptions are extremely powerful in determining what the pupils will take with them from a lesson (see, for example, Donovan and Bransford 2005). These preconceptions range from children's understanding of the 'way the world works and how people are likely to behave' (Lee 2005: 31) to substantive knowledge that pupils have amassed at home or elsewhere. We know that pupils are 'consumers' of the past; they come into school with historical knowledge gained from a range of sources such as previous learning in primary school, TV, the media, books, films, museums, and from encounters with those in their families or in their local communities (Phillips 1998). By failing to connect with the history they learn outside the classroom, history taught in school may be rejected and alternative narratives constructed (Barton and McCully 2005; Traille 2007; Epstein 2009). We return to many of these issues in Chapter 10.

Understanding history as a discipline

As we have seen in Part 1, history in schools is about more than substantive knowledge. As Slater once described it, there is a 'crucial distinction between knowing the past and thinking historically' (Slater 1989: 15), which echoes the distinction drawn in Chapter 1 between lower case history and upper case History. Thinking historically means being able to analyse sources from the past in ways that take account of the context in which they were produced; it means being able to select critically from these sources in order to construct some kind of account and it means understanding the status and limitations of such accounts. This requires pupils to think in ways quite unlike their other subjects. It means setting aside common-sense understanding and acquiring a different, more counterintuitive mindset. In this section we consider four dimensions of historical thinking: understanding the nature of evidence and, particularly, that truth and certainty are unavailable; understanding that people in the past were not like us; understanding about change over time and, finally, understanding historical interpretations.

The nature of historical evidence and lack of certainty

The work of Denis Shemilt has made a significant contribution to our understanding of how pupils view evidence in history (see, for example, Shemilt 1987). Shemilt argues that pupils who have a limited understanding of the role of evidence in history may suppose that history is simply about uncontested facts which are there to be discovered. They may draw no distinction between the information provided in a textbook and the evidence found in primary sources and indeed may never question how we know about the past. A more sophisticated understanding recognizes that history is constructed from evidence but may have a very limited view of the forms evidence takes and assume that all evidence is some kind of testimony, written with the express purpose of leaving evidence for later generations to discover and therefore likely to be inherently biased and unreliable. This makes it difficult to construct historical accounts because the historian is engaged in an – ultimately impossible – search for truth. At the higher levels of understanding in Shemilt's model, pupils understand that it is necessary to infer from sources and that the evidence that can be gleaned may not be obvious on first inspection. They understand that not all evidence is testimonial but rather that much of it is simply left with no view of posterity. Pupils working at the most sophisticated level will abandon altogether the notion that historians can attain some kind of truth and instead settle for history as a reconstruction. Put more simply, pupils' understanding of what constitutes history ranges from seeing history as a given, to something which needs to be discovered, to something that needs to be worked out and, finally, to something that is a potentially flawed reconstruction.

Thus, depending on the nature of pupils' misconceptions, it is possible that they might entirely fail to grasp what history is, how we come to know about it or why we should study it at all if it is irrecoverable. In one school we visited, the Head of Department explained that a key problem she encounters is that the pupils do not think history is real but is in fact entirely fictional. The following exchange with a mixed group of Year 8 pupils, all from a 'bottom set' in history (determined by their literacy and language achievements), demonstrated uncertainty about *what* to write and *how* to answer; it was not just the act of writing itself that was difficult for them.

Box 5.2 Discussion with Year 8 pupils from a low-attaining set

Interviewer: So do you have to be clever to do history?

All: No.

Girl 1: Otherwise we wouldn't be doing it would we?

Girl 2: But we're in sets.

Girl 1: Some of it's hard but some of it's really easy.

Boy 1: But I only like a little bit of it – I only like it when you colour and watch films.

Interviewer: Someone said they liked doing pictures but not writing – is history hard because of the writing?

All: Yes.

Girl 3: There's loads of writing.

Girl 2: And sometimes we have to figure it out for ourselves.

Boy 2: …what to write and everything… And it gets a bit hard – I can't really do it.

Interviewer: Does that mean you don't have to do that much for yourselves in other lessons?

Boy 1: But it's harder [in history] because we don't know much about it.   ·

Girl 2: It's probably the hardest lesson we do.

Boy 1: Because in maths you've got more stuff to work it out. In history it's harder because you've got nothing to work it out with.

Interviewer: Do you mean rules and stuff?

Boy 1: Yes, it's easy.

Interviewer: So are you better at maths?

Girl 1: History can be right hard because you don't know about the past. They don't really tell us a lot about it so we're sometimes stuck.

According to these pupils, history is hard because it requires 'figuring it out for themselves' without formulae that can provide 'the answer'. The lack of certainty frustrates pupils and they struggle with notions of what is 'true' and what is not, particularly when different pieces of evidence are contradictory. This may be because most school subjects are based around certainty. In science, for example, when the science experiment does not produce the expected result, pupils are often asked to record what should have happened rather than what did happen because the latter requires a more difficult explanation about why the results were as they were. History does not offer pupils such certainties. Chapter 6 offers further reflections about a series of 'myths' or misconceptions that pupils hold about evidence and some possible strategies with which to address them.

Understanding that people in the past were not like us

A further challenge for pupils is how to interpret events and actions in the past using a different frame of reference from the one used in the present. 'The past is another country – they do things differently there' (Hartley 1953) is a constant refrain within the history literature and pupils can find it difficult to empathize with people holding different sets of beliefs, values and attitudes. Michaela, in Box 5.3, is unusually insightful about the nature of the challenge and believes that her young age is part of the problem, echoing her peer in Box 5.2 who thought that not knowing enough was the major problem. To 'put yourself into the mindset' of people in the past, you cannot make assumptions about what is relevant – you have to 'take it all into account' (see Box 5.3). To make matters worse, for pupils, this also means trying to empathize with adults in the past when they find it challenging to empathize with adults in the present (Husbands and Pendry 2000). As a consequence of these and other challenges, they often fall back on a deficit view of people in the past who were somehow 'less developed' or more 'stupid' than we are (Lee and Ashby 1987). Where they do attempt some kind of empathy, it is often very stereotypical (he was a king, so he must have thought that) and generalized (all Germans were Nazis). Moving pupils on from these simplistic views is not always easy: trying to understand what made someone a Nazi is already challenging for some; understanding that there were different degrees to which some Germans were truly 'Nazi' and that the response of the German people to Hitler was actually highly nuanced and complex is very challenging indeed.

Box 5.3 Michaela thinks about the challenges of history

Interviewer: People say that history is difficult – is history difficult?

Michaela: Yes, I think especially with us being so young. In history, when it gets to A level you have to put yourself in the mindset of the group that you're studying, like the economy and religion and stuff – their point of view on it is completely different to how we're experiencing it in the modern day. And being so young, I personally find it hard to see how other people would see it; you have to consider everything even if it doesn't seem relevant. You have to take it all into account and I find that hard because I'm not used to doing it.

Change over time

One of the teachers we spoke to finds that her pupils have difficulty with chronology and, in particular, a sense of scale and how one period relates to another. This is a common problem and in part is perhaps the inevitable result again of simply not knowing enough. A particular aspect of time that poses challenges for pupils regards change over time. Pupils often equate change with events, assuming that what changed is the same as what happened, rather than understanding that there are different kinds of changes (slow, rapid, political, economic, concurrent, enduring and so forth) and that change has to be seen in a broad context in order to be understood (e.g. see Lee 2005). Pupils can also be reluctant to give continuity the same degree of attention as change: if nothing changed, why bother finding out why? Other research suggests that pupils often equate change with progress, which results from their general view that life is getting better (Barton 2008).

Understanding historical interpretations

Many of the problems that pupils encounter with evidence recur when grappling with secondary interpretations of the past produced by historians and others. If pupils believe there to be some kind of fixed past then both evidence and the accounts crafted from it are deeply problematic. Indeed, the job of the historian becomes virtually impossible if pupils hold firm to the view that there is only one possible 'version' of the past but, to access that, you need the views of eye-witnesses. Even then, problems persist, because the evidence that eye-witnesses leave behind is not consistent so the only possible route to 'truth' is if you were there yourself, which is, of course, impossible. When attention shifts to the 'interpreter', pupils frequently attempt to behave as a 'neutral' historian, focusing their attention on finding the 'bias' that would fatally undermine an account. The major breakthrough in pupil understanding will only happen when pupils accept that there are valid reasons why accounts differ because the kinds of things that historians are generally interested in are not the kinds of things where consensus is possible. Being there is no help when analysing the rise and fall of a nation or the increasing or decreasing popularity of a government, for example. Following on from that, pupils need to understand that accounts of the past cannot be *copies* of that past: even accounts of a single lesson by pupils who were there will differ (Lee and Shemilt 2004).

Progression in history

The well-versed debate about the relationship between historical content and historical skills, conducted mainly in the media and never taken seriously by teachers, is now largely dead and gone. It is commonly accepted that one is entirely dependent on the other. Knowledge about the past underpins any attempts to build conceptual understanding and to engage in the processes of constructing and analysing that past. Similarly, knowledge by itself holds little meaning unless it is situated within some kind of analytic framework and the nature and origin of that knowledge remains a mystery without some conceptual understanding of where it comes from and how it is constructed. Although assessment rarely addresses knowledge directly, it is clear that progression in history is determined by an understanding of history's key concepts and processes supported by sufficient contextual knowledge (Counsell and the Historical Association 1997). The reverse may also be true – that an understanding of second-order concepts can help pupils make sense of the topics they study (Lee 2005).

There are a number of progression models available to teachers in history. The most common is that set out in the national curriculum Attainment Target which deploys generalized statements to describe the overall level of achievement of a pupil at the end of a key stage. Due to internal assessment requirements in schools, many departments are forced to use the Attainment Target to 'level' individual pieces of work and to inform targets which will boost pupil progress. This is highly problematic for several reasons and we will discuss this further in Chapter 8. Awarding bodies write examination mark-schemes which assume models of progression on a question by question basis, but any insight into more general issues of progression must be inferred and is not explicitly explained. Finally, there are research-based, concept-specific models of progression which provide insights into the kinds of more and less sophisticated understandings pupils display when asked particular types of questions or given particular types of tasks to complete. None of the models available is perfect: the Attainment Target is a blunt instrument, providing statements at a level of generality which, while indicating the *sorts* of things pupils should be able to *do* as they make progress, give us little insight into how pupils' actual *thinking* develops. The research-based models, on the other hand, provide valuable insights into pupils' thinking about history and helpfully suggest the kinds of ideas that actively prevent them from making progress, but make no claim to indicate a sequence of learning that pupils will work through in order to make progress: they can only help us to understand where a pupil is within his or her model at any one time or, strictly speaking, in any one task.

The absence of a definitive and authoritative guide to how pupils make progress in history is no surprise and it is probably impossible to achieve due to the sheer number of variables. It is likely, for example, that the historical context itself will make a difference: how well pupils know and understand a topic will have a profound impact on how well they cope with tasks about causation or change or evidence. The task itself and the way understanding is assessed is also likely to be key, as psychologists have argued for many years (e.g. Donaldson 1978). How well a topic or a concept is taught is likely to have a considerable impact on pupil understanding. All these variables make it difficult to have confidence in any single model of pupil progression. All that can be realistically claimed is that pupils are likely to hold certain levels of understanding about history at a given point, supported by some general notion about the kinds of knowledge and understanding that need to be developed over time. Exactly *how* the pupils move from a less to a more sophisticated understanding of history is less well understood.

One thing that does seem clearer is that the awarding bodies have not got this quite right. Many of the teachers we met were frustrated by the limited opportunities within GCSE specifications to build in sufficient progress. One teacher openly stated that the best way he could prepare his pupils was by teaching them the 'formula', something he found deeply unsatisfying. The 'gobbets of information' on the examination paper were especially unpopular. Such is the seemingly dire state of GCSE that several teachers now believe that there is too great a disjunction between GCSE and A level – possibly more pronounced than in most other subjects. A discussion with a group of sixth formers at the end of their AS year indicated that history, in particular, was very different to what they expected coming out of GCSE. They felt at A level there was much more emphasis on independent study and reading whereas those studying science subjects felt that these carried on much the same as the year before. One student described the jump in history '...it feels like I've done two completely different courses because it is completely different at GCSE and now at A level because at A level they want you to analyse whereas at GCSE they want you to tell the story which at A level is just...NO!'

It is interesting to note in this context that it is generally not necessary to have studied history at GCSE in order to study it at A level, unlike in mathematics and science subjects where content was described by the pupils as more 'linear' and the need for prior knowledge and skills is more explicit. But if this is the case, it suggests that progression between Key Stage 3 and A level is primarily one of substantive rather than disciplinary knowledge which most teachers (and examiners) would reject. If progression from Key Stage 3 to 4 to 5 was more securely managed, it might be possible to argue that a GCSE in history *was* necessary in order to progress onto A level; however, it is difficult to see the current progression map for 14–19 in history as sensible for learners.

Conclusion

This chapter has explored reasons why history can be difficult for pupils and has also raised questions about how the progress of pupils' understanding can be measured and understood. The challenges of history are part of its appeal: without them, it would be less interesting, less compelling and less important. Nevertheless, history can and must be made accessible to all and this is explored in greater detail in Chapter 10. Understanding the barriers to learning about the past and taking a proactive approach to exploring pupils' preconceptions – coupled with a conviction that all pupils can and should learn about the past – are vital components of successful history teaching.

Part 3
Teaching history in schools

In this section we use the insights of the first two sections to examine the building blocks of classroom practice in history. Of course, effective practice emerges from these building blocks used together, but we introduce them separately. We begin by exploring the essence of historical enquiry and its relationship to the evidential base of the discipline, arguing – following Herodotus – that all historical understanding emerges from a process of active enquiry. In Chapter 7, we explore the other essential second-order concepts of the discipline and the way they intertwine with substantive historical knowledge to shape learners' historical understanding. In Chapter 8 we consider the way history is communicated in the classroom, exploring the way different communicative modes operate and the idea of multimodality, before moving on to assessment. In Chapter 9 we take the ideas from the three preceding chapters and explore how they can be drawn together in long-term plans. Finally, we consider the concept of inclusive practices, drawing on Part 2 and previous chapters in Part 3 to consider how the subject can be made accessible to all.

6

Evidence and enquiry in history teaching

History is enquiry: an attempt to answer specific questions about the past. Historians do this by drawing on sources of evidence, which is the foundation of all historical knowledge; it is through the relics of past societies that we have access to the past. Pupils in history classrooms also use sources, not because this enables them to behave just as historians do, but because without them, the way that history is created remains a mystery and the status and worth of the knowledge generated by historians (and others) cannot be evaluated. Throughout this chapter we argue that evidence and enquiry must go hand in hand and that without the overarching focus of an enquiry, sources of evidence are without purpose and pupils become bored and disillusioned.

What is historical enquiry and why does it have a place in our classrooms?

Strictly speaking, the term 'historical enquiry' is tautological: as we saw in Chapter 1, the first historian, Herodotus, used the term 'historia', which literally meant 'enquiry'. Enquiry, therefore, is what history *is*: attempts to answer specific questions about aspects of the past through an investigation of a range of sources. These sources are mined for relevant, reliable evidence that enables the historian to create an account about the particular aspect of the past he or she is investigating. In so far as pupils can ever get close to what historians do – and there are inevitably limitations – it is when pupils are engaged in genuine enquiry that this becomes more attainable. This is reflected in successive versions of the national curriculum which gives enquiry an increasingly central role. In early versions of the national curriculum, enquiry was linked directly to the use of historical sources, which makes sense given that enquiries require sources of evidence to investigate.

Historical enquiry, however, goes beyond the critical use of sources of evidence, and the 2007 national curriculum acknowledged this, decoupling enquiry and evidence and requiring pupils not simply to draw on evidence but also to 'identify and investigate, individually and as part of a team, specific historical questions or issues, making and testing hypotheses', and to 'reflect critically on historical questions and issues'. It is a reminder that sources of evidence are a means to an end and it is the end itself that is important: the ability to provide a credible answer to a credible question. Credible questions – and indeed answers – can mean different things to different people, but one might also say a significant question, a meaningful question, a useful or important question.

Enquiry revolves around questions. Just as Herodotus set out to answer a specific question about the Persian Empire, so pupils set out to answer questions, normally that their teacher has posed, about an aspect of the past, drawing on various sources of evidence to construct some form of answer which is substantiated. Enquiry therefore puts the pupil at the centre: this is not about the teacher imparting knowledge but about pupils finding answers for themselves under the teacher's direction and, in this sense, it fits with current notions of effective teaching and learning based largely on constructivist theories of learning. Other subjects have adopted similar enquiry models and there are particular parallels with geography where there is a move towards conceptualizing 'enquiries' as sequences of, say, four to five lessons based around a single enquiry question, which build up to a substantial outcome. A geographical enquiry has been described as a journey towards solving a puzzle or constructing an answer. A good enquiry question should have both 'pith and rigour' and 'should set up issues or challenges which can be unpacked in the enquiry sequence' (Taylor 2009). This approach is already well established among history teachers in the UK (Husbands *et al*. 2003) and the term 'an enquiry' often refers to a sequence of lessons based around a single enquiry question (Riley 2000). Box 6.1 suggests criteria for effective enquiry questions.

Box 6.1 Criteria for effective enquiry questions in history

Does the enquiry question:

· capture the interest and imagination of pupils?
· place an aspect of historical thinking, concept or process at the forefront of the pupils' minds?
· result in a tangible, lively, substantial, enjoyable 'outcome activity' (i.e. at the end of the lesson sequence) through which pupils can genuinely answer the enquiry question?

Source: Riley (2000)

The 'purest' form of historical enquiry in history classrooms is often found at A level. Variously described in exam specifications as an enquiry, a personal study, coursework or an investigation, these units all share the same characteristics: pupils identify a question and set about answering it through the use of secondary and primary sources. The extent to which the pupils' choice is a free one currently depends on the awarding body, but on the whole, there is much greater freedom for pupils to identify their own question, albeit under teacher supervision, than at earlier points in their school careers, where the questions selected by the teacher or the examiner normally dominate. This process is not entirely absent from earlier key stages, however, as the work of Burnham shows (2007).

What is evidence?

Pupils find it difficult to engage with the evidential base of history. Some pupils believe that the past itself never existed: the evidence for it lives in the present and cannot, therefore, possibly have been created in the past (Dickinson and Lee 1978). As we began to explore in Chapter 5, pupils commonly hold a series of misconceptions about historical evidence which are likely to prevent them from developing a clear understanding of the relationship between the evidence which survives and the historical past which generated it. First, however, it is helpful to be clear about terms such as source, evidence and information because confusion about the similarities and differences between them can muddy the waters for both pupils and teachers.

Imagine a lesson about children's lives in the nineteenth century. There are many potential sources of information that a teacher might draw on: him or herself, the textbook, Dickens's novel *Oliver Twist*, the film and musical *Oliver!* based on Dickens's book, testimony from children who worked in factories at the time, drawings from the time, a recent TV documentary about Victorian life and parish records. All are sources of information on which the pupil in a history classroom might legitimately draw as part of an enquiry. Some of the sources are secondary, created not by participants at the time, but by people in subsequent times who offer interpretations of the past. Some are primary, created at the time, mainly with no view to posterity but for many different purposes. At the beginning of the enquiry, pupils will need some kind of starting point, some basis from which to move forward, achieved through the exploration or presentation of factual information – information about which there is general common agreement. This may include information about dates, social class and the existence of factories and child labour, all vital contextual information that is the precursor to more sophisticated thinking. At this stage, the emphasis is on established 'fact' rather than on the nature and status of the information used. Everyone has to start somewhere: experienced historians, embarking on the study of particular archival material for the first time, need to establish what is already 'known' and accepted about the subject matter. Once this groundwork has been laid, however, it is necessary to move on from established 'fact' and towards claims that can be made about the topic. So, to return to our example, once pupils have some knowledge about time, place and context, they can start to investigate questions about the past that go beyond 'fact'. A possible question might be, for example, 'Did children have no fun in Victorian Britain?' As soon as this question becomes the driving force of the lesson, and pupils turn their attention to answering it, the sources of information at their disposal take on a new significance. Then comes a critical point: will the pupils continue to use the sources of information uncritically – in the way they used the 'facts' or background already provided – as purveyors of 'correct' or 'incorrect' answers, or will they start to use them as historians do, and explore issues of utility and reliability? Sometimes, the former happens: in order to break up the monotony of a textbook or perhaps to appear to be 'doing' sourcework with pupils, teachers might present pupils with a variety of sources, either primary or secondary, from which pupils will extract 'information' without paying attention to its nature and status. From the pupils' perspectives they are simply being asked to deal with 'text' and it matters little whether the text is a textbook, an extract from a nineteenth-century factory inspector's report or a translated sixteenth-century diplomatic letter from the Venetian ambassador: in each case, it provides 'information' and the basis of decisions to use it or discard it are not rooted in a firm understanding of the nature of historical evidence. In other classrooms, pupils will be encouraged to subject the sources of evidence to proper critical scrutiny: is it *relevant* to the question and therefore *useful*? Does it provide *reliable* evidence to support my answer? How does it *compare* with the other evidence I have analysed? How *firmly* does the evidence support my answer? Following such treatment, pupils will then make decisions about what *evidence* to draw from the sources in order to support an argument or claim. In this case, for example, pupils may discard some of the contemporary drawings of factory life on the basis of who drew them and why, whereas they may draw heavily on parish records about child mortality. In other words, they may understand that sources tell us things about the past that may not be immediately apparent: the drawings should not be taken at face value as unproblematic 'information' about the past. The local records do not 'tell' us anything at all: they are simply a basis for inference.

Box 6.2 Common myths held by pupils about sources of evidence in history

Myth 1: Primary sources are more reliable than secondary sources

Obviously this is untrue, but it is a myth commonly held by pupils. Primary sources were created for many reasons and some of these reasons had nothing to do with objectivity. For example, consider a political speech from the nineteenth century, crafted to put forward a very particular perspective. A secondary source on the same period at least aspires – one hopes – to a certain level of objectivity and will be based on more than one primary source. The answer is that we have to be careful how we use all sources, primary and secondary. The key point is that we must consult multiple sources.

Myth 2: All sources are either 'primary' or 'secondary'

Because the primary or secondary nature of a source is not a property of the source itself, but is established only when we know what the source is being used for, it follows that whether a source is classified as 'primary' or 'secondary' derives from its place in a particular enquiry. All sources are primary for something or other (a school history textbook published this year is a primary source for anyone studying history education today). Furthermore, some sources defy categorization. Consider a TV documentary about World War II containing original film footage. It might be worth abandoning the terms 'primary' and 'secondary' in the classroom because they serve little practical purpose and serve only to strengthen pupils' misconceptions.

Myth 3: Primary sources are biased and this makes them useless as evidence

This myth is based on the mistaken view that all primary sources are a form of witting testimony. In fact, there are many different kinds of primary sources, and many were not created in order to advance any kind of view or argument – for example, census records, wills, physical artefacts.

Myth 4: Historians spend much of their time evaluating the reliability of sources (mainly in order to fish out the unreliable source and discard it)

This myth is perhaps the most significant. Are we asking pupils to evaluate sources in the belief that this turns them into historians? In fact, historians spend relatively little time evaluating sources for bias. There are a number of reasons for this:

- Many sources are not biased in the sense of a deliberate attempt to put forward a particular viewpoint (see Myth 3, above).
- Even where bias may exist, it may be irrelevant to the historian who is perhaps more interested in the very existence of the source in the first place.
- Historians may be interested in a source precisely because of its bias.

Myth 5: It is possible to build up an understanding of the past through primary sources alone

In a nutshell, we all have to start somewhere and for most of the time, that means secondary sources. How can we make sense of primary sources without a reasonably secure knowledge and understanding of the period and topic under scrutiny? For many pupils, of course, the first secondary source they encounter on a given topic is the teacher.

Myth 6: It is pointless trying to answer questions about the past because only people who were there know for sure (Lee 2005)

The biggest flaw here is the assumption that it might be possible for people in the past to agree on what happened. Not only are different people likely to disagree even about fairly basic matters, such as what they saw happen, but historians are generally interested in the sorts of things that a single person at the time would have difficulty answering, such as the long-term changes to religion or the complex causes of a revolution.

Source: Based on Barton (2005) and modified by Kitson (2008)

These are important points because it is only when pupils begin to use sources to find evidence for something specific that the sources really begin to matter and the task in hand becomes worthwhile and challenging. Pupils who routinely use sources outside the scope of a challenging historical question are destined never fully to understand what evidence *is*, for it is only when sources are mined for evidence to answer a particular question that 'proper' use of 'disciplinary' history is made (Wineburg 2007). Denis Shemilt found, early in the School History Project's life, that pupils found it difficult to 'distinguish between information provided in the main text of a book and sources included within the book: both were seen as identical quarries of undisputed facts about the past' (Shemilt 1980, quoted in McAleavy 1998: 12). This may, in part, be a by-product of the layout of modern history textbooks, where sources intersperse the text, often in a double page format. It is fairly easy to spot lessons in which source material is being used uncritically as more (unproblematic) 'information': either the provenance of the source is not provided or it is irrelevant, usually because the sources are not being used in the context of an enquiry.

From the pupils' perspective, what helps them to evaluate sources effectively? Pickles (2010) has explored the relationship between the way pupils handle sources, the strength of their contextual knowledge, their understanding of the nature of evidence and their ability to think empathically about the context in which the source was produced. She concludes that the expertise with which pupils handle sources exceeds their application of routine 'source skills' – where pupils ask questions about provenance, reliability and usefulness – and includes, for example, prior knowledge and a *conceptual* understanding of the nature of evidence in history. In a similar vein, Wineburg has provided useful insights into the ways historians 'read' historical sources and how this is dominated by the deployment of their contextual knowledge (Wineburg 2007). Without this contextual knowledge pupils may struggle to go much beyond an uncritical consumption of historical sources as information.

Why use evidence in history classrooms?

As we have seen, an enquiry-based approach to learning history helps pupils to be active in the construction of knowledge and to understand the way history is 'made' through the use of evidence to support claims. Without experience and understanding of the nature of historical evidence, history becomes a set of mysterious assertions to be learned by heart and 'rote-learned history can serve only the interests of quiz contestants' (Fines 1994: 125). Using evidence *in the context of an enquiry* therefore achieves two major aims simultaneously: it affords pupils an insight into what history *is* and it also enables them to play an active role in the learning process and the construction of knowledge. At the very least, 'school pupils' historical knowledge ought to rest on an open tradition of enquiry that enables them to understand the nature and status of the knowledge they acquire' (Ashby, quoted in Howson 2007).

As we began to explore in Chapter 2, history teachers frequently find themselves having to defend history's place in the curriculum and the skills required in the critical use of sources seem to hold out the possibility that history provides pupils with genuine 'life skills': to be able to judge when something is worth serious consideration, and to do other than take things at face value, are tremendously useful skills for young and, indeed, not so young adults. Keatinge, in 1910, insisted that the development of critical faculties through problem-solving work could play an important role in the moral development of young people and regarded historical skills and ways of thinking as highly transferable (McAleavy 1998). Wineburg summarizes one of history's key roles well when he writes:

> In a world dominated by emotional appeals, quotations ripped out of context, incendiary language and journalistic analyses that aim at extinguishing sobriety rather than cultivating it, the role of such *unnatural* historical thinking has never seemed more imperative.
>
> (Wineburg 2007:11)

The extent to which evidence is used in unique ways is an interesting question, however. Wineburg's claims about historical thinking may well be applicable elsewhere in the curriculum. Certainly, evidence is used in subjects such as science, geography and English frequently and insufficient work has been done on the similarities and differences in the way pupils are expected to work with it in these different contexts.

In science, for example, a key difference (compared to history) is that pupils create their own evidence (or 'data') and this is tightly controlled by the teacher; in practice, explicit considerations of reliability rarely appear much before A level. Thus in science, evidence is something that can be created and that brings with it a level of certainty – at least at Key Stage 3 – that history could not. In English and history classrooms, the same poem, novel, play or film might be used – but potentially quite differently. Clearly, then, concepts of evidence exist across the curriculum and there will be some critical examination of it in subjects other than history. The precise way that pupils think about evidence in history, however, is likely to be quite particular, as is the sheer range of different types of evidence potentially found in history classrooms.

Using evidence in the context of historical enquiries

Where it's gone wrong

Although the use of evidence in classrooms was intended, at least in part, to enliven the study of history, this has not always been the case. Assessment practices at Key Stage 4 and A level have not always encouraged the sensitive use of evidence. Given that evidence needs to be used within the context of an enquiry to give it meaning, the possibilities of assessing pupils' understanding about the nature of historical evidence in formal examinations and single 'one-off' exercises are limited. Instead, examination questions about evidence have often been formulaic, with an emphasis on superficial judgements about reliability and utility, the brutal shortening of sources – making it harder to make meaning of them than it would be with a more lengthy extract – and inadequate background information on either the topic or the provenance of the source. As McAleavy laments, 'Do historians in reality spend most of their time agonizing over bias, reliability and the provisional nature of their findings?' (McAleavy 1998:13). Although the pressure of the final examination does not exist at Key Stage 3, similar problems can arise, not helped by the simplistic notion of progression contained within the national curriculum Attainment Target. 'Sourcework' has often become an end in itself, rather than as a means of grappling with a real historical issue and reaching independent conclusions. Faced with questions which explore what sources *cannot* tell you rather than opportunities to use evidence properly in order to extract what they can, pupils can become understandably cynical (Byrom 1998). News of the problem reached across the Atlantic and one American academic has written that 'British history educators even have a name for this practice: "Death by sources"' (Barton 2005).

When it goes right...

Despite this, there are ample grounds to believe that the effective use of evidence in history lessons is not only possible but realizable in practice; indeed, from the evidence of classroom success it is possible to identify four circumstances in which evidence makes a critical contribution to pupils' understanding of the past.

Using evidence in history lessons is likely to be most successful if the following criteria are met.

Sources are used to answer meaningful questions about the past

As this chapter has already explored, sources and the evidence drawn from them are of little use outside an enquiry question. Without an overall question, smaller questions about reliability and utility are fruitless. Some enquiries might shine a spotlight onto the nature of evidence in history (see Box 6.3) while others may focus on other aspects of history such as change and continuity but still involve extensive and critical use of sources. Others still may not involve much engagement with primary or secondary sources at all – an enquiry on the causes of World War I in Year 9, for example, might depend more heavily on factual information which is then organized into different shapes and patterns by the pupils in order to craft a causal explanation.

Box 6.3 Enquiry questions that focus firmly on the nature of evidence in history

- What can...tell us about...? e.g. What can a town's buildings tell us about Victorian minds?
- Can we be sure that...? e.g. Can we be sure that Guy Fawkes was guilty?
- Why is it difficult to tell...? e.g. Why is it difficult to tell if there was a 'Blitz spirit'? (Counsell 2000b)
- How much can...tell us about...? e.g. How much can the Bayeux Tapestry tell us about the Battle of Hastings?

Source: Kitson (2008)

Sources are placed (carefully) into context

Teachers face two dilemmas about the historical context of sources. Too much contextual information limits the possibilities of sources being 'squeezed' for evidence because pupils feel they already know all there is to know and are less likely to hunt for new information or viewpoints, while too little contextual information provides an insufficient basis for making judgements about sources' value, in which case pupils resort to essentially formulaic responses. It seems likely that there is a relationship between a pupil's skill at handling sources effectively and his or her contextual knowledge (see Counsell 2000b and Pickles 2010) but the precise point at which contextual information should be introduced varies according to teachers' aims. Thus, in a lesson sequence on the Kingdom of Benin, it might be highly effective to ask pupils to draw conclusions about what they know *for sure* about life in Benin and what they can *infer* on the basis of a series of objects, or pictures of these objects, such as the Benin bronzes. This activity would have no meaning if the pupils already knew about life in Benin. In this case, the contextual knowledge emerges from the artefacts and is fleshed out by subsequent activities which involve analysing how historians describe life in pre-colonial Benin; indeed, in this case, pupils are modelling the activities of early investigators who themselves had little contextual knowledge about Benin. More typically, however, pupils are provided with contextual or background information before they begin to interrogate historical sources.

The second dilemma is that, by providing too much contextual knowledge, the teacher may not only be limiting the use that pupils might make of a source, but may also be unwittingly exacerbating a misunderstanding that the truth is out there and the sources are just a distraction from all those right answers that the teacher/textbook/TV documentary can provide.

Evidence is used to construct accounts of the past

The best way of helping pupils to understand this is to give them experience of creating their own historical accounts from a range of sources. This is, after all, what the national curriculum requires teachers to do. Too often, the final stage of using evidence to create a meaningful outcome is omitted. This was the point made by Byrom (1998) when he outlined an activity in which pupils had to *resolve* contradictions and discrepancies across a range of sources about the Peasants' Revolt by producing their own, 'best fit' account. The activity was made accessible by ensuring the pupils had sufficient background knowledge – provided by a TV documentary – and by making it clear which source was regarded as the most reliable by historians. Thus, some of the groundwork was already done for the Year 7 class and they then set about spotting the differences between the sources and using a variety of analytic tools – cross referencing, exploring the provenance of the sources, comparing them to what they already know – in order to produce their own account. The point here was to enable the pupils to experience a sense of achievement by creating an end product, where considerations of bias were a means to an end and not the end itself. What makes this activity so effective is that pupils are being *constructive* and regarding the sources as a solution rather than a problem (McAleavy 1998).

Local history can provide rich resources in this context. The potential for pupils to identify a question, to locate a variety of historical sources – often in their original form – and to create their own accounts is considerable. In an edition of *Teaching History* dedicated to 'Local Voices', McFahn, Herrity and Bates each describe a local enquiry in which pupils explore what caused the Swing Riots in Hampshire through the case of the Mason brothers and local court records, consider how typical Eastleigh was as a railway town using evidence from Hampshire County Record Office and reconstruct Iron Age life using their own school grounds as evidence. There is something about the rawness of local history sources, the lack of previous historical study (and therefore consensus) and the geographical immediacy that makes local history ripe for wonderful evidence-based work (McFahn *et al.* 2009).

Evidence is used to challenge, engage and delight

Sources in history come in many forms and the installation of projectors, computers and interactive whiteboards has greatly increased the ease with which teachers can explore a range of sources with pupils, including pictures, film clips and audio recordings. Despite this, a sense persists that the 'proper' work of the historian begins when the written sources are consulted.

One reason for this is that written evidence is the most prized by historians and there is a vast quantity of it. It is easy to obtain and relatively easy to use in the classroom. It is also easy to incorporate into examination papers and textbooks (often written by the same people). While it is understandable – and indeed desirable – that written sources be used extensively in classrooms, it is regrettable that a richer variety of sources is not always used more fully. The pages of *Teaching History* are replete with accounts of the use of a wide range of source material, including music (e.g. Sweerts and Grice 2002, Mastin 2002 and Butler 2003), pictures (e.g. Card 2004), oral history (e.g. Edwards 2006, Johansen and Spafford 2009) and the local environment (e.g. McFahn *et al.* 2009). Interestingly (and somewhat disappointingly), there is relatively little written about the use of objects in secondary history teaching, as it is more common at the primary stage.

Conclusion

A process of enquiry lies at the heart of what it means to 'do history' and evidence, if it is to be used effectively in classrooms, must be related very directly to enquiry questions. To understand the nature of evidence in history is to understand the nature of history itself and pupils need careful support to achieve this. Some of the most vibrant, engaging work in history classrooms in recent years can be found in Key Stage 3 classrooms where, free from the constraints of public examinations, teachers have devised challenging, intriguing enquiry questions which focus on particular historical concepts and which involve pupil investigation to answer. One of the biggest challenges facing history education currently is how to build these approaches more successfully beyond Key Stage 3 in ways that also support rigorous and consistent assessment.

7

The key concepts of history teaching

What are history's key concepts and why do they matter?

Academic and popular history deals mainly with the substance of the past – content, arranged according to the historian's perspective and interpretation. Historians rarely write about the limitation of the evidence they use, nor do they frequently reflect in their prose on the nature of causation or change in abstract ways (Lee 2005). The history that they write, however, is underpinned by their understanding of these ideas – evidence and its relationship to accounts, causation and notions of underlying causes and triggers, and change over time with accompanying notions of continuity, regress, progress, fast change and slow change. These key concepts – also known as second-order or procedural concepts – provide the foundation of history: the framework or structure around or through which history is constructed. Without these concepts, history lacks disciplinary rigour and becomes a story without shape, structure and the constraint of accepted procedures. By working within them, (most) historians sign up to an agreed way of working.

Box 7.1 Extract from *Rough Crossings*

Ten years after the surrender of George III's army to General Washington at Yorktown, British Freedom was hanging on in North America. Along with a few hundred other souls – Scipio Yearman, Phoebe Barrett, Jeremiah Piggie and Smart Feller among them – he was scratching a living from the stingy soil around Preston, a few miles northeast of Halifax, Nova Scotia. Like most of the Preston people, British Freedom was black and had come from a warmer place. Now he was a hardscrabbler stuck in a wind-whipped corner of the world between the blue spruce forest and the sea. But he was luckier than most...What were they doing there? Not just surviving. British Freedom and the rest of the villagers were clinging to more than a scrap of Nova Scotia; they were clinging to a promise.

Source: Schama (2005)

The extract in Box 7.1, from *Rough Crossings* (Schama 2005), reads like a story and, indeed, the historian Simon Schama deploys lyrical language to create atmosphere. But this is not a story in the conventional sense; it is disciplinary history. The first clue comes at the end of the second sentence, where a footnote leads us to information about Schama's evidential base, in this case a manuscript copy of Clarkson's journal. The link to evidence is made clear, but Schama does not expound the reliability or otherwise of this source; we take it on trust that he has deployed critical tools in the analysis of his documents and that he has taken note of anything within the sources that need especially careful treatment. The extract also provides a clue about the focus of the book: this is not just the story of a man, it is an account of how he came to be in North America. We infer, at this stage, that the book is going to be about slavery, about those who achieved freedom and the reasons that lay behind their journeys: it is going to deal in some way or other with causation. We also know that this account is going to trace a period of time, possibly quite a lengthy one, and that Schama is more than likely going to deal with change and probably continuity too. Finally, we can see Schama's efforts to understand the people about whom he writes: his awareness of contrasting climates, for example, and the evocative description of the location suggest a willingness to enter a different world which, we suspect, will lie at the heart of this powerful book.

At no point in the extract does Schama explicitly mention causation, change, the limitations of evidence nor his attempts to empathize because he has no need to: they are implicit throughout his account. In school, however, teachers need to make these things explicit in order for pupils to understand what history *is* and the ways in which they can try to *construct* it for themselves. It is also by making these things explicit that pupils are more likely to understand how to get better at history, for without them, getting better becomes a question merely of knowing more 'facts' and that, while crucially important, is not enough by itself.

We have dealt with evidence in a separate chapter partly for convenience and partly to emphasize its relationship with enquiry. In this chapter we focus on the other key concepts which underpin historical thinking. We start with the understanding that the past and the present are not the same and that people in the past were therefore different in their attitudes and beliefs in ways that were determined by the contexts in which they lived. An ability, therefore, to understand context and the impact this had on beliefs and attitudes, while rejecting simplified labels and recognizing the levels of diversity among people in the past, is crucial. We have called this, by way of shorthand, an **understanding of people in the past**, a designation which includes concepts such as chronological understanding, empathy and diversity. But even when historians feel that they are coming closer to understanding people in the past, they pose further questions: why did things come to be that way and how did things change or remain stable over time? We call this category of concepts **describing and explaining the past** and it includes the concepts of cause, consequence, change and continuity. Finally, there is a set of concepts concerned with how history is constructed in the present which we have called **interpreting the past**, which includes the concepts of significance and interpretations. These categories are simply heuristic; in practice understanding people in the past is, for example, a prerequisite for successful work on causation.

In schools, the importance of the key concepts is twofold. First, they introduce a level of engagement and challenge which goes beyond 'knowing facts', and provide opportunities for teachers to analyse and assess progression in more sophisticated ways. Second, they provide insights into what disciplinary history – the history of historians – really is, particularly when accompanied by the underpinning concept of evidence. In practice, all the concepts are linked but it is increasingly common practice for history teachers to focus *primarily* on one second-order concept in any given enquiry.

We have so far neglected to say very much about a different kind of concept in history which relates more directly to content. Substantive concepts are used to refer to the way 'people and societies work' (Lee 2005) and include, for example, political concepts such as state, government and power and economic concepts such as trade, wealth and tax. These concepts can cause difficulty for pupils because they are abstract in nature and their meaning can shift over time. The similarities and differences, for example, between the Industrial Revolution and the French Revolution or between the Roman Empire and the British Empire make such terms hard to pin down. 'The Church' can refer to both an entire institution and a tall building made of stone.

Understanding people in the past

What is empathetic understanding?

The 2007 national curriculum for history, under the rather broad and unhelpful heading 'chronological understanding', states that pupils need to develop 'a sense of period through describing and analysing the relationship between the characteristic features of periods and societies'. A sense of period could mean knowing about the clothes that people in the past wore, or the dwellings in which they lived in order to create an 'introductory package to which a label such as "Tudor" can be attached' (Dawson 2004: 16). Certainly, such details are enormously helpful, but only in so far as they can help us to reach a deeper sense of period which affords insights into the beliefs and attitudes of people in the past – understanding them 'from the inside' (Partington 1980, as quoted in Dawson 2004: 16). Collingwood, as early as 1946, argued that historians cannot assume that people in the past shared our outlook and that every attempt should be made to understand the past on its own terms. This is what a 'sense of period' is really about and is fundamental to making 'sense' of the past. At the heart of what it means to 'think historically' lies a disposition to understand that people in the past were not quite like us and that the impact the historical context had on their beliefs, attitudes and behaviours was profound. This can be, as Wineburg argues, counterintuitive, but it is essential if teachers are serious in their attempts to help pupils understand the past (Wineburg 2007). Barton and Levstik (2004) argue that the ultimate prize is that the present is seen in its historical context, too, and that life today is not regarded as the only 'norm' that is possible, or indeed desirable. This is an immensely difficult goal, but at the very least, history teaches children that it is possible to live without a television or a personal computer and that comfort and wealth can often be at others' expense.

The word that is generally employed to describe this endeavour is empathy or empathetic understanding. There are other terms, such as perspective recognition, which helpfully implies that this is not about us 'taking on' the perspectives of others, but rather is about us recognizing and understanding these different perspectives (see Barton and Levstik 2004). Empathy is a term that has received a bad press because of ahistorical tasks that demand only presentist, superficial views (see Box 7.2, for example). 'Good' history, however, is impossible without empathy, though that is not to imply that empathy in history is straightforward. Lee writes that empathy develops when we 'entertain' ideas very different from our own (Lee 2005). Lee uses the term 'entertain' to emphasize that empathy is an achievement and not a process, but the term somehow suggests a lack of engagement by the pupils, implying that they tolerate the view of others in the past rather than attempting to understand them properly. This reflects debates about the precise nature of historical empathy in the classroom, and the extent to which pupils can empathize with others in the past at all. Chapter 5 has already outlined why this can be difficult for pupils – as it is for adults. Empathy may involve 'using the perspectives of people in the past to explain their actions' (Barton and Levstik 2004: 208), but it does not mean pupils imagining themselves in the shoes of others, or somehow identifying personally with people in the past. Nor does it nec-essarily require an emotional response, such as sympathy, for the people studied.

Box 7.2 Moral issues and the past: Nazi Germany

In 1930s Germany there were those who defended the Jews (at great personal cost), those who aided the Nazis and those (the majority) who were bystanders. What would you have done?

This all makes *historical* sense. Pupils can struggle with the strangeness of the past and it can be challenging for them to empathize with adults today, let alone in past times (Husbands and Pendry 2000). Cunningham, in her work with four British teachers, concluded that framing empathetic tasks in personal rather than historical terms – 'how would you have felt?' rather than 'how would the German woman in 1936 have felt?' – 'more frequently led to presentist responses' (Cunningham 2004: 27). So there is much to be said for viewing empathy as a purely cognitive achievement: it is about piecing together, on the basis of fragmentary evidence, some understanding of the perspectives of people living in a very different time and place from our own. Such a view would reduce the kinds of ahistorical tasks such as the one in Box 7.2. It would be a shame, however, if such an approach ruled out the possibility for some kind of emotional and personal connection to the past and if pupils were not encouraged to care about the past as fellow humans, albeit humans who acted in peculiar ways. How can this be achieved alongside appropriate cognitive challenge?

Teaching strategies for empathetic understanding

Empathetic exercises in history education have often been associated with the exer-cise of historical imagination – such as 'Imagine you are a soldier in a World War I trench…write a letter home.' Exercises like this may well produce unhistorical fiction characterized by anachronisms in which the experiences of every soldier in the war are deemed to have been the same and in which the starting point is the pupil's own life. Such exercises may, however, have value en route to something more challenging and rigorous. The task as described here is primarily about a description of what it was like in the trenches. This is an acceptable question to ask about the trenches as long as it is not the *only* question being asked. Cunningham's work suggests that by putting the question into the first person, responses are more likely to be anachronistic, but a teacher might skilfully use whole-class discussion to move pupils on from thoughts about how *they* would have felt about trench warfare to how soldiers at the time might have done. More challenging questions about experiences in the trenches towards which pupils might be working over a period of a few lessons are exemplified in an outstanding enquiry about the experiences of a single private, Reg Wilkes, which still requires understanding of people in the past but which also requires a more sophisticated understanding of the role of evidence (Evans *et al.* 2004). Overall, then, writing a letter home from the trenches is problematic if seen as the only outcome from a series of lessons on trench warfare, not only because it is likely to produce dubious history but also because it is not very challenging. However, there may be a role for this type of task or discussion as a way of helping pupils to *care* about the past. Teaching through real individuals from the past is also a powerful way to do this and avoids the first person problem altogether. If pupils are to achieve some emotional engagement with the past, this might be achieved by emphasizing the closeness in age between the pupils and the soldiers and by using the story of Private Reg Wilkes. Emotional connection with the past, carefully handled, can be powerful and helpful as demonstrated by the pupil who, having learnt about trench foot, asked 'did their feet ever get better after they got home?' (Cunningham 2004:28).

Many of the teachers we visited talked about the importance of empathy. In one school, the teacher said it was what 'made me interested in history'. We observed examples of when pupils were encouraged to write or think about what it was like at the time and two Year 7 pupils told us independently that history made them aware of how different life was years ago and how difficult compared to now. That seemed to us to be a worthwhile conclusion to have drawn. One of the tasks the pupils engage in is to produce a play based on the lives of women factory workers in the Lawrence and Scott's munitions factory in Norwich during World War II. In doing this, they have to empathize with the lives of women workers and make links to local history.

Box 7.3 includes some tasks which are more or less tightly focused around empathetic understanding and which may be helpful to you in thinking about this issue. It is worth noting, however, that empathy is more often a necessary component of other achievements in history than an end in itself: it underpins our use of evidence, it radically influences our assessment of motivation and its role in causation and it enables us to be more nuanced and authentic in the way we talk about the past. There is some evidence to suggest that group discussion is a powerful way to develop empathetic understanding and that a teacher's restraint in allowing pupils to get it wrong in the first instance can be helpful. Indeed, as Ashby and Lee write, 'it does not matter if all the partners in a discussion are equally wrong, provided that they are wrong in different ways' (Ashby and Lee 1987: 86). What such discussions can illuminate are the preconceptions that pupils bring with them to the classroom. This seems especially important when attempting to understand people in the past. If pupils assume that people behaved differently in the past because they were stupid (what Ashby and Lee term the 'divi' stage), the teacher will need to deploy particular strategies or take a particular tack in discussions in order to move the pupils on (Ashby and Lee 1987: 68).

Box 7.3 Empathetic understanding and questioning

A.   What must it have been like to be a slave on the Middle Passage?
B.   What did women think of Hitler in 1930s Germany?
C.   What motivated Ghandi?
D.   You are a doctor treating Charles II. What remedies do you recommend and why?
E.   Why was the Medieval Church so important to people's lives?

Diversity

Diversity is profoundly linked to a 'sense of period' and to empathetic understanding. If empathy is about understanding people in the past, diversity is a way of making that understanding more nuanced and complex: it gives empathy some edge. Although variations of it have been present since the Schools Council History Project talked about 'similarity and difference' in the 1970s, it has never had quite the status of a 'key concept' before. The 2007 national curriculum defined the key concept of diversity as 'understanding the diverse experiences and ideas, beliefs and attitudes of men, women and children in past societies and how these have shaped the world'. This definition is helpful in so far as the parameters set are very broad: it is hard to conceive of many topics that would not provide opportunities to explore diversity thus defined. It does not, however, provide much clue about what understanding diversity – as opposed to knowing it existed – actually *means*. The addition of 'how these have shaped the world' is also unhelpful in its apparent segue into change and continuity or significance: it shifts the focus onto the outcome of diversity rather than the nature of the diversity itself. The explanatory notes are a similarly mixed bag for those seeking guidance. They state that 'Pupils should explore cultural, ethnic and religious diversity and racial equality' which seems to imply that this is a content issue, rather than a conceptual one, and one that is limited in scope. A scheme of work, including units on, say, Islamic history, the slave trade and SS Windrush, might be felt to cover sufficient territory, though its episodic nature is unlikely to introduce pupils to the complexity of and reasons for human ideas, attitudes, experiences and actions that lie at the heart of diversity as a concept.

While teachers may be comfortable developing enquiry questions that foreground causation or evidence or change and continuity, it is less clear what an enquiry question focusing on diversity might be, and what an increasingly sophisticated understanding of diversity among pupils might look like. Part of the solution lies in exploring the dimensions of diversity in terms of complexity, difference and typicality. 'Difference', for example, together with 'similarity', provide helpful intellectual tools for 'thinking about better and worse ways of identifying or characterizing groups of people' (Counsell 2009:2). Certainly, this is the nub of diversity. It is of little interest simply to show that diversity existed; the historical challenge lies in characterizing what that diversity was – *how* people were different in their thoughts, words and deeds and *how far* they were different. Perhaps above all, diversity is about understanding the past as inhabited by real people, an understanding that emerges only from a secure knowledge and understanding of the particular context in which the people under scrutiny lived. In that sense, diversity forces teachers and pupils to examine the complexities of the past.

History is, of course, about studying people in the past. It seeks to understand what motivated people, how they responded to particular experiences and what might account for the actions they took. In this way, learning history provides insights into human nature and behaviour in ways that are revealing of us, sometimes unpalatable and often complex. People's attitudes and actions in the past cannot be limited by notions of race, ethnicity and religion, important though these are, not least because these ideas are themselves historically conditioned, so that there are always both general and local factors, quirks of personality, and influences of gender and class at work.

The complexity – and therefore diversity – of human behaviour cannot be explained by a checklist of factors and it is precisely this that makes history so interesting. In practice, groups which behave differently from the way one might expect given their religious/ethnic/cultural make-up are more interesting to historians and learners than those which behave more predictably. Similarly, fractious groups are often of more interest than cohesive groups: not all German Christians in the Third Reich behaved in the same way towards Jews, for example. Notions of multiple identities are common today and there is a widely held assumption that one cannot be defined by a single 'group'. In Britain, the layers of identity that influence beliefs, attitudes and actions include gender, colour, faith, locality, region, family, language, class, ethnicity and so forth. On top of these layers come those shaped by experiences as a child, in school and as an adult; individual responses can never be identical to anyone else's. Matthew Bradshaw recently wrote of an exchange he had with his university tutor while a student. On being puzzled about the existence of two apparently contradictory views on Oliver Cromwell, the tutor replied 'Oliver Cromwell was human'. Perhaps we should not be asking our pupils to choose between Cromwell as 'hero' and 'villain': perhaps we should allow them to consider the possibility that he was both (Bradshaw 2009).

The challenge for the historian – and for the history teacher and student – is to understand how all this complexity might speak to bigger issues. It is not generally possible nor, on the whole, desirable, for historians to operate at an individual or even a group level. Biographers do, of course, as do those historians who focus on a single town, village or family. But generally speaking, historians are more interested in making bigger claims about the past, generating the challenge of how to reconcile the tension between diversity and the need for generalizations. Box 7.4 provides one way of exploring this tension with Key Stage 3 pupils.

Box 7.4 Diversity and generalization

STEP 1 Test the generalisation

It is easy for people to get away with sloppy thinking when they make generalisations. So you test the generalisation to make sure it is based on sound evidence. If not you will need to reject it or change it.

Based on your completed diagram, do you think this generalisation is justified? Are there more emigrants in the economic area of the diagram than anywhere else? Is this the most common reason?

How would you complete this sentence:

The generalisation that people emigrated for economic reasons is (completely/only partly/not at all) true.

STEP 2 Strengthen the generalisation by adding supporting evidence

Choose one example from the diagram that shows how economic factors motivated the emigrants. Complete these sentences to show there is truth in the generalisation.

People who emigrated for economic reasons included … (name the people and add details to explain their situation). Another example of people who shared this motive was … (add details to explain their situation).

STEP 3 Strengthen it further by showing that you know it is not the whole story

A generalisation never tells the whole story. But you can strengthen it by showing the exceptions. Some people might think this undermines the generalisation but the opposite is true: if you can show that there are some emigrants who do not fit this pattern, but that it is mostly true, you strengthen your argument.

How would you complete these sentences:

Economics was not the only reason. For some emigrants the main reason was … (add an example of why these people moved). Or …

STEP 4 Check your language

Generalisations can be made much more accurate by carefully selecting words like *many, some, majority, minority, often, sometimes, occasionally, probably, possibly.*

Look at the following examples. What would happen to the sentences if you took out the phrases highlighted in yellow? Would they still be true?

Life for many working people in Britain in the mid-nineteenth century was not good. The majority found it hard to manage on their low pay, and sometimes unemployment cut even that.

The emotional pain of leaving was probably hard for some. Only a minority of emigrants ever returned.

Source: Culpin *et al.* (2009: 109)

Explaining and describing the past

Cause and consequence

Exploring why things happened is often the area of historical thinking teachers feel most comfortable with and is, on the face of it, the area that seems easiest to assess. The first national curriculum, for example, included reference to the multi-causal nature of events, different types of cause and consequence, the relative importance of different causes and consequences and the inter-connectedness of causes. This way of thinking about cause and consequence, supported by helpful work on how to help pupils structure written explanations (Counsell 1997), has been enormously influential on the way teachers think about and teach this concept. This section explores these ideas a little further and offers some principles and strategies for successful practice.

Historical explanation and causal reasoning

Historical explanation involves exploring the relationship between at least two dimensions: the intentional and the contextual (Chapman 2008). The intentional dimension focuses on individuals and the 'hopes, intentions and beliefs' that shaped what happened in the past (Chapman 2008). Thus, Gavrillo Princip assassinated Archduke Franz Ferdinand, Wat Tyler marched to Blackheath, Luther posted his 95 theses onto the door of the Church in Wittenberg and Eden withdrew troops from Egypt and the Suez Canal Zone. The fact that they chose to do these things certainly shaped the course of events in the past and reflected their own beliefs and intentions. However, their actions were also profoundly influenced by their context: where they were, what resources they had available, what support they could muster and the prevailing attitudes at the time. As Chapman states, 'Contexts enable and constrain: they make acting and thinking possible' (2008). Fundamental to any explanation about why something happened, therefore, is a consideration of both the intentional and the contextual. Furthermore, Chapman emphasizes that in order to analyse causation in this way, pupils need to

> understand that the world can be thought about in many different ways and that there is nothing necessary or 'natural' about the way 'we' see things now. Past actors lived in mental worlds that were differently structured from ours.
>
> (2008)

The sorts of misunderstandings that pupils are likely to have about causation are summarized in Box 7.5. Any of these misunderstandings could restrict pupils' progression in the way they think about causation. Underpinning several of these misunderstandings is the notion that a cause is a particular 'thing', whereas in fact, causes are relationships between 'things'. For example, the assassination of Archduke Franz Ferdinand was not, by itself, a cause of World War I; in isolation, it would certainly have triggered some kind of response but that may have been restricted to the imprisonment or execution of Gavrillo Princip. That it led to war was the result of the causal relationship between it and other factors, including Serbian nationalism and Austrian's relationship with Germany. Thus, causes are not causes in isolation: they only become causes when they interact with other causes, whether intentional or contextual. Exploring causes in this way takes us back to those early ideas about causation in the first national curriculum because pupils will be forced to consider multiple causes and the connections between them, which in turn open up the possibility of the relative importance of causes.

Box 7.5 Misunderstandings that pupils might have about causation

- People in the past behaved and understood things as we do (presentism)
- Things happened because people wanted them to (voluntarism)
- Things happened in a straightforward linear way, like billiard balls colliding (mechanical causality)
- Each element in a sequence of events is equally important
- Things happened for a (single) reason (monocausality rather than multi-causality) – often the reason closest to the event chronologically
- Things that happened were bound to happen (determinism/inevitability)

Source: Based on discussions with Arthur Chapman and on Lee (2005)

Principles and strategies for teaching causal reasoning effectively

(i)   Explore ways in which causal relationships operate

This involves exploring categories of cause with pupils and helping them understand causation as a web rather than a linear chain. It is easiest to divide categories of cause into types: first, descriptive causes, which can be classified by 'content' (such as religious, financial, political, social and so forth) or by 'time' (such as long-term and short-term) and, second, explanatory causes, which can also be classified by their role in explaining patterns and events (such as triggers, catalysts, preconditions) or by their importance (such as 'enabling' and 'determining' causes). Ultimately, it is explanatory categories that are most helpful in understanding causal relationships: 'content' categories – such as economic, political and social – certainly have a potential role to play, not least when constructing extended written explanations which avoid a chronological narrative, but they do not help pupils understand the way causes interlink to make something happen. Similarly, long-term and short-term categories, which are always difficult to define precisely, tend only to be helpful when related to the explanatory category of role. For example, long-term causes may include preconditions whereas among short-term causes will be triggers and possibly catalysts. To make judgements about the relative importance of different causes and causal relationships, it can be helpful to distinguish between those which are 'enabling' and which make an event or particular consequence more likely or possible and those which are 'determining' and determine the event or consequence by making something actually happen (see Lee *et al.* 1996, Coffin 2006 and Chapman 2008). Another way of thinking about this is through the terms 'necessary' (x was needed for y to happen) and 'sufficient' (x was enough to make y happen).

There are numerous strategies which help pupils understand these categories and, as a result, develop their understanding of causation. Card sorting activities have become well established as a way of helping pupils physically to manipulate causes in order to explore relationships between them while also being reminded of factual information. Christine Counsell provides one of the most sophisticated ways of using a card sort for a causal analysis about the murder of Thomas Beckett through effective use of a set of cards and a piece of sugar paper (Counsell 2004a). First, pupils create a relative continuum of causes inside a 'zone of relevance' which focuses attention firmly on the particular question being asked. Second, pupils experiment with a short-, medium- and long-term diagram by placing particular cards nearer to the middle of the sugar paper (with the event at the centre). Third, pupils sort the cards freely in order to discern or create 'big points' (which might become topic sentences) from 'little points'. Fourth, once the cards are organized under headings, pupils are asked to 'lump' categories together or split them into two smaller categories. Fifth, and relating back to the 'zone of relevance', the teacher changes the question in order to demonstrate to the class the way in which this changes which cards are most relevant and which are not relevant at all. The outcome of just a few of these activities is likely to be a familiarity with the information on the cards, a sense of the different ways the information can be manipulated and a way into writing (or thinking about) a causal analysis that is a far cry from a chronological narrative. Diamond nines activities are variations on a card sort with considerable potential (Chapman 2003): nine causes are written onto a diamond-shaped card and the cards themselves sorted to make a big diamond with the most important placed at the top. This forces pupils to make decisions about relative importance and can also be used to explore other kinds of connections, although one disadvantage is that only nine causes can be dealt with at any time.

Analogies can be deployed to considerable effect. Chapman's story about Alphonse the Camel and Frank the Camel-killer is a great story with which to explore the different categories of cause set out above in a humorous and accessible way (Chapman 2003). Thus the fact that poor Alphonse, who dies of irreversible back collapse after Frank places a straw on his back following years of overloading, worked in a mountainous area could be seen to be a long-term cause or precondition. The straw was certainly a trigger but whether it was therefore the most important cause is a matter for discussion. Pupils can also debate how each of these factors related to Alphonse's physical strength and condition, or which were intentional factors and which contextual. However, it is important to position analogies such as this carefully in an enquiry: too early, and the pupils will struggle to draw any connections between the analogy and the actual historical question, be it an explanation of the abolition of the slave trade or of the victory of William in 1066.

Equally powerful are questioning strategies, which depend on adopting an appropriately quizzical tone in interrogating the past. Causal thinking depends on pupils being asked to think about causes in novel ways, so teachers need to ask questions such as whether x made y more likely to happen, whether x made y happen or would x have happened without y. Counsell (2004a) notes that such questions stand effectively within successful enquiry questions. She outlines how she refined a question about the murder of Becket in order to ensure it served the function she wanted it to: a move away from apportioning blame (which 'Why was Becket murdered?' might encourage) and a first step to analysing wider issues of the monarchy and the Church. She also wants a question that will engage and motivate Year 7. The result – 'Why did Henry and Becket's quarrel turn bitter and fatal?' – provides just the right focus and intrigue necessary. Many causation questions would benefit from similar refinement. It is more interesting and challenging to ask 'Why did war break out in 1914 and not before?' rather than 'Why did World War I break out?' Counter-factual (what if?) questions can be helpful when discussing the relative importance of causes and causal relationships. A simple way to do this is for teachers to provide a list of causes (perhaps on cards) and ask pupils which one(s) might be removed in order to prevent the event happening (for example: 'What if Harold's troops had not been tired when they arrived at Hastings?').

All of these strategies help pupils to see that causal relationships are not linear and that events happen because of a tangled web of causes all interacting with each other. Many of the strategies outlined above would be helpful for exploring complex causal relationships and a good old-fashioned spider diagram is not a bad place to start, either. Woodcock (2005) also uses visual aids to demonstrate that causes neither occur sequentially, each bumping into the other until the event happens, nor that all causes are of equal importance (see Box 7.6).

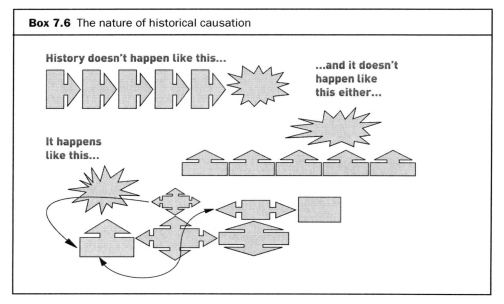

Box 7.6 The nature of historical causation

Source: Woodcock, J. (2005:7)

(ii) Explore the relationship between language and history

The principle that teachers should *explicitly* explore the relationship between language and history applies generally, and not simply to teaching about causation, although there is particularly interesting research on language and causation. Clark (2001) has explored ways in which pupils can be encouraged to talk about causes and causal relationships, including ways that they might describe and justify the links they make between causes, whole-class debates around counter-factual questions and assessment of pupil understanding though oral presentations using video, all of which provide linguistic contexts in which understanding can be developed. Woodcock (2005) provides advice about approaches to introducing the vocabulary of causal reasoning to pupils and argues that understanding of this language in itself helps pupils to think about causation in particular ways, i.e. that the 'linguistic' really does release the 'conceptual' (Box 7.7).

Box 7.7 Examples of Woodcock's terminology of causation

Central... Contribute... Exacerbate... Allow... Latent... Trigger... Incite... Spark... Significantly... Nevertheless... Despite... Further... Foundation... Birth... Beginning... Element... This compelled... Encourage... Develop... This nurtured... Preceding... Consequently... Impede... The root of... However... This led to... In addition... Prevent... Deter... This was the source... Erupt... Bring about... Fundamentally... Underpin... Discourage... Support... Origins... Foundation... Principally... Motivate... Drive... Influence... Permit... Reflect

---

Source: Woodcock (2005)

In order to increase familiarity with new vocabulary, there is much to be said for short, focused written tasks of only two or three sentences to build confidence and develop the principle of explanation. Evans and Pate advocate the use of what they call the PEGEX model (point, example, explanation) to encourage pupils to go beyond mere identification of a cause and to explain it: why was it linked to the outcome and how does it connect with other causes (Evans and Pate 2007)? A neat acronym such as PEGEX is easily remembered and increases pupils' confidence and ability to do what history teachers are constantly asking them to do: to 'explain their answers more fully'.

(iii) Motivating pupils to answer the question

Perhaps the best way to motivate pupils to answer a causation question is to make the event that is 'caused' real to them. If they are to spend several lessons exploring the causes of the English Civil War, they need to know why this is worthwhile. It is likely to help them to understand that the Civil War divided families and led to one of the most shocking events in our history – the execution of a king, an event which had profound implications for the way the country was ruled thereafter. By showing them images from the time, or even a clip of Alec Guinness, in role as Charles I, acting out a dignified and rather moving death (see http://www.youtube.com/watch?v=k88K8AMVcgg), pupils at least have a sense of the calamity of the event and a reason to want to find an answer to the question 'Why did this happen?' Howells recognizes this and argues that 'there is no point seeking causes for an event which is still abstract or vague to the pupils' (1998: 17). Similarly, Clark writes that

> Our department now believes that the consequences of a chain of events generally need to be shown first. This helps to focus the mind on what they are explaining the causes of. Without understanding the importance of the Nazi war machine

and the Holocaust, for example, the relevance of understanding Hitler's rise to power seems vague. Again, pupils need to feel the need to build an argument if they are to attempt true historical explanation.

(Clark 2001: 27)

Change and continuity

The central character in Simon Mawer's 2006 novel *Swimming to Ithaca* is a historian whose mother is dying. He wonders when her dying began: 'It had taken eighteen months, Or four years. Or a lifetime. Like any piece of history, it all depends where you want to draw the start line...A life is the history of a death'. Change and continuity are perhaps the underlying organizing dichotomies of history: the ways in which the past was different, and the ways in which it is the same as the present are endlessly complex issues in both lower case history and upper case History: it depends where the start line is drawn and the perspectives adopted. Historians have used a range of more or less complex analytical frameworks to explore the ideas of change and continuity in the past – indeed, there seem to be an almost disproportionate number of historical monographs with the subtitle including 'change and continuity in...'. For some historians, the idea of change – as progress or regress, as the interplay of events – describes the entire enterprise of history: history is the study of change over time. Social and economic historians have borrowed extensively from the ideas of anthropology and sociology, examining the deep structures of continuity in kinship, tradition, ritual and belief systems which change gradually over long periods of time. The French historian Fernand Braudel has been especially influential in articulating the triple model of *la longue duree*, the deep, slowly changing routines of history, often expressed in the relationship between traditional communities and the land, *l'histoire conjoncturelle*, the cycles of change over a generation, often influenced by technology and the economic cycle, and l'*histoire événementielle,* the day-to-day rush of events much loved of politicians, journalists and chroniclers (Braudel and Matthews 1980). Braudel's influence is perhaps seen most strongly – and best exemplified – in the work of Emmanuel Le Roy Ladurie who used long-term tithe, wage, tax and rent records, together with the use of economic and anthropological theories to argue that the history of Languedoc was '*l'histoire immobile'*, marked by waves of population and economic growth and decline that in essence changed very little over centuries while wars and revolutions raged (Le Roy Ladurie 1978). The relationships between change and continuity are always difficult to probe and to understand: famously, it is said, the Roman Catholic church thinks of change in terms of centuries.

If, for historians, the interplay of change and continuity, processes and structures is central to what it is to understand the past, for pupils change and continuity are particularly difficult ideas to fathom (Counsell 2010). The evidence available suggests that pupils think almost automatically in terms of change in binary terms: the past is different from the present, things are not the same as they were in the 'olden days'. What has changed, therefore, is much the same as what happened, and changes are seen as events. For many pupils, the foundational point is almost that the past is temporally 'shrunk': because their understandings of the past focus on events which stimulate change, the past is a sequence of changes, one after the other

(Shemilt 2000). Understanding change and continuity as teaching challenges, therefore, involves at least three different dimensions: developing an understanding of the relationship between the past and the present, understanding patterns of change and continuity within and between past societies, and understanding that the concept of change provides a language with which to understand the past. Each of these is itself complex. Although few pupils have difficulty in understanding that there are differences between the past and the present, they face challenges in understanding continuities between the past and the present. For most, the idea that change is generally for the better is an almost automatic assumption, so that a past without iPods, mobiles, social networking and even TV must, by definition, have been a denuded place to live. Teaching can frequently if inadvertently fail to engage such assumptions. Indeed, a history focusing on events and change is likely to play into this belief. Of course, explicit comparisons between the past and the present can help, but more important are likely to be teaching approaches which convey the richness of past societies. It is still the case that too little history teaching makes explicit reference, in even an ambient way, to the art, music and material culture of past societies which might help pupils to build up a textured understanding of past societies. Ian Dawson makes the point that recall or key events, people and dates is likely to be enhanced if understood as part of long-term thematic stories such as 'Who held power – king or parliament?' or 'How have working lives changed?', but it is also the case that these thematic structures provide a way of understanding the complexity of past societies – itself a stage on the way to understanding that the relationship between the past and the present may be more complex than pupils might believe (Dawson 2008).

Rather more challenging for pupils is the idea of change *within* historical periods. Again, teaching can inadvertently encourage the belief that the past was patterned by periods of extensive continuity with short bursts of historical change: teachers' use of the language of periodization ('the medieval castle', 'the Roman Empire', 'the Victorian town', 'the American West') can too often lead pupils to suppose that change within these periods was relatively insignificant. On the other hand, without a clear sense of period pupils are unlikely to develop an enduring map of the past. The national curriculum requirement is that pupils study history as a mixture of overview and depth studies in which pupils are required to consider the 'nature' and 'extent' of change. This requires explicit teaching strategies, and the key task is to develop 'nested' understandings of different periods. Sometimes this involves mapping different concepts within a period, so that pupils can explore the relationship between them over a series of lessons; at other times it might involve explicitly breaking a period down into shorter, manageable units. Steven Barnes outlines one possible such strategy explicitly focused on the enquiry question 'How far was the period 1750–1900 an age of progress?'. Pupils worked in pairs on a sequence of paintings and sorted information about the years 1750–1800, 1800–25, 1825–50, 1850–75 and 1875–1900 under three heads – political events, economic events and social events. Thereafter, they used three devices to *make judgements* about the experience of change – an analytical timeline on which for each of the periods they made a judgement about things which showed evidence of progress and things which showed evidence of things getting worse, a large swingometer placed on a display board in the classroom again examining things which got better and things which got worse, and a graph. One pupil, commenting on the graph, wrote 'I expected progress to be a straight line but it isn't, it goes up and down' (Barnes 2002:12).

Finally, the language of change is itself challenging. Changes may take place in many aspects of the historical past – political, cultural, social, technological – and the relationship between them is often difficult and intellectually challenging to unpick (Lee and Shemilt 2004). Rachel Foster (Foster 2008) set out a six-lesson enquiry on the American civil rights movement which sought to problematize change and continuity for a Year 9 group. Foster worried that the conventional approach to teaching saw black Americans as victims of Reconstruction and the era of the Jim Crow laws who 'passively waited for a "Great Leader" to deliver them'. Foster recognized that historians themselves use the idea of change as a metaphor for describing historical processes, and she spent some time trying to find a metaphor which her pupils could use, before finally coming up with the idea of a car journey. Pupils were asked to suggest factors which could speed up or slow down a journey and these ideas were used to shape an investigation of things which could affect the 'speed, rate, nature and direction of change'. This done, pupils began to design and produce their own maps of the car journey between the end of the Civil War and the 1960s, with pupils puzzling about how to depict white violence on their road maps. Pupils became increasingly inventive in their use of metaphors on the road map. Although 'many pupils were not able to translate their visual and oral ideas into writing', the activity enabled pupils to understand the complexity of change and the extent to which the way it is described is one of the challenges for historians (Foster 2008:7).

Interpreting the past

Interpretation

As we saw in Chapter 5, pupils often believe in a fixed account of the past, making it hard for them to explain the existence of two credible but contrasting accounts of the same topic. Indeed, pupils might reject entirely the possibility of two worthwhile accounts because only one account is possible: the one that mirrors 'what actually happened'. If one of the accounts is accepted, the other will be explained away by problems with the historians themselves: perhaps one has reason to favour a particular 'side' or is writing further after the events, if only by a few years. Worse still, some pupils may reject the possibility of a modern historian's account telling us anything useful at all because no one alive today could have been there so how is it possible to know what really happened? After all, they might argue, the testimony left behind is fatally flawed.

This section explores ways to overcome this mode of thinking. McAleavy's definition of 'historical interpretations' remains one of the best: 'A conscious reflection on the past and not the ideas and attitudes of participants in past events' (McAleavy 1993:10). This definition has the benefit not only of clarifying what an interpretation is but also what it is not, a distinction that was not always apparent in history classrooms after the introduction of the national curriculum. 'Interpretations of history' was one of three Attainment Targets in 1991, a radical move that ensured a firm focus on history as a construction and something that could therefore be abused, but it was, and can still be, often handled as a verb rather than a noun. Thus, teachers believed they were 'doing interpretations' when, in fact, pupils were interpreting evidence for themselves and engaged in enquiry and using evidence – separate strands of historical concepts and processes in any version of the national curriculum since its inception. The popular enquiry question 'Was Oliver Cromwell a hero or a villain?' is a case in point. Often billed as an 'interpretation' question by teachers, it is more likely to take pupils back to contemporary evidence (Mastin and Wallace 2006) and would need rephrasing as 'Why has Oliver Cromwell been seen as both a hero and a villain by historians?' in order to give it a tighter 'interpretations' focus. The confusion is understandable given the close relationship between interpretations and evidence, not least because in order to evaluate an interpretation it would be prudent to consider the evidence used to inform it. To engage properly in 'interpretations', however, the focus should be on analysing interpretations produced some time after the event, rather than on the production of an interpretation by pupils. An interpretation might include historians' accounts but it could (and should) also embrace other, more popular forms of history including historical fiction, films, songs and documentaries as well as pictures and historic sites such as museums and palaces.

It is important for pupils to understand how historical interpretations arise because to understand the nature of interpretations is to understand the nature of history: history *is* interpretation. That is not to say that any one interpretation of the past is as good as another, however, and there are grounds on which to judge the relative value of another interpretation of the past, including the way in which evidence is handled, the way in which it accords or conflicts with other accounts, the relationship with established fact and the internal consistency of the argument. A study of historical interpretations should aim to move pupils 'beyond a view that "anything goes" and towards an understanding of how the validity of claims about the past can be assessed' (Chapman 2010:99). Nevertheless, history *is* constructed: it exists only because someone saw fit to marshal and analyse evidence in order to answer particular questions about the past and therefore understanding the process of this construction is central to understanding what history is. In addition, there are further reasons to study interpretations beyond the subject itself: it could be argued that understanding both that the past itself is open to particular uses *and* that any claims that people make, whether about history or something else, can and should be evaluated in terms of their evidential base and their underlying purposes, are extremely helpful skills or dispositions for the 'critical citizen' (Wrenn 1999).

Given what is known about pupils' understanding in this area, teachers' aims can and should be defined with some precision: pupils need to consider how interpretations differ, why they differ and whether one interpretation is better than another. How interpretations differ is the most straightforward, though a vital step along the way. Why they differ requires a substantial step up. Comparing and evaluating competing interpretations might be illuminated by asking questions about, first, their evidential base and second, about the 'baggage' of the historian (Howells 2005) or what Carr called 'the bees he has in his bonnet' (Carr 1961: 23). It should be clear at this stage that even the point of addressing why interpretations differ and whether one is better than the other will elude pupils if they persist in seeing the past as fixed and capable of yielding only one true 'story'. In the light of both the theoretical basis for studying interpretations and the practical knowledge we have about pupils' understanding of them, it is possible to identify a number of challenges facing teachers and some possible solutions (Haydn *et al.* 1997).

First, pupils need help in understanding how evidence is used to form the basis of an interpretation – and therefore to understand the difference between the two. One approach might be to consciously ask pupils to reach their own conclusions on the basis of evidence and then to compare and analyse the differences between the pupils' accounts, perhaps by asking them to identify facts and opinions. This is an example of how classic enquiry work can also shed light on the nature of historical interpretations. A variation of this task is to deliberately provide conflicting evidence to, say, different sides of the classroom and ask the pupils to reach conclusions. The difference between the two groups is a helpful illustration of how interpretations differ partly because of the evidence selected by the historian or film-maker. Other activities are designed to illustrate the differences between historians. Richard Cunningham, for example, edited a biographical video of Elizabeth I so that all the vignettes of historians appeared sequentially (Cunningham 2001). The differences between a series of eminent historians, all drawing on much the same evidence, not only provided pupils with an insight into how history works but also reassured them that the differences between their own views of Elizabeth were not weakened by being different to their friends' views. Shoham and Shiloah outlined a similar kind of activity where pupils examined four accounts of Baron Rothschild's 'guardianship system' and used these as a way of exploring the difference 'between evidence and the conclusions drawn from it' (Shoham and Shiloah 2003:32).

Both Cunningham and Shoham and Shiloah refer to the importance of pupils distinguishing fact from opinion. Once pupils understand that historians select facts from the evidence to support their opinions, conflicting accounts based on a similar evidence base become more comprehensible and pupils move beyond seeing a valid interpretation as something which simply replicates the past and tells us 'how it was' and start to understand that the facts, by themselves, explain little of interest or importance. Archaeology is a helpful way into this: there is little that we know for sure about Stonehenge so the notion of 'telling it how it was' cannot apply. So how are we to make sense of the stone circle other than to use what we do have to form opinions which change over time (Chapman 2007)? It is important to convince pupils that opinions are good things and indeed are what drive history as an endeavour. Opinions can – and should – be evaluated, but history is, to all intents and purposes, a set of opinions supported more or less well by evidence.

Historical interpretations differ for many reasons. Once pupils have started to understand the relationship between historical interpretations and evidence, they will become more receptive to the possible reasons why historians using the same evidence might form different opinions. This takes us on to Carr's buzzing bees and the need to 'study the historian before you begin to study the facts' (Carr 1961). This can also take pupils down some dead ends if not handled carefully; it is not uncommon to find reductive approaches where pupils are forced to make facile statements about one historian being more trustworthy than another because he is older or younger, British or non-British, a university lecturer or a school teacher and so forth. Howells (2005:32) also warns against too simplistic a view of the evolution of interpretations over time given that 'no one interpretation…dominates any one era' and that 'historians are not Pavlovian dogs responding to world conditions in predictable ways'. Nevertheless, one of the factors shaping any interpretation is, to a lesser or greater extent, the time in which she or he is writing and Howells (2005) helpfully provides some questions which tackle interpretations in the long term in ways that might do justice to the complexity of the issue (see Box 7.8).

Box 7.8 Good enquiry questions which focus on 'interpretations'

How might the Civil War change how we view Elizabeth?
Why have historians emphasized different reasons for the English Civil War?
When was the English Revolution?
Does 1640–60 deserve the title 'The English Revolution'?
Why are popular historical views of Charles II so different from those of academic historians?

Source: Howells (2005:33)

Chapman's work on assumptions is also illuminating here: once pupils are trained to spot the underlying assumptions of an account, they are better equipped to critique it (Chapman 2006). Put simply, the approach involves pupils identifying a claim made by the historian (e.g. Gellately's claim that there were very few secret police in Nazi Germany), the assumption underlying it (this was known at the time) and the conclusion that the historian therefore draws (that people were not afraid of secret police surveillance). By analysing – and evaluating – the underlying assumption, it might be more possible for the pupils to evaluate the conclusion. In Gellately's case, for example, pupils might challenge the assumption that people did know this at the time (after all, there's a reason they were called secret police) and therefore challenge the basis for one of Gellately's claims (Chapman 2006). This approach helps to overcome another kind of 'dead end' in pupils' thinking, what Chapman refers to as the '"schools of history" approach…[which] usually results, as many examiners know, in garbled versions of the same summaries coming back to haunt us in pupil answers' (2006: 12).

Pupils need to know enough about a topic to engage seriously in analysis of it, and this is as true for historical interpretations as for any other concept. Unless knowledge about the topic is reasonably secure, it is unfair to expect pupils to engage seriously in understanding the different ways it has been interpreted. However, as we began to explore above, the time in which the interpretation was created may well also be of importance, creating additional challenge for pupils. Jane Card calls this 'double vision' (Card 2004) and her example of a Victorian painting of Lady Jane Grey's execution is apposite: pupils need to know both about the sixteenth and nineteenth centuries in order to make proper sense of the painting. Work on King John has also explored the impact of the context of the interpreter (Banham 2000). In many cases, however, the interpretation is likely to be relatively modern and it may be knowledge of a genre which is just as important, for example knowledge of how and why films or computer games are made.

Several of the schools we visited use film as a way of tackling historical interpretations and there are a number of reasons why it is important to explore a range of popular interpretations as well as more traditional historians' accounts, the most important of which is that pupils are more likely to encounter these popular forms outside school than they are to pick up a history book. Using film can also be highly engaging, providing pupils with the kinds of alternative forms of communication they enjoy. Banham and Hall's work on J.F. Kennedy provides a good example of how an enquiry can focus on a single film very profitably (2003; see also Klein 2008) and Brown and Wrenn's work notes that with proper planning and effective teaching, pupils in Year 6 can compare and evaluate the different treatment of Alexander the Great by a modern historian and the filmmaker Oliver Stone (Brown and Wrenn 2005).

Assessment of pupils' understanding of interpretations often generates formulaic answers which either summarize the views of different 'schools' of history or make spurious claims about the value of one interpretation over another based on misconstrued or at best undeveloped ideas about the bias of historians. More valid assessment will enable pupils to explore the ways in which the past has been interpreted differently, the reasons for these differences and, if appropriate, some evaluation of the interpretations themselves. That is not to say that activities focused on spotting 'problems' in an interpretation are always well conceived. Commercial films are unlikely to demonstrate historical integrity and a focus on 'what they got wrong' as an end in itself is fairly pointless. More interesting are the ways that the film-maker has cherry picked from the past, the reasons for doing do and the success of the result in terms of constructing a convincing narrative. Therefore, the particular outcomes of any activity may depend on the nature of the interpretations themselves as well as the progression that a department has built into its long-term planning.

Significance

History teaching has always been concerned with significance – with teaching young people about significant events and people from the past. However, it is only in recent years that the concept of 'historical significance' has received explicit attention in research and professional practice. This recent prominence might be explained by a growing need to 'sell' history to pupils as important or relevant (Hunt 2000) or by a concern with helping pupils to broaden their perspective on the past, though it may also have grown out of work on historical interpretation which seeks to challenge and extend pupils' thinking about the nature of historical judgements. The position of significance in this chapter, alongside interpretations, underlines its status as a 'meta-concept' (Counsell 2004): because one task for history teachers is to explore the significance of causes or changes or diversity, the idea of significance sits above these concepts and draws on any of them. Crucially, significance, rather like diversity, is not about content choice: a teacher cannot claim to have 'done' significance by choosing to teach about aspects of the past they believe to have been significant. Instead, the emphasis is on significance as a judgement made at the time, in subsequent periods or, most commonly, today, with the recognition that significance is not fixed and is not a property of a person, event or development itself. The Great Fire of London cannot be characterized as 'significant' *per se:* it is significant within a study of urban development but less so in the context of political organization (Lee and Shemilt 2004). Judgements about significance are also often highly personal: significance to one person is not significance to another and this depends on many factors, from our own preoccupations and knowledge to the questions being asked and context in which judgements are made. Hence, significance *is* interpretation and is relative, contingent and shifting (Lomas 1990).

The way progression in pupils' understanding of significance is currently understood reflects these assumptions, but significance is also frequently embedded in curriculum guidance and syllabi. In such documents, significance is a taken for granted assumption underpinning the selection of content. One purpose of successful history teaching is to subject these assumptions to scrutiny. A starting point might be for pupils to use explicit criteria to make their own judgements about what is significant or the extent of its significance; later, pupils might devise and use their own criteria. At a more sophisticated level still, activities might help pupils to recognize that historians' judgements about significance change according to the question being asked, the criteria being used and the circumstances in which that judgement itself was made. Despite this admittedly complex understanding, teachers should not lose sight of the power of the concept to illuminate why it is that studying the past matters, even if in different ways to different people. As Brown and Woodcock write (2009: 6), 'significance is about *making meaning* of the past and it's also about why people care, or have cared, about the past' [emphasis added]. While the ambition to explore the different and changing ways that significance has been attributed to particular people, events and developments in the past is a worthy one, this should not distract too much from a more immediately pressing and useful ambition: that pupils consider the value of what they are learning. Consequently, in what follows, emphasis is placed on earlier stages of thinking about significance which involve pupils making their *own* judgements about significance as a powerful way to demonstrate history's importance.

Box 7.9 Sets of possible criteria with which to judge significance

Partington (1986, as cited in Phillips 2002)
Importance – *at the time*
Profundity – *how deeply people's lives were affected*
Quantity – *how many lives were affected*
Durability – *for how long people's lives were affected*
Relevance – *how the event has helped us to understand the present*

Phillips' GREAT mnemonic (Phillips 2002)
Groundbreaking
Remembered by all
Events that were far reaching
Affected the future
Terrifying

Dawson's criteria that Year 7 might use (from a Year 7 textbook – Dawson 2003: 31)
A person might be deemed significant if she/he:
Changed events at the time they lived
Improved lots of lives or made them worse
Changed people's ideas
Had a long-lasting impact on their country or on the world
Had been a really good/bad example to people of how to live

Counsell's 'five Rs' (Counsell 2004a)
Remarkable – *remarked upon at the time or since*
Remembered
Resonant – *some connection to lives today*
Resulting in change
Revealing – *helps us to understand other things about the past*

Box 7.9 summarizes some of the different schemes of criteria that have been suggested as ways of supporting pupils' thinking about significance. Some are relatively context-specific – Phillips, for example, devised his set of criteria for the Great War – and none claim to be definitive. Counsell's five 'Rs' were devised with specific reference to the term 'historical' which accompanies significance in the national curriculum and she uses her criterion of 'revealing', for example, to illuminate one of the reasons that Josephine Butler might be deemed *historically* significant. All of the schemes in Box 7.9 are, in some way or another, questionable: it could be argued that the criterion of 'revealing' provides little basis from which to judge relative significance, because much in the past can be revealing of attitudes and values in the past and Dawson's inclusion of a criterion that to provide a model of how to live one's life is a possible reason to be deemed significant might be queried by some. But to quibble with the particular criteria is to miss the point: none of them was intended to be deployed whole and each provides a starting point rather than a definitive list. What these criteria can do is demonstrate that significance can be about more than the impact of something on today which, though critically important, is not the only way to assess significance. As Counsell argues (2004a), the Tolpuddle Martyrs did little to affect us directly today, but that does not mean that they should be consigned to the scrapheap of history.

It is possible to use the discussion above to offer some specific guidance about the ways in which teachers might develop pupils' understandings of significance. Four strategies seem particularly promising. In the first, teachers ask pupils to decide *why* something or someone is deemed to be significant. The challenge is not to decide whether a particular aspect of the past is significant, but rather to explore why it is commonly agreed to be so. This might include trying to discern the kinds of criteria that have been used by others to ascribe significance to an aspect of the past, and the examples in Box 7.10 draw widely on different attributions of significance – by comedians, governments, popular memory and historians. In a second strategy, pupils might be asked to decide *whether* an event or person is significant, or to judge the extent of the significance. Pupils might be asked whether and why Darwin is worth knowing about, how significant the Thirty Years War was, or how far Henry VIII's 'break with Rome' actually changed lives. A third strategy might be to ask pupils to *compare* the significance of historical events, either events which are close in time or context, or events which require considerable breadth of knowledge. For example, pupils might be asked whether the siege of Lucknow or the massacre at Amritsar was more significant, or whether the Battle of the Somme or the Battle of Waterloo was more significant. A variant might be to ask pupils what three things pupils should learn about the seventeenth century or the westward expansion of American settlers. Finally, pupils might study how judgements about significance have changed over time, being asked to think about why no one appeared to bother much about a given event until recently, or why some historical events once considered important are now rarely studied.

Box 7.10 Possible enquiry questions and activities which help pupils to develop an understanding of significance

---

What have the Romans done for us?

Write to the government and demand that the Industrial Revolution stays on the history curriculum.

Why was World War I called the 'Great War'?

Design a statue/coin/stamp/memorial commemorating the life of X.

What does studying Josephine Butler reveal about Britain in the nineteenth century? (Counsell 2004a)

What 'age' was the twentieth century?

Of course, a single topic might lend itself to several of these approaches. Allsop's work on the song 'We didn't start the fire' by Billy Joel (Allsop 2010) addresses – or potentially addresses – all four. He asked pupils to discern the criteria used by Joel to identify 118 events, people and inventions referred to in the song and then to apply these criteria to the last twenty years in order to select events, people and inventions which would bring the song up to date. There is plenty of scope here for pupils to modify and change Joel's criteria themselves and to challenge his judgements for the earlier period by considering, for example, how a British perspective would have generated different choices, or by exploring how his rock star status or the nature of the song itself influenced the choices made. At this point, work on significance starts to relate to historical interpretation, which is inevitable when reaching higher levels of thinking in which the relative nature of significance is explored.

Our final example brings us back to our core message, which is to use significance as a way to consider the value of studying the past. In a six-lesson enquiry about Darwin, already described briefly in Chapter 1 (Box 1.1), a decision to focus on significance generated a number of possible enquiry questions. Three of them covered similar ground to those contained in Counsell's five 'R's: did Darwin's dangerous idea change the world, was Charles Darwin a remarkable man, and what can a study of Charles Darwin tell us about the nineteenth century? Two of them required pupils to consider *why* Darwin is regarded as significant: what's so special about Charles Darwin, and what should everyone know about Charles Darwin? The final two addressed the question of *whether* Darwin is significant – or at least significant enough to appear on a banknote: why is Darwin on our £10 note, and should he stay on it and, finally, how and why has Darwin been remembered?

Any of these questions might have worked well and possible activities immediately suggested themselves in many cases: pupils might have designed a memorial to Darwin or redesigned the £10 note; they might have made a case either to remove him from the £10 note or to keep him on it; they might have put together a public exhibition about Darwin. The question that was finally selected – 'What's worth knowing about Darwin?' – focused attention very firmly on why Darwin should be studied at all, moving pupils on from simply deciding whether he is significant and instead encouraging them to explore why, which resulted in some interesting debate about whether, for example, his role as family man is 'worth knowing about' when compared with his 'big idea'. The activity which drew the enquiry together asked pupils to create a one-minute introduction to Down House – Darwin's home for most of his adult life and now owned by English Heritage – which encapsulated what is worth knowing about Darwin to a general audience. Pupils had to be ruthlessly selective in what they chose to include from the previous four lessons, using Dawson's criteria (see Box 7.9) as a starting point before refining them as they planned their presentations. The fact that each pair of pupils responded in different ways to the task was an illustration of how views about significance are not fixed: somebody's assertion that Darwin is worth knowing about because he delayed publishing the *Origin of Species* in order to collect more evidence is not 'wrong', even if someone else thought this missed the point entirely. At the heart of the enquiry was a determination to justify learning about Darwin at all, but the enquiry nevertheless revealed something about the relative nature of significance, too.

Conclusion

This chapter explores the ways in which pupils understand, describe, explain and interpret the past through the lens of key, or second-order, concepts. These concepts – change, continuity, cause and consequence, diversity, empathy, interpretation and significance – transform history from a body of knowledge to a form of knowledge, providing prisms through which to view the past. To these we must add evidence: understanding the nature of historical evidence is a conceptual issue, not a skill, and is arguably the most fundamental of all the concepts in helping pupils understand what history *is*. History is one of the only subjects with concepts that are 'content-free' and in this sense they have an integrity and purity that is part of what makes history so distinctive, engaging and challenging. These key concepts are not fixed – they will continue to evolve, as will our understanding of the way pupils make sense of them – but they must continue to sit side by side with the content knowledge of history in all history curricula if we are to take forward the considerable progress made since the 1970s in transforming history into a dynamic, engaging and suitably challenging subject.

8

Communicating and assessing history

The past is out of reach. Our understandings of it are always partial and restricted: restricted by what evidence we have and what perspectives we adopt. Historians have accepted as a commonplace that while some things are incontrovertible – no account of the past can acceptably declare the Saxons the winners of the Battle of Hastings, nor the French the victors of Waterloo – the meanings of the past are subject to endless interpretation and reinterpretation: what it meant, for example, for the Saxons to lose at Hastings in terms of the politics of the post-Conquest elite, or the longer term development of language, culture, social institutions and trading routes, are questions for historians to debate endlessly. These debates are coloured by the evidence available, the weight given to different sorts of evidence, the nature of the questions historians pose of that evidence and the assumptions which are made about the social practices and belief systems of the people being studied. This is true both of academic history and of history in schools: in both, there is a need for accuracy in the deployment of acknowledged fact, but both are also about processes of meaning-making and communication. For all these reasons, knowledge and ideas about the past must be tested and compared, brought into the open – communicated – so that they can be evaluated and assessed. Communicating and assessing history are integral to developing knowledge about the past in schools.

Talking, listening, reading, writing – the importance of language in history

However history classrooms are organized, and whatever the pedagogic approach to the teaching of history, there are four principal ways of communicating – or 'communicative modes' – in the history classroom: talking, listening, reading and writing. The ways these modes of communication are used matters because 'words, for both teachers and pupils, are the most powerful tool we have in thinking about history' (Husbands 1996: 97), and the ways in which they are encountered in the history classroom shapes the ways in which pupils make sense of the past: pupils do not encounter 'the past' in the classroom but the descriptions and accounts of the past which are framed by language. It is, of course, possible to see these modes of communication as separate from each other, and to consider talking and reading as distinct routes to understanding, but in practice they are closely intertwined. In this chapter we explore these modes both separately and together to think about the ways in which they can shape teaching and learning.

History classrooms are both linguistically rich and linguistically dense. Teacher talk, questioning, pupil responses, textbooks, evidence, written texts all provide modes through which the past is communicated to pupils and through which they present their understandings of the past. In classrooms we find registers – registers of the present, through which teachers establish some points of contact with pupils and pupils communicate with each other, registers of the past which – to some extent – pupils need to master in order to make sense of the past, and the registers of History as a discipline – the language of time, change and causation which historians use frequently. Individual words and expressions crop up and are deployed differently in these different registers: language changes and shifts its meaning. Words like 'revolution' meant something very different in the sixteenth century from their later meaning in the eighteenth, nineteenth and twentieth centuries; words like 'monarchy', 'empire' and 'parliament' shift their meaning in different historical periods; the word 'period' has an abstract and difficult meaning, but also – for pupils – an everyday meaning which might refer to a 'lesson'. Some words move rapidly between concrete and abstract: the word 'free' had a specific, often technical meaning to a Roman citizen and a quite different meaning to a contemporary teenager; the word 'crown' is an object worn by a 'monarch' in some 'periods', an abstract term referring to the powers of the 'monarch' and a dental treatment. Words in all these cases signify meanings which lie beyond the words themselves. What all this means is that the four communicative modes – talking, listening, reading and writing – are deployed in different ways both to develop pupil understandings of the past (lower case 'history') and their facility in communicating their grasp of historical thinking and reasoning (upper case 'History'). Given the complexity of this, images, whether still or moving, diagrams and charts have been supports to the main purpose of generating linguistically mediated understandings of the past. The range is huge, from contemporary visual sources to heuristic diagrams which 'represent' an abstract historical idea: the pyramid of authority and obligation in feudal England, or the simplified map of the 'triangular trade' in slaves and sugar in the eighteenth century, for example. The availability of digital resources via the internet opens up the possibility of accessing a much broader range of primary and secondary resources than was previously possible, and web 2.0 technologies create the possibility for thinking in more creative ways about the communication of history in school. However, in many respects extending the communicative range to the visual and symbolic, although intended to simplify the processes of communication, can add a further layer of complexity. The relationships between the different ways teachers and pupils communicate in history classrooms need some careful thought.

Talk is perhaps the principal way in which teachers mediate the past for their pupils: teachers narrate, explain, and ask questions, offer conclusions and summaries. Talk is also one of the principal ways in which pupils articulate their own responses to the past: pupils talk to teachers and to each other, answering questions and advancing ideas. Whole-class question and answer, in which teachers ask questions and individual pupils answer, remains a staple of history teaching as much as of other subjects. For all its dominance, this classroom technique has its sharp critics as a tool for the development of the communicative modes of speaking and listening. Whole-class question and answer does not, by and large, require pupils either to listen carefully nor to form clearly thought out responses. Most classroom research suggests some routinely characteristic features of such exchanges: teacher talk is punctuated with questions requiring short answers emphasizing recall; pupil strategies are principally confined to second guessing teacher demands, few pupils contribute, and those who do tend to do so relatively frequently, and few responses demonstrate extended thinking. In its standard form the dominance of whole-class question and answer does not develop the skills of advanced listening nor oral argumentation on which higher order cognitive responses depend (Andrews 1995). In this sense, much teacher-led classroom practice neither *models* the cognitive processes it is intended to promote nor does it *train* pupils in these processes. International evidence does suggest that this is not an automatic consequence of whole-class teaching (Alexander 2000). There are a range of alternatives which have been explored. In some classrooms, in order to prevent the situation in which a well-informed few answer all the questions, teachers do not ask pupils to raise their hands to volunteer answers; in others, teachers build in 'think' time before questions are answered; in others, questions are sequenced carefully to move pupils towards higher order thinking.

Bloom's taxonomy has been widely used in schools and has enjoyed a recent resurgence as teachers search for ways to build progression into their lessons, particularly through questioning. Both Bloom's original taxonomy (knowledge, comprehension, application, analysis, synthesis and evaluation) and his revised taxonomy (remembering, understanding, applying, analysing, evaluating and creating) define what 'lower order' and 'higher order' thinking entail and this can be a useful tool in moving beyond simply recall-type questions. However, as with any such tool, it benefits from a light touch, not least because each subject throws up its own characteristics. 'Understanding' the context in which a source was written and empathizing (not explicitly contained within the taxonomy) with its author may require a sophisticated insight into the nature of the past and of history which is multi-layered and far from 'low order'. 'Evaluating' a source may be more or less challenging depending on its nature and the confidence with which pupils may place it in context. Furthermore, if the taxonomy is applied too assiduously, teachers may restrict learning opportunities – the phrase might go something like 'They're a bottom set, so they're doing well to get as far as understanding' – and there is plenty of research to show that teacher expectation is a powerful factor (positively and negatively) on pupil outcome (Rubie-Davies *et al.* 2006). Overall, Bloom's taxonomy is a way of looking at knowledge, not a structure for teaching. The overuse of the taxonomy as a basis for questioning implies an assumption that pupil learning itself proceeds through a linear progression which is independent of context (Husbands 1996).

Of course, it is not only teachers who talk in history classrooms and if we are to take seriously constructivist theories of learning, it is imperative that pupils are provided with opportunities to explore their thinking with others. We saw many examples of activities designed to generate pupil talk in history lessons on our visits and evidence to support the view that a 'noisy classroom is a thinking classroom' (Rudham 2001). Pupils might talk in pairs, threes, or fours, they might be regrouped from 'home' groups into 'expert groups, or 'snowball' from a pair to a four. They might engage in class debates which are structured to ensure maximum participation and historical rigour (e.g. see Luff 2001; Hammond 2002), enact role-plays and teach each other. Underpinning all such activities is a belief that pupils learn through exploratory talk and that through the sharing of ideas, understandings are made, shaped and refined.

History is frequently regarded as one of the two or three subjects which make the most extensive reading demands on pupils. Principally, there are three reading activities which are found regularly in lessons: pupils read questions which are set by their teachers and to which they must respond, drawing on teacher exposition or texts; they read secondary textbook accounts of the problem or situation, either alone or through some form of reading aloud; and they read versions of primary historical sources as a basis for making some form of (normally) written response. The extent to which reading is used creatively to promote historical thinking – and, vice versa, to which history is used to support and extend literacy – is more problematic. Most reading in history lessons is 'transactional', focused on the extraction of information for subsequent evaluation from relatively short texts. This is despite the many potential reasons for reading in history that exist. Consider these A level reading tasks, for example (based on Kitson 2003):

- Read pages 24–27 and make a timeline of the key events of Hitler's rise to power.
- Read Chapter 3 and make notes on Nazi policies towards women.
- Read Gellately's article and summarize his argument about the German people and the Gestapo.
- Read the extracts from Kershaw and Fest and note the similarities and differences in their views about Hitler's long-term ambitions.
- Select a relevant book in the library to supplement your existing knowledge about the Police State.

In these examples, there is reading for basic factual information, reading for a sense of chronology, reading for interpretation/argument, reading for comparison and reading to expand existing knowledge. We would argue that reading tasks become much more purposeful when the reasons behind them are made clear and the nature of any scaffolding or activity is related to that purpose. In terms of the tasks above, it is likely that pupils would want detailed notes for the first two, summaries for the next two and much briefer notes for the last (or even annotations of existing notes). Implicit in all this is the notion of progression. The type of reading that is appropriate at any given time is determined by the types of reading already completed. It would be unwise to set a piece of complex 'academic' writing before the student has gained a firm grasp of the topic through more accessible reading and class discussion.

Often, source material is extensively rewritten and simplified in order to make it accessible to readers, which, though at times a necessity, can remove the drama from a text and make it less inviting to read (see Box 10.3, Chapter 10). We argue that pupil motivation is a critical factor in opening up texts and we agree with Counsell (2003a) when she challenges a misconception that to read a text means to understand every word in it (and thereby spending much time with a dictionary or a glossary). Instead, Counsell wants pupils to see texts more holistically: 'By focusing on the text [rather than on the individual words], and on the text as window into the word, we can get a deeper return' (Counsell 2003a: 3) and, not surprisingly, has encouraged the reading of lengthier texts and questioned the likelihood of anyone being motivated to read gobbets. Counsell exemplified this in a series of examples for Year 7 in 2004 where she draws on a range of techniques to encourage pupils to read lengthy extracts by the Roman poet Horace, by the modern writer of children's books, Kevin Crossley-Holland or by the historian Eileen Power. In each example, an entire sequence of lessons is built around a text and Counsell uses powerful ways to motivate pupils to read, and to read for much more than information. So Eileen Power provides pupils with a model of shaping and styling an argument, Crossley-Holland provides an insight into writing historical fiction (as well as an insight into the impact of change in the sixteenth century) and Horace provides an opportunity to question an historical source and extract anything of historical value from it. Similarly, Woolley explores ways to use a Thomas Hardy short story as a foundation to a study of the nineteenth century. By using a range of DARTs activities (**D**irected **A**ctivities **R**elated to **T**ext) – many examples of which remain highly popular and effective – she made a lengthy text, used in a lower achieving Year 8 class, accessible and engaging. For example, she arranged pupils into groups to hunt through the text for examples about particular themes such as crime and punishment; pupils used a layers of inference chart to capture information, inferences and questions about the text and she used the text as a starting point for pupils' hypotheses (Woolley 2003). Indeed, not only did the use of *The Withered Arm* engage pupils but it made the rest of the topic engaging too, because pupils were testing out the hypotheses made from Hardy in future lessons. Much of this boils down to a basic but vital message: make sure that the reason to read is made explicit, the text itself is engaging and the activities designed to motivate and support the reading are effective.

Oscar Wilde once said, 'Any fool can make history. It takes a genius to write it.' A substantial proportion of time in history lessons is spent writing and there is evidence to suggest it is one of the aspects pupils find most difficult and least enjoyable (Haydn 2005). The nature of the writing carried out in history lessons differs to some extent across key stages, but the range is likely to include what Coffin (2006) describes as 'recording genres' and the more challenging 'explaining and arguing genres'. Pupils might complete charts, answer comprehension-type questions, write essays or newspaper reports, put together a TV documentary or create a piece of historical fiction: the potential range of writing tasks is extremely wide. Despite this, Peter John's research suggested that much pupil writing required short answers and Coffin finds that historical recount – a form of recording – predominates above the construction of more challenging historical accounts. Although Coffin's analysis of classroom work suggests that pupils' writing – and the talking on which it depends – does demonstrate increasing abstraction and a shift from reliance on time as the main organizing factor of text, as students move through the genres, she argues that much remains at the level of recording rather than aspiring to develop argumentative skills. She argues that 'if teachers have precise labels for distinguishing genres, as well as a way of talking about the kinds of meanings that different genres foreground and the lexical and grammatical resources for expressing those meanings, then they are in a strong position to provide explicit guidance to students in their reading and writing of historical discourse' (Coffin 2006: 92).

Coffin's argument – that pupils would benefit from greater support in learning how to write in particular ways depending on the genre – makes a great deal of sense. Many history teachers have embraced ways of supporting pupils in writing analytically – usually to enable them to write a fairly traditional (and often impressive) essay – by providing various supporting mechanisms such as charts, card sorts, writing frames and so forth (see, for example, Counsell 1997). The writing of historical fiction has also received much attention in recent years (see, for example, Martin and Brooke 2002 and Hillyard 2010) and again the emphasis has been on understanding the structure and defining characteristics of this type of writing, using models and whole sequences of strategies to enable pupils to write compelling stories which demonstrate a degree of empathy with the past and a firm grasp of period detail. What both these types of writing – analytical pieces of extended writing and historical fiction – have in common is a requirement to devote time to developing pupils' understanding of what the genre requires and developing their skill and confidence to write in these particular ways. In our experience, especially at Key Stages 3 and 4, but also at A level, writing is often something that is taken for granted, something that just 'happens' when pupils have learnt what they are to write about. At Key Stage 3, this is partly because of a shortage of time: with only a lesson a week in most schools, and a lot of history to teach, it can be hard to prioritize teaching pupils how to write in particular ways. Teaching history through substantial enquiries lasting several lessons (possibly a half term), as outlined in Chapter 6, can help teachers find a way through here because time (perhaps a lesson or even two) can be built into the enquiry to produce a good quality outcome whether written, visual or oral. This tends to happen more naturally at A level and to some extent at GCSE too: written outcomes are set as a way of pulling together sequences of lessons. Of course, writing is not only about final outcomes – pupils will write in order to record information or to practise particular skills in most lessons – and nor is it only about writing at length, but in order for pupils to shine at writing in Coffin's 'explaining and arguing genres', they need to be taught how to do so.

Communicative modes in the history classroom

Over the last fifteen years, understandings of the place and nature of language in the classroom have changed markedly. Instead of seeing talking, listening, reading and writing as different activities, they have been explored in relation to each other and in relation to other communicative modes in the classroom. The work of Gunther Kress and others has explored the potential of multimodal approaches to understanding learning exchanges in classrooms and begun to shift the way communication is understood in classrooms (Hodge and Kress 1988; Kress and van Leeuwen 1996, 2001). In traditional approaches to communication, the assumption has been that communication chiefly took place through the medium of Language. Language made full communication possible (Kress et al. 2001: 2–7): that is, communication was seen as 'monomodal'. Kress and his colleagues make a theoretical distinction between representations (what an individual wishes to represent about the thing being represented) and communication (how this is done in the environment of making his representation suitable in a specific context). The basic unit of meaning in semiotics is the *sign* – a unit in which a form has been combined with a meaning, or in which a form has been chosen to carry a meaning. A sign is a form (a signifier) which is fused with a meaning (that which is signified). A white cloth may be a sheet, or a flag of surrender; a white cloth with a red cross a St George flag, a Crusader banner or a Red Cross flag. For semioticians, understanding – or expressing meaning – is a process of sign-making, and 'the sign-maker uses existing materials to make a sign' (Kress *et al.* 2001: 7); in the same way, pupils in history lessons use existing materials – from teacher talk, from textbooks, from documentary or other sources – to produce their own sign, the product of their learning. In a history lesson taught to Year 9 (13-year-olds) examining the challenging question of what was the 'key turning point' of World War II, the teacher handed out a worksheet with some short extracts from history textbooks. He projected onto a whiteboard screen a single slide which incorporated a series of signs – a Spitfire, a searchlight scanning the sky, a landing craft, a Russian tank and so on: the images were 'signs' which signified events in World War II. These signs were signifiers for events – the Battle of Britain, the Blitz, the siege of Stalingrad, D-Day – which carried meaning in the context of the lesson. Over the images he played mp3 extracts from two Churchill speeches – 'We shall fight them on the beaches' (May 1940) and the 'End of the beginning' speech (November 1942). In the lesson, pupils were asked to translate these signifiers into patterns of meaning to communicate their understanding of the topic. This sort of engagement is not atypical: pupils are required to master a set of signifiers – whether presented visually or orally ('the monarchy', 'revolution') – into communicative forms which convey their understanding of the past.

Understanding and communicating about the past pose obvious semiotic as well as cognitive challenges: resources act as signifiers for complex constellations of historical ideas. Historical sources provide fertile grounds for sign-making. Frequently this is obvious. The so-called Ditchley portrait of Elizabeth I was painted in about 1592 by Marcus Gheeraerts, and is widely used in classrooms. It is not merely a representation of the queen. It was commissioned by Sir Henry Lee of Ditchley in Oxfordshire, and the queen stands on a map of England with one foot at rest near Lee's estate. The portrait is a lavish collection of signs: it celebrates Elizabeth's divine powers. A jewelled heavenly sphere hangs from the queen's left ear, signifying her command over earth and sky. The sphere had been Lee's emblem when he fought as Elizabeth's champion in the annual Accession Day tilts. The background of the portrait appears odd – it is split between blue, clear sky on the left, and a threatening stormy sky on the right, indicating the message of royal authority over the forces of nature themselves. A widely reproduced print from 1650 purports to show the execution of King Charles I in January 1649. A large crowd is assembled before the Banqueting House. On the scaffold, the executioner holds aloft the head of the king. In the foreground, some of the crowd are shown having fainted. The print is often used in textbooks and classrooms as a (quasi-photographic) representation of this iconic event in English history. At the top of the picture, the king's torso – his head still attached – appears in a small panel, around which clouds swirl and the heavens open, welcoming Charles, king and martyr: the picture is a *sign* which carries assumptions about the event and its significance for royalists. Some of the significance of both these images is inaccessible to us because we do not understand the signifier in the context of the signification system of the period. In some lessons, such images might be used as an illustration, which robs them of their potential to open up wider understandings about the world view of artists and audience. History classrooms become richer when looked at through multimodal lenses and when it is accepted that learners are routinely asked to place their own understandings of signs and signification alongside signification systems from the past. Fifteenth- and sixteenth-century paintings from contexts as far apart as Tudor London, Renaissance Florence and Mughal India were dense with signification and iconography. In the classroom, work can be done to use understandings of this iconography to access value systems of the past. For young people used to reading similarly complex images of celebrities who have carefully positioned their image through choice of pose, clothing, accessories and settings this can be very powerful, as two semiotic systems meet.

There are a number of practical consequences of adopting a multimodal approach to understanding interactions in the history classroom. First, any historical topic in the classroom involves the understanding of a series of linguistic, visual, textual and digital signs. History teachers have become adept at deploying linguistic signs, the complex and rich, often subtly shifting meanings of concepts, concepts deployed in different ways in different periods and often in different ways in the same period (Husbands 1996). Less attention has been given to multimodal signs in the history classroom, to the complexities of unpacking visual and aural signs in historical material. But doing so enables pupils and teachers to think differently about the ways these signs operate and to consider the relationships between them. Secondly, pupils bring to their work a semiotic system which both helps, because of the facility in understanding sign systems, and hinders, because of the cultural and temporal specificity of this sign system. One of the creative challenges for the history teacher is the mediation between the cultural references which underpin that being studied, and the cultural references of learners.

Multimodal approaches also open up thinking about the range of signs and sign systems to which pupils can be exposed in the course of their historical learning, and make us think more rigorously about the relationships between linguistic modes and non-linguistic modes. Although it has not been unusual to show a film extract as part of a unit of work on history, systematic thought has frequently not been given to the ways in which young people might *use* the film in developing their own understandings. Given the range of communicative modes available at the beginning of the twenty-first century, it would be appropriate to consider the ways in which young people are asked to represent their understandings of history in particular communicative contexts, and to think systematically about the relationship between writing, which has a central place in understanding and representing complex ideas, and its functions in a variety of settings.

Assessment: making judgements

Assessment is an integral component of communicating in the history classroom: through assessment judgements, teachers communicate their appreciation of pupils' work, and provide a basis on which pupils can modify, correct or adjust their understandings as a basis for deeper understandings. Of course, the term 'assessment' is over-used in Anglophone education: teachers make assessments of individual pupil contributions in informal classroom exchange; they make assessments of more formal pupil submissions, normally in writing, which are completed after a sequence of lessons; they make assessments of pupils' progress over a period of time and they make assessments of pupils' level of attainment, which are reported to other audiences. And this teacher assessment activity is framed by a wider infrastructure of assessment: the frameworks of assessment provided by the national curriculum, and the patterns of assessment devised by external awarding and examining bodies. All of these activities involve the exercise of judgement about the qualities of contributions and all involve communication about these judgements to pupils and others. In recent years, academics and policy-makers have worried about the relationships between the different functions which assessment serves in these different activities. There have been extensive pressures to *contextualize* assessment. For example, the English Qualifications and Curriculum Authority urged in relation to primary teaching that judgements should take into account 'strengths and weaknesses in performance across a range of contexts and over a period of time, rather than focusing on a single piece of work' (QCA 2007c). There has been interest in the transparency of assessment to aid comparisons across schools and to enable parents to 'benchmark' their child's performance, by providing apparently clear statements of expectation in, for example, the national curriculum 'level descriptors' within the Attainment Target, or the exceptionally detailed mark schemes published by examining bodies (Box 8.1). Perhaps most radically there has been emphasis placed on the role of formative assessment carried out in everyday classroom practices so that teachers can base moment-to-moment decisions they make about the lesson and future lessons on evidence about pupil learning (Black and Wiliam 1998). All of these principles are sound: assessment should be contextualized, transparent and grounded in classroom practice, but it is equally important to note that assessment activities do inevitably involve the exercise and communication of judgement.

The best assessment practices are embedded in realistic contexts: the best way to assess whether someone can ride a bicycle is to ask them to ride one. In some subjects, authentic assessment contexts are easier to establish than in others. Authentic assessment contexts pose some obvious challenges for history teachers: pupils are asked to demonstrate their understanding of the past at one remove, through oral or written assessment which is – by definition – inauthentic in context. The 'authentic' past is unrecoverable; understandings of the past are always partial. This challenge of authenticity is a profound one for history teaching: it is relatively easy to ask pupils to provide the date of the Battle of Waterloo, or to sequence later nineteenth-century American presidents, but these very simple questions in themselves generate little valid evidence of a pupil's historical understanding. Such knowledge may be *necessary* but it is far from sufficient. For this reason, assessment in history has sought to become more authentic through the posing of more challenging questions. Some of these may be relatively conventional in focus – for example, asking pupils to explain the causes or consequences of a particular event, or asking them to account for the significance of a specific action or piece of evidence. Others may be more challenging: for example asking pupils to consider what alternative courses of action were open to a particular historical figure or to explore competing interpretations of an event. These tasks derive their authenticity from the ways in which they require pupils to identify, select, organize and present relevant knowledge to shape interpretations of an historical event or episode. However, classrooms also impose inauthenticity on pupil responses because of pressures of time or an insistence that some communicative modes are more 'useful' for assessment purposes than others. This frequently means that assessment opportunities in history lessons are either trivialized to factual recall questions or formalized to written work produced under time pressures.

In history teaching, contextualized and authentic assessment is that which asks pupils to think about their work *in context*. This can be achieved in a number of ways. Pupils might be asked to jot down – perhaps on a small whiteboard – their initial thinking about a problem before sharing it, so that time to reflect on a causal relationship or a challenging moral choice facing a historical figure is built in; they might be asked to think through and propose a hypothesis or generate ideas on the basis of having read some source material or seen a video. As Barzun and Graff point out, 'a note is a first thought' (Barzun and Graff 1970); in classrooms, this can be modelled. Most important of all, however, contextualized and authentic assessment needs to be located in the context of historical enquiries which span sequences of lessons, and the enquiry itself needs to sustain the assessment focus. The enquiry 'Why did the Romans come to Britain?' generates a series of investigations which are relevant to the explanation of an action, such as the Roman invasion of 43 CE, but equally rules out of authentic contextualization a series of different investigations, such as 'What was Roman Britain like?', which may divert the enquiry. Assessment of pupils' learning in this enquiry is likely to be developed over a number of tasks, a number of lessons as pupils develop ideas and present conclusions which help to conclude the enquiry.

It is almost a truism that it is difficult to establish whether a task has been completed successfully without clear and transparent performance criteria: such criteria help teachers and learners to understand what success and progress towards it look like. Assessment practices have increasingly reflected this, but in doing so they confront a challenge. In order to set out clear performance criteria, learning targets need to be atomized with precision. However, in practice, very little learning, or evidence for learning, presents itself in these atomized ways. This makes transparency in assessment a ferocious technical challenge. The English national curriculum has sought to resolve this in a number of ways over the twenty years of its existence, with the number of Attainment Targets varying between different versions of the curriculum. In its current form, the national curriculum sets out a single Attainment Target for history. At Level 5, the level expected of the majority of pupils at the age of 14, the Attainment Target requires that:

> Pupils show increasing depth of factual knowledge and understanding of aspects of the history of Britain and the wider world. They use this to describe features of past societies and periods and to begin to make links between them. They describe events, people and changes. They describe and make links between events and changes and give reasons for, and results of, these events and changes. They know that some events, people and changes have been interpreted in different ways and suggest possible reasons for this. Using their knowledge and understanding, pupils are beginning to evaluate sources of information and identify those that are useful for particular tasks. They select and organize information to produce structured work, making appropriate use of dates and terms.
>
> (QCA 2007b)

As an approach to defining performance criteria, the national curriculum Attainment Target has some merits: it aspires to be comprehensive, but it is defined at a high level of abstraction and connections – or, indeed, weightings – between the different components of the Attainment Target are undefined. Much of what is said is difficult to pin down: it is possible to 'describe features of past societies and periods' at any number of levels of conceptual sophistication, and to produced 'structured work' at any number of levels. Some of these difficulties can be addressed through exemplification of the level, and much work has been done on this. But other difficulties are more fundamental. The national curriculum Attainment Target pulls together assumptions about the development of pupils' *substantive* historical knowledge and progression in their grasp of *second order* concepts, without resolving the relationship between them. At Level 4 – the level expected of most pupils at entry to secondary education – the history Attainment Target opens with an expectation that pupils 'show factual knowledge and understanding of aspects of the history of Britain and the wider world. They use this to describe characteristic features of past societies and periods, and to identify changes within and across different periods'. The relationship between Level 4 and Level 5 is not immediately apparent. In relation to causation, the Level 4 descriptor requires that pupils 'give some reasons for, and results of, the main events and changes'. As we have seen in Chapter 7, progression in understanding causation is more complex than is suggested by these summary statements. To some extent, a broad brush statement of expectation in progression may be seen as helpful and supportive of professional judgement; but it is difficult to see that such an approach supports a clarification of what progression in history looks like. By way of contrast, Box 8.1 sets out a different *approach* to transparency in assessment criteria. Here, one A level awarding body has set out the standards 18-year-olds need to achieve at the grade A/B boundary and the grade E/U boundary. The underlying approach here is different: an assessment objective is defined and a series of performance expectations are set. However, in doing so the objective – itself a *partial* statement of what levels of expectation look like – is atomized into a series of strands which can be mapped onto pupil work and used to derive a view of levels of performance.

What all this suggests is that the drive for transparency in assessment criteria is exceptionally complex. Acknowledging such complexity is one stage in developing professional strategies. There are, however, a number of observations which can be made. The first is that the tensions between holistic and atomized accounts of what successful learning in history looks like are exacerbated in settings where there are pressures to describe performance against imposed levels too often. Because there is a tension between atomized and holistic descriptions of performance, veering too often towards one rather than the other is likely to be unhelpful. The second is that there are particular issues in relation to assessment in history which need to be addressed. Unlike most other school subjects, the second order concepts which define progression in understanding exist independently of the substantive knowledge they support: understanding, for example, the causes of the Wars of the Roses does not necessarily 'progress' onto an understanding of the causes of World War I. However, this does not mean that the reverse is true, and that there is not a concept – here 'causation' – which underpins understanding of specific contexts. In history, the substantive knowledge and second order concepts exist in dynamic relation to each other, so that assessment opportunities need to reflect the tension. Finally, it is important to recognize level-based assessment for what it is: a shorthand attempt to capture what it means to make progress in understanding. National curriculum Attainment Targets were created to assess pupil performance holistically at the end of each key stage, and are exceedingly blunt instruments with which to assess individual pieces of work (see, for example, Burnham 2009). Discussions with teachers in schools suggest that the pressure to assess pupils against national curriculum levels is widespread; in some settings, the pressure is redoubled by the identification of sub-levels to create the impression of more finely tuned assessment. Such practices restrict the type of work that pupils undertake in history to mainly written forms that can easily be assessed and moderated. Requirements to 'level' pupils seem to apply indiscriminately to all subjects, despite the fact that the core subjects may have three lessons a week per teaching group compared to history's one. There is little evidence that levels have integrity when applied to individual pieces of work (Oates 2010). Assessment strategies are often flawed, revealing more about the nature of the task and the teacher than the potential of the pupil (Donaldson 1986). There is no reason why a pupil should not do worse in an assessment during Year 9 than at the beginning of the year: the task itself will be different as will the historical context, the challenge of the language and the clarity of the teacher, but pressures on teachers – from parents, schools and the pupils themselves – to present a picture of consistent progress can make variation problematic. Burnham and Brown capture this when they observe, in an account of assessment 'without levels', that 'getting better often cannot be seen as finding the next increment. It is about revisiting, reshaping, reconnecting' (Burnham and Brown 2004: 11).

Box 8.1 Performance levels at GCE A level – *Edexcel, Objective1*

- Recall, select and deploy historical knowledge appropriately, and communicate knowledge and understanding of history in a clear and effective manner.
- Demonstrate their understanding of the past through explanation, analysis and arriving at substantiated judgements of:
  - key concepts such as causation, consequence, continuity, change and significance within an historical context
  - the relationships between key features and characteristics of the periods studied

A/B boundary performance descriptions	E/U boundary performance descriptions
Candidates characteristically:	Candidates characteristically:
(a) recall, select and deploy accurate, relevant and detailed historical knowledge appropriately	(a) recall and select some relevant historical knowledge appropriately
(b) show evidence of understanding through analysis and explanation and reach appropriate judgements about key concepts	(b) show some evidence of understanding through analysis and/or explanation and attempt some judgements about key concepts

(c)	show evidence of understanding through analysis and explanation and reach appropriate judgements about the relationships between key features/characteristics of the historical period	(c)	show evidence of some understanding through analysis and/or explanation and attempt limited judgements about the relationships between key features/characteristics of the historical period
(d)	communicate clearly and fluently, using appropriate language and structure, using standard conventions of spelling, punctuation and grammar	(d)	convey meaning clearly, although powers of expression may be limited and there will be errors in spelling, punctuation and grammar

Source: Edexcel (2009)

The most powerful motivation for development in assessment in the past decade has come from 'assessment for learning' research (Black and Wiliam 1998). Black and Wiliam drew on extensive international research to demonstrate that external, summative assessment was ineffective in promoting improvements in teaching and the quality of learning. The widespread use of high-stakes testing approaches appeared to distort learning, to encourage pupil and teacher gaming and to demoralize learners. In particular, over-emphasis on marks and grades, far from motivating learners, encouraged them to cultivate tactics and behaviours which produced the best marks rather than to develop their own learning; as a result, in these circumstances learners tended to play safe and to avoid putting themselves into situations where they might fail – avoiding challenging questions, for example. At the same time, high-stakes testing tended to encourage teachers to teach to the test, and to adopt teaching styles which met the needs of testing: an emphasis on short-term recall, and marks and grades. Finally, repeated emphasis on the importance of testing and the key focus of assessment demoralized learners, particularly lower attaining learners. Black and Wiliam outlined a compelling case for assessment *for learning*, placing the quality of feedback at the centre of the learning experience. There are two critical aspects of assessment for learning which history teachers need to grasp. One is the idea of metacognition and the other that of formative assessment. Metacognition – effectively the skills of thinking about thinking – equips learners with the intellectual tools and habits of mind to take responsibility for understanding their own learning (Black *et al.* 2003: 97). Formative assessment is 'usually informal, embedded in all aspects of teaching and learning' and involves using assessment techniques – notably questioning – to drive pupils' thinking, so that the assessment activities, embedded in teaching, 'provide information to be used as feedback by teachers and by their pupils...to modify teaching and learning activities' (Black *et al.* 2003: 2). This frequently involves finding ways to involve learners themselves in their assessment. Box 8.2 provides an example of one approach from an upper school in Suffolk.

Box 8.2 Self-assessment in practice in one school

Where are you now? Shade in a block in each column that best describes where you are now

Historical understanding	Using evidence	Communication	Personalized learning
You can analyse and explain a range of historical ideas – causes, interpretations, significance, diversity, change	You can support your answers with relevant evidence	You organize your work carefully and use historical words to explain your ideas	You show independence in the way you work
You are able to reflect on a range of different ideas and come to your own decisions and conclusions about the historical idea being studied	You can use sources together to help reach a conclusion or judgement	You organize your response to a question into clear and well-structured paragraphs	You can work independently with no extra help
	You can use the sources to support your key arguments	You can draw clear and balanced conclusions	You show that you can formulate your own questions and investigations
	You can give reasons why a source is useful and reliable	You use a range of complex ideas and words accurately	You collaborate with others and help to direct their learning
You can describe the historical idea being studied	You can comment on how a source fits into the period you are studying	You organize parts of your writing clearly using historical words to explain key ideas	You are able to work independently but with occasional guidance
	You carefully select information from a range of sources to support your argument	You structure your answers in class discussion linking key points together and using historical words and ideas	You can answer key questions with your own ideas and you are starting to think about your own questions
	You start to think about sources as more than just information – they may be incomplete or biased	You can reach a conclusion	You can work well as part of a team

	You use some relevant examples to support your answers	You can write answers to questions with short and clear points using historical words	You can work with other pupils but you prefer to be directed to particular tasks
	You use some relevant examples to support your answers	You can answer questions in discussion using historical words and ideas	You can answer questions if you have been given clear guidance

In practice, assessment for learning has proved extraordinarily challenging to implement in the classroom. There are several reasons for this. The first is that the circumstances which make it tempting for teachers – and learners – to focus on assessment *of* learning have by and large remained in place. High-stakes external testing at GCSE and at A level remain central features of the educational scene and have powerful backwash effects on earlier stages of the curriculum; in the same way, experience of testing at the end of primary school has a 'forward wash' effect on learner expectations of the sort of assessment practices they are likely to encounter in secondary schools. The second is that while assessment for learning has had an impact on teachers' classroom thinking, partly because of the difficulties already referred to, teachers have tended to adopt those aspects of assessment for learning which are most easily adapted to existing practices. Thus, feedback on written assignments has often become more extensive, with greater attention to annotating pupil written work, but these are assessments of pieces of summative work rather than the short-term, minute-by-minute assessment to inform teaching decisions and pupil work which advocates of assessment for learning emphasize (Black and Wiliam 1998). Peer and self-assessment have become somewhat more popular – but along with assessment for learning more generally have been deployed in the context of the 'levelling' of pupils' work, as if providing pupils with frequent sub-levels – themselves largely meaningless to pupils – and target levels will somehow transform the learning that takes place. As we have seen above, such practices in fact run contrary to the findings of Black and Wiliam. Successful assessment for learning practices involve disrupting some conventional assumptions about the relationship between teaching and learning, so that teaching approaches routinely collect information about what pupils know and understand, enabling teachers to adapt provision to support the next steps in learning. This involves careful thinking about learning objectives, questioning strategies and short- and medium-term learning plans.

Many of the strategies characteristic of assessment for learning generally can work well in history, including 'no hands up' question and answer, thinking time for pupils, self-assessment. However, some of the strategies to check pupil understanding, particularly at the end of lessons, can be too narrow to serve history's purpose well without some modification. Exit cards, for example, where pupils write down what they have learnt in the lesson before they can leave, or the use of mini-whiteboards or flash cards to indicate which answer is right, suit lessons where right and wrong answers abound.

In history, that is more problematic. A lesson about the nature and extent of change in nineteenth-century Britain is difficult to assess with a flashcard or post-it note on the board: to agree that life changed a lot or to assert that it hardly changed at all is to miss the point entirely when the key learning of the lesson is about the complexity of change, and its differential impact. Assessment for learning techniques need to be adapted in ways which advance, rather than divert, subject understanding.

9

Long-term planning: making history more than the sum of its parts

Arnold Toynbee is now best remembered for his twelve volume analysis of the rise and fall of civilizations, his comprehensive rebuttal of 'the dogma that life is just one damned thing after another'. For Toynbee 'human affairs do not become intelligible until they are seen as a whole'. If pupils are to understand that learning history is rather more than accumulating knowledge about a series of unconnected periods in the historical past, the subject needs to become more than a sum of its parts: it needs both structure and rationale. Pupils need organizing ideas and patterns which help to frame understanding and may offer an enduring framework for thinking. In this chapter we explore what these might be in three connected ways. First, in terms of the overall rationale which might underpin long-term planning; second, in terms of the ways pupils might develop a 'big picture' of the past and third, in terms of the ways pupils might make progress in their historical knowledge and understanding.

An event in and out of time: the restoration of Charles II

Let us start with an event familiar to most historians: the restoration of Charles II. What mental images does it conjure? Where does it sit in your own mental map of the past? Does this mental map place emphasis on what came before or after – is the event cause or consequence? These and other questions are shaped not only by knowledge and understanding of the past but also, potentially, understanding how the past relates to the present; no two people would make the same meaning of this event. Nor is our choice of event significant: it could have focused on any historical phenomenon.

Box 9.1 illustrates how one of us 'made sense' of Charles II through childhood and adulthood. If teachers want any understanding of Charles II to go beyond the initial childhood presentation of the 'merry monarch' accompanied by stories of Nell Gwynn, they must place him into a bigger picture of history. For history graduates this might come quite naturally. For example, Charles II may immediately suggest political turmoil (Civil War, Republic, Restoration, Glorious Revolution), social upheaval (plague and the Great Fire) or religious reaction (Act of Conformity, Popish Plot, Exclusion Crisis). Each of these interpretations invoke mental maps of Britain's past which would perplex the average 13-year-old, but which are central to making sense

---

Box 9.1 The 'meaning' of Charles II

He was restored on 29 May 1660. When I read this in my encyclopaedia aged – what – 8, 9, I decided this was a good thing as it happened on my birthday and I identified with the event (how thoughtful of him, I thought). In fact I remember defacing my encyclopaedia to add 29 May to the regnal year '1660' on the chart of kings and queens. In some way this got me into history. I remember a novel – again, I would have been about 10 – which began with the Battle of Worcester and the escape of Prince Charles. I forgot about the so-and-so, and when we did A level I immediately associated with the bolshy side – the parliamentarians, then (even better) the Levellers and then (better still) the Diggers. I realized that this was at odds with my childish sense of May 29 and I decided that the defeat of the republic was a Bad Thing. It was only at university that I realized what a duplicitous swindler Charles II was, but it really took Iain Pears's novel *An Instance at the Fingerpost* to finish him off for me – the power of childish misconception.

---

of any historical period or event. The task of the history teacher is not simply to teach what happened – one damned thing after another – but to bring pupils to some more rounded sense of the past which carries meaning.

Overarching goals and content choice

As we have seen in Chapter 1, the choices that history teachers must make are endless. Prescribed content in the national curriculum decreased between 1991 and 2007, which, while welcomed by most, has increased the pressure on teachers to create courses at Key Stage 3 which have clear, distinctive rationales and which somehow connect with the rather different approaches taken in examination specifications. What is more, teachers are required to develop and teach ambitious and wide-ranging curricula at Key Stage 3 in (typically) one lesson a week. One of the teachers we spoke to referred to the difficulty of fitting in 'medieval, early modern, industrial and twentieth century periods, as well as doing depth, breadth and thematic studies!' Meanwhile, concerns have been raised about pupils' lack of 'the bigger picture' in history, whereby pupils have some sense of how the topics they learn about relate to each other. This concern is often coupled with a dissatisfaction about what pupils know and a yearning that they should know about certain other things. Of course, one person's ideal big picture is not another's. Nevertheless, the desire for pupils to place their study into some kind of wider perspective is not misconceived, though it is important to be realistic about what is possible with particular age groups and within the time that is allocated to history in the school curriculum. The 2007 national curriculum attempted to address the lack of 'big picture' understanding by suggesting a number of themes that teachers might bring out in their teaching and by requiring history to be taught 'through a combination of overview, thematic and depth studies' (QCA 2007b: 115), all of which were familiar terminology to history teachers in England.

History teachers currently have a great deal of choice about what is taught at Key Stage 3 but less so at later key stages where, for the minority of pupils who study history, content is prescribed by examination specifications. Choice at GCSE has become particularly restricted, largely because of the ungainly struggle between awarding bodies to make courses profitable. Choice at A level opens up again, though it is still usually limited to tried and tested historical content. It is therefore only at Key Stage 3 that secondary history teachers tend to have genuine choice about what they teach, albeit within some kind of overarching framework.

Evidence suggests that teachers draw on different kinds of rationales when choosing what to teach, which range from the practical, such as the availability of resources or established habits, to the contextual, based on a set of assumptions about what particular learners might enjoy and need, to the more ambitious, which take seriously the idea that *what* and how teachers teach has the power to convey powerful messages about both the past and the present (Husbands *et al.* 2003; Kitson 2005). Some history teachers do have very clear overarching goals that inform their long-term planning. A teacher in Northern Ireland, for example, believes firmly that her classroom is where sectarian views about the past, and therefore also to some extent about the present, are challenged and where pupils are required to engage with alternative perspectives about past events for reasons that are very much rooted in present-day divisions (Kitson 2005). Similarly, a teacher in a school in England believes strongly in the links between history and citizenship. She says: 'I've got a mission to get kids to see politics not as party politics but…that they should feel empowered, that they're not an individual on their own, that it matters, they have a say', and both her choice of topics and the way she teaches them reflect this goal. When teaching about Northern Ireland, for example, she hopes that 'kids [will] extrapolate from that and…think more widely and hopefully get…an interest in the world they live in'(Husbands *et al.* 2003: 128). It is unlikely (and undesirable) that a single aim would dominate what and how history is taught, but some sense of overarching goals is likely to lend greater coherence to long-term planning, even if they are often undermined by shorter term objectives such as assessment.

However, teachers are not always able to articulate a rationale for including one part of history while excluding another, not least because the national curriculum appears to have set in motion a powerful definition of the 'canon' twenty years ago which stubbornly persists today. Even unit headings that have long disappeared from official curricula remain in many schools: 'medieval realms', 'making of the United Kingdom' and 'expansion, trade and industry.' The Battle of Hastings does not always have to be the starting point for planning a Key Stage 3 scheme of work: 'the key to coherence and progression is planning backwards' (Dawson 2008: 16). In other words, teachers must know what they want pupils to 'take away' from a study of history *before* starting to put together a long-term plan. The extent to which teachers ought to be determining these 'take aways' will be explored later in the chapter.

Box 9.2 summarizes the initial thinking of one history department in east London as it tried to grapple with the 2007 national curriculum and its emphasis on themes. Several overarching goals are discernible here. One addresses the development of a sense of 'big picture' history. The department clearly saw in the 2007 curriculum an opportunity to build up a series of narratives which by the end of Key Stage 3 might be fused into a sense of how different elements of the past fit together and are mutually dependent on each other within a broad chronological framework. This is the aim which underpins the themes of each year. Beyond that, the choice of themes and topics within each overarching theme is interesting. There are attempts to make direct connections to the pupils' lives and the role of the individual – especially in the first two themes – is emphasized. There is a desire for pupils to engage critically with the past and relate it to the present – the third theme, for example, is clearly designed to evaluate the extent of progress and the ways this can be measured. The range of specific topics extends from local to national to global, with an attempt to be genuinely wideranging in scope, both temporally (for example, by including the Egyptians, more commonly found on primary school curricula) and spatially (for example, linking London to the United States, India and the Middle East).

Box 9.2 Long-term planning in an east London school

A significant aim is to respond to the need for 'the bigger pictures' in history and to try to help children 'orientate' themselves in time. Key Stage 3 schemes of work are being rewritten around the themes of :

Term 1 (each year): Identity – 'How important is identity?'

Term 2 (each year): Voice and Representation – 'To what extent have people had a say?'

Term 3 (each year): Progress and Technology – 'How far has "progress" improved our world?'

These themes will encompass social, cultural, economic and political ideas and will be mapped against the key concepts. Areas covered will include:

· A local study, London's identity, national identity, popular culture and teenagers
· The growth of democracy, suffragettes, slavery e.g. Egyptians, Romans, Indians as well as transatlantic, liberty in the USA including civil rights movement
· Science and superstition, medicine – Medieval and Islamic, scientific revolution, industrial revolution, World War Two, Cold War, last fifty years – Holocaust, genocide, Middle East, the environment

---

Organizing the content: big picture history, themes and chronology

It is unlikely that any of us remember much of what is taught at school in the long term, at least in terms of specific detail, and this is as true for history as for any other subject. Albert Einstein is quoted as having commented that 'education is what remains after one has forgotten what one has learned in school'. This is one of the arguments underpinning skills-based approaches to the curriculum – that *what* is learnt is less important than *how* it is learnt and what *skills* are honed along the way. In this case, one of the current concerns among history educators – that children have a poor sense of the 'big picture' of the past and are largely unable to connect seemingly isolated episodes (QCA 2005; Ofsted 2007) – would seem irrelevant: if we are destined to forget what we learn, then presumably any content will do. However, there are other ways of characterizing 'content' and its longevity in the minds of pupils. Counsell (2000a) has distinguished between what she calls 'fingertips' and 'residue' knowledge, the latter being the knowledge that lingers when the detail starts to fade. Similarly, Byrom writes of an occasion when he happened upon an old history essay written years before: not only did he have no recollection of writing it, but neither did he remember anything at all about the subject matter, in this case, Phillip II's Angevin rivals. Does this mean that his knowledge doesn't matter? He goes on to explain that what does matter are the 'landmarks' – and that 'the more landmarks I have in my knowledge of the past the deeper my understanding is likely to be' (Byrom 2003: 13). Not only is the discipline and skill involved in thinking historically enduring; so are the patterns and shapes about the past that emerge from a study of that past.

In the first revision of the history national curriculum in 1995, explicit encouragement was given to incorporate 'depth' and 'overview' into long-term planning, made possible by a reduction in content specification. An overview can mean different things. It might be restricted by time, by place, by theme, or it might be an overview of something altogether bigger such as in Gombrich's *A Little History of the World* (2005). The exact nature of 'overviews' in the 1995 national curriculum was left open, though such overviews were by no means intended to be solely chronological and geographical. Primarily, overviews were intended to allow pupils to develop a broader understanding of the past, which could include setting events and changes in a broader spatial or temporal framework or broadening out the social and cultural context. In the wake of the 1995 curriculum, extensive work was done on the interplay of such overviews and depth studies. Dale Banham, for example, illustrated how an overview – in this case of kingship in the Middle Ages – might be *revealed* through a depth study of King John, deploying that memorable phrase 'the overview lurking in the depth' (Banham 2000: 23). Michael Riley's work on how to position overview and depth studies was also important, for example his suggestions that two overviews might book-end a series of depth studies or that an overview might be the product of a sequence of depth studies (Riley 1997).

Alongside the notion of overviews were thematic studies and the two have often gone hand in hand. The GCSE course devised by the Schools History Project included 'studies in development over time' which traced, for example, the history of medicine or energy from prehistoric to modern times. Covering such a broad time span inevitably involved overview blended with depth studies of, for example, key individuals such as Galen, Vesalius and Pasteur. Within the overall theme of medicine, further themes were (and still are) explored, such as the development of surgery, natural versus spiritual cures and the impact of war. This was – and still is – a highly sophisticated and complex unit to teach, combining chronological and thematic overviews and depth studies, though its role in developing 'big picture' understanding of the past has since been questioned by one of its architects (Shemilt 2000). At A level a requirement was introduced in 2000 to teach a unit spanning at least one hundred years, usually part of the 'synoptic assessment' of the syllabus, creating topics such as the economic development of Germany, 1870–1990. A more thematic approach to teaching history was encouraged in the 2007 national curriculum, though in this case the themes were considerably broader than the GCSE studies in development or the A level synoptic units. That is not to say that teachers were not attempting to discern themes in their teaching at Key Stage 3 before this, but it happened *ad hoc*. The pamphlet published by the Historical Association in 1997 to support teachers planning the Twentieth Century

World Key Stage Unit 4 assumed that teachers would not only wish to approach the teaching of Key Stage 3 chronologically, but to bring out particular themes in their teaching such as popular protest, overseas expansion and the treatment of poverty. It was not expected that these would be taught as discrete themes but that teachers would draw attention to the themes as they emerged to enable and support pupils to 'articulate analogies and anomalies' (Counsell *et al.* 1997:7).

Since then, greater emphasis has been placed on teaching thematically at Key Stage 3 and Ian Dawson's work has been particularly influential. Dawson uses the term 'thematic stories' to describe his practical approaches to long-term planning which support pupils in identifying, tracking and understanding 'stories' in the past. Dawson makes a powerful case for linking together the sum of what is taught at Key Stage 3 into a number of 'thematic stories' (Dawson 2004). These might focus on warfare and unity, religion and human rights, and social life and empires, for example, and should be 'tell-able in one lesson: a summary which enables pupils to see the whole story at once' (Dawson 2008: 15). These 'stories' will be revisited throughout the key stage and pulled together with some strong end of year or end of key stage concluding activities. By doing this, Dawson believes that pupils may develop a more sophisticated understanding of chronology and be better equipped to 'trace patterns of change and continuity across long periods of time' (Dawson 2004: 17). It may also, he argues, enable pupils to challenge hopelessly anachronistic comparisons between past and present. More broadly, it can give new meaning to individual enquiries by ensuring that bigger stories do not 'lurk, unseen' and enable pupils to develop 'a coherent big picture of the past' (Dawson 2008: 14) while making history more accessible by allowing pupils to capitalize on their emerging understanding of, say, political structures, by providing clear opportunities to revisit and revise this understanding (Counsell *et al,*. 1997).

A helpful illustration of Dawson's thinking involves Thomas Becket. The story of Becket is taught in many secondary schools, not least because it is such a powerful narrative. It could be possible to claim some link between Becket and the shifting balance of power between monarchy and church, but the role of the Becket murder is rarely linked to this kind of 'bigger picture'. Dawson argues that, in order for Becket to have some meaning beyond the event itself, the question ought not to be 'Why was Becket murdered?' but rather, 'Why was Henry whipped four years after Becket's murder?' The answer, of course, is that Henry had to secure church support against the rebellious barons, which suggests a rather less powerful monarch than the story of the murder itself might suggest. Dawson's choice of the word 'story' to describe this approach is significant in two ways: first, it denotes the power of narrative in our teaching and second, it emphasizes that each narrative is but one possible 'story'; not fixed, but open to interpretation and modification (Dawson 2008). There are some limitations as well as advantages to this approach. First, the stories are pre-selected; it is not the pupils themselves who decide what the stories are or should be and their responses to an enquiry will be shaped by the theme it is intended to illuminate (for example, see Brooker 2009; Jones 2009). In other words, if the theme is power and democracy, then this is the lens through which certain events, changes and developments will be viewed. Second, although a thematic story explores particular ideas or concepts over time, their meaning does not necessarily remain fixed: democracy in ancient Athens was different from democracy in the UK today (Jones 2009). Third, organizing history into stories could imply a level of determinism: what happened led inexorably to particular outcomes and the 'end' of the story. This is not, however, what Dawson intends: he uses the term story to emphasize that this is but one possible narrative and indeed writes that the story, told in outline at the start of the term, can be 'exploded' through pupil enquiry (Dawson 2008).

Box 9.3 sets out a summary of possible Key Stage 3 planning approaches in response to the 2007 national curriculum. All three have organized the substantive history into themes, based on those suggested in the 2007 national curriculum, but they are markedly different in the way they handle chronology and the way they have arranged the themes. In Model A, pupils study one theme each year, covering aspects of medieval to modern history. In Model C, pupils move chronologically from the first millennium to the present across the key stage, encountering one of five themes in each term. It is too soon to say what impact these different approaches have on pupils' understanding of the past and the evidence about how pupils best develop a coherent big picture of the past in general is inconclusive. Intuitively, it may make sense to teach chronologically but it should not necessarily be assumed that teaching chronologically is the best way to help pupils understand about one period in relation to another (Barton 2009). On the other hand, it should be possible to pull out themes and patterns in the past through a broadly chronological framework as long as the teacher is able to move nimbly between themes and relate each topic to them appropriately.

Box 9.3 Key Stage 3 long-term plans

Model A: Thematic and chronological within each year

Year 7	Living and believing 1066 to now
Year 8	Power and protest 1066 to now
Year 9	Conflict and co-operation 1066 to now

Model B: Thematic and wholly non-chronological

	Autumn = changing lives and attitudes, medieval to modern	Spring = power, conflict and co-operation, medieval to now	Summer = Civilizations and empires, medieval to now
Year 7	Daily lives	Rulers	Islam and the wider world
Year 8	Hearts and minds	Challenges to power	British Empire
Year 9	Moving stories	Impact of war	Britain and India

Model C: Wholly chronological with themes integrated throughout

		Themes running throughout, with each allocated to one or two terms:
Year 7	The first Millennium and Middle Ages	Everyday lives and beliefs Movement and settlement
Year 8	Islamic empires to Industrial Revolution	Power, democracy and the UK Empire
Year 9	Slave trade to now	Conflict and co-operation

Source: Historical Association (online)

Historical consciousness and frameworks

Implicit in all work in this area is a sense that the elements of history education need to be connected and inter-related to some form of 'big picture' – a 'map of the past' or a sense of the passing of historical time. It is argued that this might help pupils to establish history 'landmarks', to make the kinds of temporal and spatial connections that characterize higher order thinking, to provide a greater sense of satisfaction for pupils and to prepare them better for further study. As we have seen, this is nothing new. The relationship between what became known as big stories and little stories, together with overarching themes, has been teased out in the pages of *Teaching History* over a number of years (see, for example, Rayner 1999; Banham 2000; Riley 2000; Byrom 2000; Barnes 2002; Sheldrake and Banham 2007). Indeed, it goes further back to the later nineteenth-century preoccupation with 'our Island story' – itself nothing more than a 'big picture' of the historical past. Despite recent work to bring out the 'big stories' of history, however, there is evidence to suggest that pupils are not necessarily developing a sense of the past – or what some call a 'historical consciousness' – which goes beyond specific topics (Howson 2009).

The Centre for the Study of Historical Consciousness defines historical consciousness as 'individual and collective understandings of the past, the cognitive and cultural factors which shape those understandings, as well as the relations of historical understandings to those of the present and the future' (http://www.cshc.ubc. ca/about.php). Everyone has their own more or less sophisticated historical consciousness which helps them (to greater or lesser degrees) to understand the world as it is and is likely to be. Its application in the field of education is highly practical. Adults will rarely engage in historical enquiry, but instead will deploy the conceptual and methodological tools developed in history lessons to deal with everyday issues – their 'social reality' (Laville 2006). This could involve exercising critical (historical) thinking when using the internet or it could be about making sense of modern conflicts and elections or envisaging future patterns of work. The more adults can bring an understanding of the past to bear on their understanding of the present and future, the more, it is argued, they can hope to make informed decisions and exercise good judgement.

A term recently used in the UK to describe this kind of functionality is a 'usable past', to denote a past that pupils can use to help orientate themselves in time, rather than the more commonly used term of 'utility', which implies a past that serves functions ascribed by others, such as being a good citizen (Howson 2009). The Usable Historical Pasts project – summarized more fully in Chapter 5 – found that pupils were poorly equipped to view the past as anything more than sporadic, random episodes and that this presented an obstacle to them using the past as any kind of basis from which to comment on the present or future. It suggests that pupils are not developing a picture of the past sufficiently 'big' to enable them to get beyond singular events and to make generalizations about patterns of change that help make sense of the world as it is today. Complexities emerge when the kind of big picture that might fit the bill is discussed. Although Rusen advocates a common European historical consciousness to support European unification, supported by 'concrete historical knowledge' (Laville 2006), this is not quite what is envisaged by academics in the UK where the work of

Peter Lee and Denis Shemilt has been most influential. Lee and Howson, for example, reject any notion of a single 'big story' (Lee and Howson 2009). Consider the story of Britain since 1066 – a story often told in secondary schools. Is it to be taught as the story of progress, of tolerance, of exploitation, or of political liberty – or none of these? The answer, of course, is that it could be some or all these things and it may not the job of the teacher to decide but rather the pupils.

In fact, the example above may not be big enough: Shemilt, for example, wants the history of human activity in the frame (Shemilt 2009). Shemilt stresses that this is a *teaching* issue: 'Left to their own devices few adolescents articulate synoptic overviews of the past from masses of data taught over weeks, month and years' (Shemilt 2009:141). He argues that the content of history lessons is more likely to build into usable 'pictures of the past' when framework overviews of the past are taught over single lesson time spans rather like Dawson's thematic stories and revisited at regular intervals, when pupils are taught how to organize historical data into 'big' pictures by being taught how to form generalizations, and when teachers themselves pose problems about the relationship between the present and the past. Sitting alongside these frameworks could be, say, thematic studies, but by relating these to a bigger picture it might be possible to 'delineate the deep currents that shape the lives of millions upon millions rather than the frothy antics of the few' (Shemilt 2000: 94). To support this big picture of the past, a particular conception of a framework has been developed. A framework could, in theory, consist of a timeline of kings and queens, a thematic story or a period study but the kind of synoptic framework proposed is bigger – dealing at the level of humanity rather than at the level of particular periods, more open to continual revision and providing an overview which is regularly revisited (Howson 2009). This is likely to be thematic – Shemilt suggests 'Modes of Production', 'Political and Social Organization', 'Growth and Movement of Peoples' and 'Culture and Praxis' (Shemilt 2009) – and able to support generalizations which go beyond specific events and deal with broad patterns of change and development.

There are both potential problems and exciting opportunities arising from this work. There are as yet few examples of teachers working through these ideas in the classroom and the ambition that lies behind them could alarm teachers who have never thought about history in this way and who, without further practical examples of how this might work, might wonder if this approach could be remotely feasible with a challenging teaching group. It may also be the case that there *are* particular stories teachers want pupils to be familiar with which create a common historical consciousness that serves valuable social functions (this is explored further in Chapter 12). Furthermore, there is an inevitable limitation to how much pupils can know: Dawson claims that 'an all embracing framework of knowledge by the end of Key Stage 3 is simply too ambitious' (Dawson 2008: 14). Finally, the goal of a big picture created out of a number of large-scale thematic frameworks that pupils respond to reflexively and in which they identify patterns and narratives for themselves is to some extent unattainable. By providing frameworks at all, some restriction has already been posed on the kind of big picture of the past that is available and the role of the teacher as mediator is likely to restrict this further. While it is highly desirable for pupils to discern large-scale patterns of behaviours and states of affairs themselves, the extent to which they can do so independently must surely be limited.

And yet, for all the potential limitations, there is something alluring about the vision painted by Shemilt, Lee, Howson and others, and it relates to its highly practical, usable dimension. If a 'big picture' of the past is possible to achieve – and even this is open to question currently – and if it enables pupils to make greater sense of the present and the future by drawing some highly generalized conclusions about the past, then there may be something here of importance. Certainly, at a time when school history sometimes struggles to expound its use both to society and to pupils, providing a way of making history more 'usable' could be vital. It certainly alleviates the problem of teaching 'one damned thing after another'. If it is ever to work, however, it must be highly inclusive and accessible to all pupils.

Perhaps thinking about long-term planning and thinking about historical enquiry are at similar junctures: in both cases there are things teachers can do – frame good enquiry questions, identify helpful thematic stories – to secure engagement and learning, but both may be enhanced if the pupils are themselves in control. By framing their own enquiry questions, pupils are likely to gain considerable insight into what makes a good question in history and are likely to be more motivated to answer it. The same may be true for pupils' big pictures: the more they are consciously constructing, revisiting and revising their own big picture of the past, the more they may understand its significance and be motivated to extend it. Of course, the role of the teacher, as ever, is critical in both cases and the idea of independent enquiry can be taken too far: the teacher sets the parameters and will need to provide both good models of enquiry questions and effective frameworks within which pupils can build up big pictures.

The concept of a synoptic timeline, taught rapidly in the first instance and regularly revisited, is a compelling one. Within this broadest of overviews, any number of frameworks – including a chronological one or those suggested by Shemilt – might work. Dawson's thematic stories, though not perfect, remain an accessible route into thinking beyond individual topics and their effectiveness might be enhanced if teachers involve pupils in discussions about what to call this 'story' and whether the nature and name of the story changes over time.

Whatever route teachers take in developing thematic stories, overviews or other kinds of big pictures, it is crucial that the smaller stories of history are not lost. Some of the existing work on blending overview and depth has already been mentioned. The challenge for history teachers is to move their teaching and pupils' thinking between the large arcs of historical time and the personal stories which often engage and interest learners. History is a subject concerned with people in the past in their infinite variety and is replete with small stories that hook pupils' interest and help us to understand what was really going on at a human level. A big picture ought therefore to be about helping pupils make *more meaning* out of the particular people and particular episodes they are studying (Rogers 2009). It should not be about turning all history lessons into overview-type surveys which remove all that is most compelling and engaging about history, but ought to be a way of helping learners to develop those 'landmarks' that Byrom described when he happened upon his old history essay on Philip II. There are many examples beyond school history of how small stories can feed into bigger pictures. The BBC's collaboration with the British Museum to tell 'A history of the world in 100 objects' (http://www.bbc.co.uk/

ahistoryoftheworld) was described in Chapter 3. The premise of the series means that the people who made the objects, used them, saw them, left them behind, are centre stage. The story of The *Ordeal of Elizabeth Marsh* in Box 9.4 provides a further and rather wonderful example.

Box 9.4 The Ordeal of Elizabeth Marsh

In *The Ordeal of Elizabeth Marsh*, Linda Colley (2007: 261) uses one obscure but remarkable woman to explore some of the biggest questions of all. Elizabeth Marsh was born in 1735 to a British shipwright father and a Jamaican mother. Conceived in Jamaica and born in Portsmouth, Marsh was, as Colley puts it, 'in motion for most of her life'. She spent significant amounts of time in a half-dozen cities and towns, from London to Madras, following her parents, her husband and, at times, her own schemes. She spent three months as a hostage in Morocco in 1769 and produced a memoir of the experience. Colley tracked Marsh's family connections to Spain, Italy, Central America, coastal China, New South Wales, Java and the Philippines; through this virtuoso historical detective work and outstanding narrative skill, Colley shows us how one woman's life in the eighteenth century illuminates the large themes of identity, cultural exchange, and emergence of a world economy.

Progression in historical thinking and understanding

As we explored in Chapter 5, pupils make progress in terms of what they know and also in terms of their historical thinking – the key concepts and processes which are of course closely linked to the content knowledge they develop. Much of this chapter has focused on the way teachers structure and present substantive knowledge to pupils but of course it is essential to plan for both kinds of progression in the long term. One school we visited said that they 'home-grow' their A level pupils 'in that the skills that are needed are begun in Year 7 and built upon in subsequent years'. This can be difficult when pupils come to the school for A level from other schools in the area with different approaches to learning history lower down as 'sometimes we have to start again, trying to undo what they have previously learnt'.

Box 9.5 contains one department's Key Stage 3 plan which is built around some excellent enquiry questions that focus on particular historical key concepts. Opportunities to revisit concepts are built in for two reasons: first, so that an understanding of a concept need not be developed in a single enquiry and second, so that sufficient opportunity is provided for pupils to achieve high levels of understanding of that concept. Any long-term plan that takes this kind of progression into account must reflect what progression in that concept might actually look like and what pupils' likely preconceptions might be. The progression that any single pupil makes is unlikely to be linear, with variables ranging from the quality of teaching, familiarity and ease with the subject matter and the power of their preconceptions, but if departments do not have a clear and shared understanding of what an increasingly sophisticated understanding of, say, significance or causation might look like, it will be difficult to build in opportunities to make progress in these areas across and beyond a key stage.

Box 9.5 Revisiting key concepts to support progression: an example

Evidence

Year 7:   What is history?

Year 8:   'William didn't conquer Britain – he created it!' Do you agree?

Year 9:   What do stories about Attelborough boys tell us about WWI?

Causation

Year 7:   Why did Norfolk farming change after 1750?

Year 8:   Why do we have a Church of England?

Year 9:   Is there any rhyme or reason to Islamic terrorism?

Change and continuity

Year 7:   If stones could speak, what could they say in Attelborough church?

Year 8:   Which protestors have changed British society the most?

Year 9:   A revolution in ideas: how big a step forward was the Renaissance?

Interpretations

Year 7:   Is Norwich castle a fake?

Year 8:   Was the Magna Carta the only 'good thing' from King John?

Year 9:   From hymns to hip hop: can songs truly represent black people's fight for freedom?

Significance

Year 7:   Why bother with Queen Boudicca?

Year 8:   Who had the more explosive impact on our country – Guy Fawkes or Oliver Cromwell?

Year 9:   What history will your children be learning?

Diversity

Year 7:   How can we hear the different voices of nineteenth-century Attelborough?

Year 8:   Did Britain change the world or did the world change Britain?

Year 9:   Who suffered the most in WWII?

Sources: Bradshaw (2009)

Conclusion

This chapter has explored difficult and challenging issues. Often, when teachers think about planning, they think about the need to plan stimulating and engaging lessons. That remains a central professional responsibility, but individual lessons also sit within a longer experience of learning, and it is this which we have set out to explore here. Research evidence suggests that for most pupils the experience of school history does not provide them with 'big picture' understandings of the past which enable them to see the present in the context of long waves of historical change. These long patterns of historical change have been crucial in shaping both the world today and the historical past more generally: the experience of child labourers in Manchester at the beginning of the nineteenth century was part of a long wave of industrialization which can be traced back to the sixteenth century and forward to the collapse of large-scale manufacturing industry in western Europe in the later twentieth century; the experi-ence of the Indian Mutiny is part of a widespread colonial encounter between Europe and the wider world which has shaped assumptions and societies in the post-colonial era. History teaching on this grand scale is demanding of teachers, but the accumulat-ing evidence suggests that a reluctance to plan and think on this grand scale is limit-ing children's ability to make sense of their past. The approaches we have discussed here – the need to think about the relationships between personal stories and wider scale historical change, the need to plan for progression in ideas and understanding as well as in the acquisition of knowledge, the need to reflect on the nature and focus of historical consciousness – provide a set of tools to stimulate thinking, and a frame of reference for long-term planning.

10

History teaching for all

Schools strive to be inclusive learning environments in which all learners have the opportunity to succeed, whether they find learning easy or difficult, whether they need additional support or extended challenges to enable them to realize their learning potential. Schools deploy a variety of tools and devices in order to help them achieve this goal, including the way the curriculum is structured, the way pupils are grouped and the way classrooms are managed. History teaching operates within the constraints and opportunities afforded by such whole-school decisions. In practice, much of the focus of schools' provision relates to pupils who need, and deserve, additional provision, whether these are pupils with special needs which require additional support to enable them to access the curriculum, or those who are gifted and require additional challenge. However, it is perhaps too easy to forget that inclusive practices have a much wider focus. In principle, all learners have individual needs, and they all experience learning in different ways that might be affected, for example, by their gender, ethnicity, social class. In this chapter, we explore some of the ways in which history teachers can address individual needs and differences, and the ways in which inclusive practices relate to the learning of all pupils.

The learners in history classrooms

For many teachers, the first knowledge they have of a pupil derives from various sources of data available to schools such as those in Box 10.1. Such data is used in different ways: it informs the ways pupils are organized into classes, for example by setting, and it supports the way teachers plan for inclusion in their classroom. Sonja may need some additional support to access certain texts and written tasks, Michael needs to be given very tight boundaries and focused tasks to prevent him from misbehaving and Jaya may need considerable scaffolding from the teacher and teaching assistant in order to access the curriculum. This data is both useful and potentially limiting: it provides information which can help teachers meet pupil needs and mitigate the prospects of under-achievement but it can also define the pupil in particular and narrow ways which may not be the whole story. Rarely is the data subject-specific, especially in non-core subjects, so it can mask particular strengths or weaknesses in understanding history, and it almost never takes account of pupils' interests or motivations. As schools have accumulated more data on pupils and have codified it in a variety of ways – through special needs registers, gifted and talented registers or logs of pupils with English as an Additional Language – they have also tended to create labels for pupils which are hard to shift. Such data is obviously extremely valuable, but it can only go so far in helping teachers to meet learners' needs. Take Sonja, for example. Having arrived in England when she was 9, her low test scores at Key Stage 2 might have been largely the result of language difficulties. However, her failure to make much progress in history lessons in Year 8 may be less to do with her language development and more to do with a lack of motivation because Sonja does not consider the past that she is learning about to be anything to do with her. In Michael's case, it is the symptom of a problem – his poor behaviour – rather than its cause that has been highlighted: in fact, Michael is bored by his work and losing faith in his own ability to do better. The pupil sitting near him, Kemal, is on the school's Gifted and Talented register and is provided with extended tasks as a result of which he attracts teacher attention and praise. Unfortunately, Michael is not on the same register and, perhaps as a result, is not challenged and acknowledged in a way that might motivate him further. Jaya was passionately interested in history at primary school, but the bottom set she is in is unruly and she no longer has the opportunities for the quiet, independent work at which she flourished in Year 6. As a potential grade E/F student, Jaya is unlikely to be allowed to take history beyond Year 9 even if she wants to because it is school policy to exclude pupils from subjects in which they are likely to achieve below a grade C.

Box 10.1 Three Year 8 pupils

Sonja
Special Educational Needs (SEN) status: Not on register
English as an Additional Language (EAL): Yes
Gifted and Talented: No
Home language: Albanian/Shqip
English Test Level KS2: 3
Maths Test Level KS2: 4
End of key stage Target (history): 4B

Michael
SEN status: School Action (Behaviour, Emotional and Social)
EAL: No
Gifted and Talented: No
Home language: English
English Test Level KS2: 4
Maths Test Level KS2: 5
End of key stage Target (history): 5A

Jaya
SEN status: School Action Plus (Specific Learning Difficulty)
EAL: Yes

Gifted and Talented: No
Home language: Persian/Farsi
English Test Level KS2: Unknown
Maths Test Level KS2: 3
End of key stage Target (history): 3B

Three pupils and three different sets of data which only partially explain their needs and the ways in which these needs might be met. Successful teaching involves going beyond the data to understand the pupils themselves. Sonja needs to be persuaded that the history she is studying carries some meaning for her personally; Michael needs to be challenged and rewarded to gain a sense of pride and Jaya needs to be allowed to work independently in order to achieve further.

What might 'inclusive history' look like?

'Inclusive practices' in the classroom are multi-faceted. The most common practice is associated with teaching approaches which focus on the achievement levels of the pupils and, indeed, this is of crucial importance and addressed in detail later in the chapter. Academic achievement is, however, one dimension of a broader issue: it is an outcome in relation to specific inputs. Teachers needs to consider pupils' starting points when they enter a classroom and their learning needs, broadly defined. Pupils have widely varying needs which impact on their learning, and these can be characterized as social, affective and cognitive. Social needs centre around the pupils' identity and cultural context, affective needs are concerned with the learners' views, feelings and characteristics and cognitive needs address the need for appropriate challenge (Pollard 2010). In each case, it is only through a combination of the available data, a determination to know the pupils as well as possible and moment-to-moment assessment of the learning taking place in lessons that teachers can implement successful inclusive practices in their classrooms. There is evidence that the more expert teachers become, the more likely they are to show 'sensitivity to contexts and situations' (Pollard 2010), and the assessment for learning movement has been helpful in encouraging teachers to root the quick decisions they routinely take in lessons in evidence about the quality of learning taking place (Black *et al.* 2003). Clearly, then, many of the issues around inclusion facing history teachers take them far beyond the subject, particularly those concerned with the affective dimension. Guy Claxton's association of successful learning behaviours with the '3 Rs' – resilience, reflectiveness and resourcefulness – is a useful way of thinking about this. Reaching the pinnacle of achievement in any field, Claxton argues, requires considerably more than talent: it requires a disposition, a motivation and a determination to learn. In schools, pupils who display some or all of the 3Rs are more likely to succeed, but resilience may be one of the hardest to achieve: 'Learning can feel like an assault on one's very own belief in oneself' (Claxton 1999: 52). Inclusive practices in any classroom, whether history or mathematics, music or French, must take account of social, affective and cognitive needs, drawing on data, on knowledge of the pupil and on routine use of assessment for learning strategies in the classroom.

There are some specific challenges of inclusion in history teaching. We know something about the ways pupils can struggle to understand the past and to think historically because of certain mental 'blockers' they experience, for example the belief that history is a copy of the past or that people in the past behaved as they did because they were stupid (see Chapter 5). If pupils are not helped to overcome these 'blockers', progress in history will be difficult. We also know that the language of history is challenging for many pupils and that the level of abstraction in history (one cannot generally 'see' a revolution) may be difficult for some. This has led, in the past, to scepticism around pupils' capacity to study history, particularly when based on Piagetian theories of learning (Cunnah 2000), but a strong research tradition suggests that, with the right kind of teaching, pupils are able to grasp abstract concepts and to make progress in understanding history both as a form and a body of knowledge (e.g. Booth 1978; Dickinson *et al.* 1984; Shemilt 1987). This has led to a consensus among most history educators that it is possible to make history accessible to all pupils while remaining faithful to its fundamental principles and aims. In other words, pupils can understand, analyze and interrogate the past when provided with the right scaffolding, tools and knowledge. Here, successful inclusive practices depend on sensitivity to the nature of history as a discipline *in the light of* the challenges pupils face.

Beyond the cognitive challenges of history, however, there is evidence that the kind of knowledge that is valued and recognized in history classrooms (or indeed by researchers seeking to find out how much pupils 'know') may be somewhat limited and far from inclusive and that this, in turn, limits teachers' capacity to engage learners. Wineberg has argued that, too often, claims are made about what history pupils do *not* know; attention currently, at least among some researchers, is shifting towards what they *do* (Wineberg 2001). A number of history educators have emphasized the importance of 'starting from where pupils are' (e.g. Seixas 1993 and Wineburg 2000) by exploring what pupils already know through developing family history, local sites, monuments, mainstream films, drama, books, and other media. They argue that history is all around us and not just in the classroom; it can be learnt from other people and not just those in school. In Northern Ireland, for example, pupils learn about the past at home – 'street history' – which they know is a different kind of history from school and which can become the dominant history if not acknowledged and explored explicitly in the classroom (Barton and McCully 2005). Similarly in England, when teaching about King John or the Crusades, President Kennedy or Hitler, it is likely that pupils will bring into the classroom the knowledge derived from films, TV documentaries or their parents. By failing to take account of what pupils already know – some of which will have value and some of which may need challenging – teachers can do little to move on pupils' thinking about those topics because school history will simply be seen as a 'version' of the past like any other and we may as well allow pupils to learn about the past from Oliver Stone.

Research in the United States suggests that 'official' (i.e. school) history and 'vernacular' (i.e. outside school) history rarely coincide. Barton and Levstik's work with 10- to 14-year-olds suggests that 'official' history of the US is aspirational and focuses on progress and achievement in the US while 'vernacular' history is more likely to address 'private prejudices' and policies that are working against social inclusion. The challenge, they argue, is to provide a framework for making 'critical sense out of both legitimating stories and alternative, vernacular histories' and to enable pupils to 'decide for themselves' which version is best (Levstik and Barton 2008: 261). Although some of the features of history classrooms in the US which Levstik and Barton describe – where exposure to the 'complexity and diversity of perspectives' is not always apparent – are not necessarily present in the UK, the authors' claim that 'history matters politically' because it informs people's political and social values is certainly true internationally. Pupils will draw on whatever version of the past they have to hand to justify or inform particular views and positions. If the version available in school seems too remote, too disconnected from the versions at home and from the TV, it may become less 'usable' and, in turn, may be cast aside in favour of less critical and less informed versions. The point here, in relation to inclusion, is that we are more likely to be effective as history teachers if we take account of the many different starting points that children bring with them into the classroom which arise out of their diverse cultural and social contexts. Pupils may learn about the past through rich oral family history traditions, or from computer games and wall murals. To dismiss these as myth, 'popular' (and therefore unworthy) history or propaganda is to dismiss the ways in which children learn: by making meaning of new knowledge by aligning it with existing knowledge. If such an alignment – whether this involves challenging or reinforcing existing knowledge – does not occur, then there is a risk that this new knowledge will be discarded or, at best, transient.

It seems likely that issues of social class, gender and race have profound and particular influences on pupils' starting points in history classrooms and on the version of the past – the one constructed in school or the one learnt at home – which pupils find most usable in explaining and understanding the present. Kay Traille's work in the UK, for example, suggests that Afro-Caribbean pupils' experience of history is not always what is intended by teachers and expected by the Afro-Caribbean community: they can in fact feel excluded and marginalized from studying the past (Traille 2007). This includes occasions when topics often thought to have a 'multicultural' appeal are taught, including slavery, which can all too often portray slaves – and, by default, black Africans – as victims. Terry Epstein's work in the US presents similar findings: when African-American pupils fail to connect with the dominant narrative in the classroom, they do two things: switch off in class and construct their own, alternative narratives that have little to do with the history they learn in school (Epstein 2009). There is relatively little work on the impact of either gender or class in relation to pupil learning in history classrooms – although the underrepresentation of women and minority groups in books and schemes of work has been explored (Smart 2010), and both are well documented in more general terms. Certainly, pupils' cultural reference points, general knowledge and vocabulary play a huge role in their ability to access the curriculum. In one school we visited, the teacher argued that history was an elite subject 'in the way it is examined' and used the example of a GCSE paper in which the word 'portrayal' was used; she felt this excluded a majority of pupils. Research on children's vocabulary in the US found that what matters in determining the number and quality of words that a child understands is relative economic advantage and not gender, race or birth order. Hart and Risley's study suggested that in the course of a typical hour, children of parents on welfare heard 616 words, while children of professional parents heard 2153 words in the same period of time (Hart and Risley 1995). It is hard to overstate the impact of this on a child's ability to access the school curriculum, including history – a subject drenched in literacy – with confidence and skill. It is also surely the case that to label children whose vocabulary is severely limited in this way as 'low ability' does not quite capture the complexities or the potential for pupils to develop given the right support.

Taken as a whole, such research raises complex implications about what being 'inclusive' means. Faced with large, mixed gender, multi-ethnic, mixed ability classes, the concept might seem daunting or overwhelming. Any response to these challenges has to focus on finding a point of connection with the past – a 'way into' a topic that is accessible and which has resonance for pupils. It is, of course, not realistic to tailor the history curriculum to every child's needs. However, there are ways to make history matter because of the many enduring and common human experiences that transcend borders: the experience of the persecutors and the persecuted, the rich and the poor, the victors and the vanquished: all are there for us to see. By drawing on pupils' prior knowledge and by focusing on human experience, we can find many points of entry. We return to the idea of finding resonance with the past in Chapter 12.

There are other powerful reasons to choose content carefully. History plays an integrative as well as a multicultural role: it is important for learners to learn the history of the country in which they live; equally, any history of Britain must be inclusive, and should acknowledge the complexity of the history of a polyglot nation of migration and transhumance over two thousand years. By studying a wide range of historical experience, learners come closer to understanding the range of human experience and are more able to put UK history into a broader perspective. In practice, the challenges of such diverse content are considerable. While it is important, for example, for learners to explore the history of slavery, its abolition and its continuing impact on the modern world, to study black Africans only as slaves, rather than in the broader context of African and Caribbean history before and after slavery is one-dimensional and likely to perpetuate stereotypes. Equally, for pupils to encounter European Jews only in concentration and death camps rather than as members of vibrant, diverse communities before 1933 is to create stereotypes and simplifications. Such simplifications are not only unhelpful, but also restrict an understanding of the significance of either slavery or the Holocaust.

An inclusive history classroom is one that takes account of a diverse society, both in terms of what is taught and to whom; content matters as much as pedagogy. Establishing what pupils already know is of paramount importance in order to identify preconceptions, misconceptions and the extent of prior knowledge. It is also critical to establish some point of connection with the pupils, whatever is being taught, with some attempt to address the 'so what?' question. Box 10.2 includes examples of how one London comprehensive school attempts to connect history to the pupils' own lives. An inclusive classroom is also one in which high-quality outcomes for learners are possible by making learning accessible: inclusion is entirely compatible with high standards of achievement, and it is to levels of achievement that we now turn.

Box 10.2 Finding the point of connection in one London comprehensive school

---

This history department uses the following strategies to engage its socially and ethnically diverse intake:

1   The pupils' own history
2   Use of story
3   Local history
4   Allowing pupils to choose aspects of a topic they wish to study.

In Key Stage 3, the department runs a 'My own history' project. The stories written by the pupils are autobiographical and involve them placing their lives into a wider context. There are opportunities for pupils to present their stories and share them with one another. Writing stories is a thread running through history at Key Stage 3 and the department plans to extend links with the English department to develop this further. Currently, they also ask pupils to write their own Roman story. Links with the locality are also important: in Year 8, pupils spend about 12 weeks exploring the history of London through the evidence of, for example, local buildings. The outcome is to produce a tour of their local area. This local history links with many other aspects of the history curriculum, for example the Industrial Revolution. The department is also planning to make links with the London Olympics. In Year 9, pupils are asked to identify an initial hypothesis in response to the question 'The twentieth century was an age of what?' The subsequent direction is partly steered by teacher expertise and partly by pupil interest. A common focus is on genocide – using the UN definition as a starting point – about which the pupils at this particular school are very knowledgeable. The topic requires some sensitive handling, but the pupils find it a highly engaging topic.

'Ability' labelling

We have tried to avoid talking about 'ability' in this book because its usage implies that ability is somehow 'fixed', a proposition that we – and many others – reject. To describe a pupil as being of 'low ability' or 'high ability' is to imply that this is a property of the pupil him or herself. It would be more accurate to say that the pupil was low or high attaining or achieving at a particular point, recognizing that it is the outcome that is being judged, not the pupil. The practice of grouping pupils by 'ability' – normally on the basis of literacy or language skills – is increasing, not least because of the policy expectation from politicians of all persuasions that the use of setting – and streaming – will be encouraged. The evidence that setting and streaming do raise standards is slight and, indeed, there is stronger evidence that ability grouping may depress the scores of the majority (Kutnick *et al.* 2005).

In some of the schools we visited, pupils in history were streamed for English and humanities according to their English subject scores, although in one school it was on the basis of modern foreign language skills. Pupils – rather than their teachers – were vocal about the mismatches that could ensue: 'We've got people in our set who shouldn't be there. Sometimes you have people who are good at history but not at English.' In none of the schools we visited did the history department determine its own teaching groups except where these were based on mixed-ability tutor groups, probably because history is not given enough teaching time to block across a year group. The history teachers we spoke to generally did not express any view on the particular issues of setting in their subject, except around the difficulties with the behaviour of 'lower ability' classes. In most of the schools we visited, teaching approaches were determined by the individual class teacher, although broad content was determined at department level. This means that in history classes that were grouped by attainment, we observed the use of very different pedagogical styles and different tasks with these different classes. Those teachers in schools with mixed teaching groups were often more explicit about the rationale for this grouping policy, although the reasons were more often linked to social, behavioural and timetabling goals rather than goals associated with learning.

An important side effect of streaming and setting is its impact on pupil attitude and motivation. Research into the classroom experiences of lower attaining sets indicates that teachers adopt more restricted teaching approaches that allow pupils fewer opportunities for innovation, creativity or even discussion (Boaler 2002; Kutnick *et al.* 2006). Often pupils are placed in these sets because of their low literacy levels, which means that there can be a tendency to over-practise and over-emphasize literacy skills at a low level through copying, cloze exercises and similar activities to the exclusion of other forms of task outcome. Repeatedly practising skills that do not come easily can reinforce pupils' sense of failure and further alienate them from a subject. During our visits to schools we also observed and were told by pupils in higher attaining sets that they were more likely to work in groups, to create plays, have debates and so forth: it appeared that these pupils enjoyed more freedom of thought and opportunities for innovation and originality and, as a result, they appeared to enjoy history as a school subject more than their peers in lower attaining sets. Once in Year 10, however, pupils are more likely to find themselves learning history in mixed ability classes (assuming that the full range of pupils have been allowed to study history at GCSE), largely because of the nature of options blocks and timetabling. Here, pupils might expect to find a greater variety of tasks and teaching approaches – in one school for example, a teacher talked about GCSE groups which had 'Gifted and Talented' pupils 'mixed with SEN' and described one pupil with SEN who enjoyed the debate and the generating of ideas in a different environment.

While 'ability' grouping appears to have little effect on raising pupil attainment and therefore is of little benefit in terms of academic outcomes, the evidence suggests that it is damaging for lower attaining pupils in terms of their self-esteem and motivation to school and learning. Pupils in lower sets are often much more challenging to teach not only because there is a concentration of pupils who may have particular learning needs but also because of those who could be described as 'overtly disaffected', or who have severe emotional and behavioural needs. Furthermore, this lack of concentration might be exacerbated where the work set is unchallenging. One history teacher, Julie – a case study in the wonderfully titled book *Learning without Limits* – is worth quoting at some length about why she opposes the practice of setting:

> Very often the type of pupils who end up in the bottom set, you look at their backgrounds, they are the ones who haven't had the help and support in the formative years, they haven't got resources at home, haven't got many books…and on top of

all that, they are placed in bottom sets, or they are told 'You can only do this.' And some pupils just accept that and they slip into this feeling of being worthless. Some fight against it and keep trying but it is very hard, isn't it, to keep trying when you are told 'Well, you are being entered for an exam where you can only get a D.'

(Hart *et al.* 2004: 137)

Since Julie's arrival at the school as a head of department, she has moved the department towards mixed ability grouping with backing from senior leadership, not least because examination results have compared favourably with those of other departments. Julie's conviction was that accessibility comes from teachers' 'judicious choices and actions' rather than an 'objective quality inherent in the relationship between particular task objectives and the characteristics of particular pupils'. In other words, she believes that teachers should not simply match particular tasks to particular learners, but rather should respond creatively to any obstacles which prevent pupils from accessing common tasks and ideas. We can generalize by saying that Julie supports a social rather than a medical model of disability broadly defined: in a 'medical' model it is assumed to be the learners' problems which prevent them from accessing learning opportunities, whereas in a 'social' model it is argued that learners could access learning provided the environment is appropriately modified. For example, a physically disabled child is no longer a 'problem' if sufficient ramps are provided; in the same way, a visually impaired child is no longer a 'problem' if provided with text of the correct size of font or suitable IT equipment. Recent legislative change has placed on schools and other bodies the responsibility to remove barriers to access. However, it may also follow that a lower achieving child is not a 'problem' if teachers make adjustments to teaching – changing the pace, simplifying instructions, allowing pupils some control over tasks and accompanying resources, making effective use of other adults – until they succeed in making their subject accessible and esteem-building.

Teacher perceptions of pupil 'ability' can have a profound impact on their practice in history as in any other subject. In one study of teachers in Northern Ireland, where the majority of pupils are educated in a selective system, there was evidence that history teachers' goals were considerably more ambitious in selective grammar schools than in non-selective high schools, particularly around sensitive and even controversial history. By contrast, teachers working in comprehensive integrated schools were more ambitious for *all* their pupils and made less distinction between higher and lower sets, perhaps suggesting that teachers choosing to teach in the small number of integrated schools in Northern Ireland have a particular educational philosophy (Kitson 2005). None of this is to argue that the challenges associated with inclusive practices are at all easy. In many ways, they challenge profound assumptions about the nature of teaching and its relationship to pupil learning, as well as assumptions about what successful practices look like. However, there is sufficient evidence that transforming practices impacts positively on outcomes for all.

Differentiating history: principles for successful practice

We have already explored some of the aspects that pupils find difficult about history lessons in Chapter 5: its lack of certainty, the 'strangeness' of the past, challenging

---

Box 10.3 Six principles for inclusive practices in history teaching

1   Make history accessible to everyone but still complicated (enough)
2   Provide opportunities for success
3   Give pupils responsibility for managing their own learning and let them decide when they need additional support
4   Find a point of connection between the pupils and the past
5   Be creative in communicating the 'golden nugget'
6   Tackle literacy issues head-on so they don't get in the way

---

concepts and, perhaps most of all, the levels of literacy often required. This section picks up those challenges and offers six principles for successful inclusive practice (Box 10.3).

Like the pupils, we have our own starting points based on some fundamental premises, the first of which is underpinned by a principle that informs the book as a whole: entitlement. We believe strongly that all pupils have an entitlement to learn about the past in ways that provide useful knowledge and develop an ability to think historically, regardless of the kind of school or teaching group they find themselves in. 'Thinking historically' includes not only a sense of the evidence from which history is crafted but also an awareness of and empathy towards the difference of others in the past. Achieving this means making history *accessible* to all without making it *meaningless*: reduce history to a series of cloze exercises, word searches or short response comprehension questions, and it becomes an unchallenging literacy exercise that fails to have meaning for the pupils. History must be simultaneously accessible and appropriately challenging, though this balance can be difficult to strike. Ben Walsh (1998: 47, quoted in Counsell 2003b: 25) captured this well:

> There is a belief in some quarters that history is too complicated. The problem with this argument is that if history is to stop becoming complicated then it must become simple. Then we are in real trouble, as in the minds of our pupils all Catholics hate all Protestants...for all time. All Jews live in Germany and are persecuted. All Indians work on tea plantations or emigrate to Britain. Similarly, all black people in the eighteenth and nineteenth century sit around bemoaning their lot as slaves until that Wilberforce bloke comes along and sets them free.

Ofsted has similarly encouraged teachers to make history 'satisfyingly difficult' (Ofsted 2007). If teachers make history too simple, it no longer serves a useful purpose, so they need to find ways to make it both complicated and accessible – what Counsell calls 'acceptable simplification' (2003b). 'Acceptable simplification' is, perhaps, easier to articulate than to implement. For Counsell, 'acceptable simplification' depends on working with the structure of history as a discipline: 'Instead of seeing subject rigour as the opposite of accessible work for the struggling pupil, we should see it as the solution' (2003b: 25). In practice, teachers frequently make tasks more difficult for learners by ostensibly making them easier: this might happen by not providing enough contextual knowledge for a task so that learners struggle with the gap between what they have been told and what they need to understand. For example, it is not unusual to see lower history sets asked to deal with the consequences of Henry VIII's divorce from Catherine of Aragon without reference to the religious divisions of the 1530s, so the history becomes, effectively, soap opera. Sometimes, tasks which are 'simplified' are presented with an insufficiently clear or well articulated conceptual focus, so that the learning focuses on a narrative sequencing rather than on a historical explanation; in other cases, pupils are given anachronistic explanations. In each of these cases the *intention* is worthy – to allow lower attaining pupils to grasp something of the history – but the consequences are counterproductive.

There are a number of possible routes to 'acceptable simplification'. One is to ensure that pupils know *enough*. To limit the amount of knowledge a pupil has is to create a number of obstacles to historical thinking (Harris 2005). This is particularly, though by no means exclusively, a problem when using source material in classrooms. Attempting to evaluate the usefulness of a source on the basis of very limited knowledge is highly problematic and, thus, longer sources can be considerably easier to handle provided they are made accessible (see Principle 6). Another approach is to start with the familiar: using a ten pound note as an introduction to Charles Darwin or a picture of a local building as a way into the Industrial Revolution or asking the pupils what they *already* know about a topic could all provide a point of reference for pupils before moving them into less familiar territory. Analogies can also be helpful (think of the report of a football match analogy to demonstrate the impact perspective has on how something is viewed), though they can also be misleading and need to be handled with care. Role play and practical demonstrations can be an enormously powerful way of illuminating a key point. The work of Ian Luff has been influential here (e.g. see Harris and Luff 2004; Luff 2000, 2001, 2003) and his imaginative and often simple techniques are very effective in a way that words on a page are not. The point of these, and other, techniques is not that they make history 'easy' but that they make the core ideas (the 'golden nuggets' – Principle 5) – and the knowledge and understanding that underpins them – accessible.

Our second principle is rooted in the conception that ability is not a fixed property of the pupil and that all pupils are capable of success if appropriately supported. One of the more unfortunate consequences of regular 'levelling' of pupils at Key Stage 3 is another label: that pupil A is a Level 3b while pupil C is a Level 5a. In other words, the pupil, rather than the piece of work that was assessed, is defined as a level. However, as we know all too well from the work of Donaldson (1986), assessment is highly problematic. A pupil may achieve a Level 4 on an essay about slavery, but could have achieved more if the instructions had been clearer, the task had been structured differently, the topic had been taught in a different way or the markscheme had been made more task-specific.

Many schools now favour a 'must', 'should', 'could' approach to learning objectives, but we are wary about applying these to lessons. Given that it is impossible, halfway into a lesson, to restrict further teaching and learning to a particular group of pupils, the 'must', 'should', 'could' model therefore assumes that some pupils will not access the whole lesson. This seems to us unacceptable; it would be preferable to design a lesson which all pupils in the lesson could access at different levels. For example, a lesson objective which states that 'pupils will explore the different experiences of slaves in America' can be accessed at a number of levels: an appreciation that experiences differed, an exploration of the way in which experiences differed and an explanation about the extent of these differences. We are fortunate that history – no matter what the topic or the concept being studied – can be accessed at multiple levels and it therefore seems to us unnecessary to set artificial ceilings to pupil achievement.

Our third principle is about placing the pupils in charge of their own learning and letting them decide when they need additional support. Pupil needs, like ability, are not fixed: they may require more support with one task, less with another. Allowing them to choose can create an atmosphere of mutual support and also of empowerment. For example, pupils might be able to choose which side of a worksheet to use, assuming that one side provides more accessible or scaffolded text, or select which colour information sheet they will read. Similarly, pupils might sometimes be given a choice about how to communicate their work so they have opportunities to be assessed orally or through creative, visual forms.

Individuals in history provide an accessible yet potentially complex entry point into the past that can work effectively with all pupils but especially those who struggle to connect with the past (Principle 4). There are many examples, but three in particular are worth mentioning because of the way they illuminate different approaches. The first is Mike Murray's use of *Ethel and Ernest*, Raymond Briggs's lengthy cartoon about an ordinary couple who live through many of the changes of the twentieth century. Briggs provides a deeply personal overview of a century from which any number of themes and events can be pursued. In this sense, the cartoon is a tool from which to blend overview and depth, but it is the role of personal perspectives that makes it most attractive. Despite the fact that the people are in this case fictional, their story makes the century more 'real' and comprehensible to pupils, leading one to ask 'Which was more important, Sir, ordinary people getting electricity or the rise of Hitler?' (Murray 2002). The second example is the enquiry about Private Reg Wilkes (Evans *et al*. 2004), already mentioned in Chapter 7, which leads pupils through his experiences in World War I using his letters and diaries. The 'cliffhanger' lesson is perfect: at the end of one lesson, the pupils see Reg's diary end abruptly around the time of the Battle of the Somme. It is only at the beginning of the next lesson that they learn that, although injured in battle, Reg survived, managing to fashion a diary from a notebook and writing shakily with his left hand. It is a compelling story and one that is made historically rigorous and engaging through an enquiry question that focuses on evidence and typicality: 'How much can Reg Wilkes tell us about the Great War?' The third example focuses on interpretation, in this case of two specific individuals, Ken and Pat, each a composite of real people living in Northern Ireland today from the Catholic and Protestant communities respectively (McCully and Pilgrim 2004). Pupils first get to know Ken and Pat before examining Irish history through their eyes and analysing why each might interpret the past differently. It is a brilliant technique for exploring the ways in which issues in the present colour our interpretations of the past.

Our fifth principle proposes that all lessons should have a golden nugget – the key idea that pupils understand and take with them when they leave the lesson. The golden nugget must be attainable by *all* the pupils and is greatly enhanced by learning strategies which communicate the key idea or concept of the lesson. If the golden nugget is that World War I was caused by a gradual build-up of tensions and the assassination was only the trigger, teachers might use the game *Buckaroo* to demonstrate how the mule only bucks when the 'causes' loaded on its back build up. Place only one item on its back – a stand-in for the assassination – and nothing happens. If the golden nugget is that Hippocrates was the first 'modern' doctor, teachers might start the lesson by handing out symptoms of various ailments to six pupils. Assuming the role of Hippocrates, the teacher invites each pupil to come to the front and visit the great doctor, making a big deal of examining them systematically and asking questions about their symptoms before prescribing cures based on the Theory of the Four Humours. If the golden nugget is about why the United States felt so threatened by the presence of Russian missiles in Cuba, teachers might use Ian Luff's simple but effective activity involving pupils throwing paper missiles (Luff 2003).

Principle 6 responds to the finding that one of the aspects of history that pupils most struggle with relates to literacy skills (Harris and Haydn 2008, 2009). Essentially, there are two challenges here: accessing information and communicating ideas. Chapter 8 has explored communication in more detail, but it is worth making some brief points here about ways to overcome literacy 'hurdles'.

First, problems with literacy skills should not prevent pupils accessing the key *ideas* of history. The previous principle focused on making the golden nugget accessible through active, creative strategies. Second, whether for reasons of motivation or access, 'warming pupils up' can be vital if they are to persist with some complex reading, speaking or writing. This generally involves 'hooking' their interest early on, perhaps through an engaging story or a puzzle which needs to be solved. Bringing pupils to the point where they *want* to find out more is vital, whether in Year 7 or Year 13. Providing pupils with challenging text 'cold' is likely to be met with some resistance. Third, a degree of scaffolding is helpful and often necessary, for example through the provision of useful phrases, sentence starts or writing frames, but they can also hold pupils back (Evans and Pate 2007): ultimately, pupils should aspire beyond such scaffolding. Fourth, immediacy and simplicity are often most effective. For example, a strategy which appears not always to work is the provision of glossaries at the bottom of sheets or in the back of books which pupils appear to consult rarely as they struggle to read and make sense of some text. A better technique might be to provide an explanation or alternative word in brackets immediately after the word in question so that the flow of pupils' reading is not interrupted. Fifth, making text 'easier' is not always a way to make it more accessible because pupils either have insufficient information from which to draw conclusions or the absence of colour and detail in the text fails to bring it to life and engage the reader. Box 10.3, from Harris 2005, exemplifies this.

Box 10.4 Two versions of Equiano's treatment

From Kelly *et al.* (1999: 15)
'I was soon put under the deck. There was such an awful stink as I had never smelt before. Everyone was crying and I was soon too unhappy to eat or wish for anything but death. When I refused food two white men tied me up and flogged me.'

From *The Life of Gustavus Vassa* by Olaudah Equiano
(http://www.wsu.edu:8000/~dee/Equiano.html)
'I was soon put down under the decks, and there I received such a salutation in my nostrils as I had never experienced in my life: so that, with the loathsomeness of the stench, and crying together, I became so sick and low that I was not able to eat, nor had I the least desire to taste any thing. I now wished for the last friend, death, to relieve me; but soon, to my grief, two of the white men offered me eatables; and, on my refusing to eat, one of them held me fast by the hands, and laid me across, I think the windlass, and tied my feet, while the other flogged me severely.'

Harris contends that any pupil, regardless of literacy difficulties, is likely to find the second version more engaging than the first, even if it appears daunting. The trick is therefore to find ways to make the second source accessible. In this case, an endless list of definitions will not do: instead, pupils need to get a 'sense' of the source. This could be achieved by, for example, the teacher reading it aloud in a dramatic fashion. It could also involve freeze-framing or some kind of DARTs activity (Box 10.5).

Box 10.5 Possible strategies to ease the literacy demands of history

Helping pupils understand the language of history
Provide alternative words, both oral and written
Explain terms; try not to take too much for granted
Make the abstract more concrete – *empire, economy, appeasement* – by use of analogy, enactment or visual representation
Provide useful phrases and words: 'It suggests that'; 'it is possible/likely that'; 'an underlying cause was…'

Helping pupils to read
Make the purpose of any reading clear: are they reading to:

- gain basic information about something or to understand someone's opinion?
- find evidence in order to answer a question?
- gain a sense of chronology?

Break text into manageable chunks through the use of sub-headings, timelines etc.
Use DARTs (**D**irected **A**ctivities **R**elated to **T**ext) where reading is clearly for a purpose such as card sorts, tables and charts, continuums, living graphs, questions to answer, preparation for a role play, a team game and so forth
Simplify the text if necessary but without removing too much colour
Ensure that pupils have sufficient contextual knowledge to make sense of what they are reading
Teacher (or pupil) reads out dramatically
Pupils freeze frame what they read

Helping pupils to write

Provide pupils with helpful models such as burgers (Mulholland 1998; Banham 1998, 2000) or the popular 'PEE' (point, evidence, explanation) mnemonic

Writing frames/some kind of scaffolding (can pupils devise their own?)

Provide clarity about purpose, style, audience, form

Provide examples of successful writing

Provide time and space for pupils to sort through and organize what they want to say. Support their attempts to organize

Vary written formats. For example, pupils use flow charts, spider diagrams and cartoons as an alternative to notes. Make heavy use of data capture instruments such as tables, charts and diagrams.

Threats to inclusive history classrooms

Examination results are crucial to schools' reputations and naturally important to pupils too. In history, however, as in other subjects, the drive to raise examination results can lead to excessively exam-oriented teaching at GCSE and A level which can, according to some of the teachers we spoke to, lead to a 'spoonfeeding' approach. Some departments make a point of doing *more* than required for the exam (e.g. Banham and Culpin 2002), but we have no evidence that this is common. On our visits, we did speak to pupils who find studying history at GCSE less engaging than in previous years, although this was partly because of the increase in the volume of writing required. The current GCSE courses have remained relatively constant since 1988, despite a number of revisions, and there are concerns among teachers about its accessibility. The introduction of tiered papers in history is one possible solution, although this was not a popular option among the teachers we spoke to. The pilot hybrid GCSE offered by OCR provides a challenging yet different kind of qualification that appeals to a range of pupils through its combination of 'standard' history and 'applied' history. Its flexibility also enables teachers to plan and assess the course in creative ways that exploit the location of the school and that meet the needs of the pupils. However, it does not meet any of the existing GCSE criteria and continues to exist only as a pilot involving a small number of schools.

One of the biggest threats to history is the current trend towards schools barring pupils from studying a subject at GCSE in which they may fail to achieve a C or above. This effectively closes off most of the curriculum for such pupils beyond the core subjects and forces them down more vocational routes. In many cases, this may be what the pupils prefer, but there is evidence of pupils who *wish* to study history further being prevented from doing so (Harris and Burn 2011).

We are also concerned about the attachment some schools appear to have to learning styles theories which suggest that, by matching teaching and learning strategies to a pupil's preferred 'learning style', achievement will increase. In fact, there is no evidence that this is the case and many of the claims made about learning styles have been challenged on the basis of inadequate evidence (see, for example, Coffield *et al.* 2004 and Hargreaves 2005). There is no neuroscientific evidence to support the claim that individuals have particular learning styles and common sense suggests that our preferences will depend on the context: to be talked at by a very dull lecturer is unlikely to help someone to learn whereas a more engaging speaker may suggest that the listener is an 'auditory' learner after all. In essence, even if there is some credibility to the theories, it simply lends weight to what we have known for many years: that good teaching is also varied. To add to the many labels assigned to the pupils is, in our view, a mistake, of little use and possibly even harmful.

Conclusion

Inclusion describes an aspiration that no child will be excluded from the ethos, culture, practices and curriculum of a school. Traditionally focused on pupils with special education needs and disabilities (SEND), it is generally accepted that inclusion extends to all pupils and touches on issues including ethnicity, gender, class, language, religion and disability. The policy of inclusion has particular resonance for history where the selection of what we teach, as well as how we teach it, directly confronts our assumptions about 'usable' or 'significant' knowledge. In this chapter we have argued strongly for an entitlement for all pupils to study history, based on our firm belief that history can engage and hold meaning for pupils when it is made simultaneously accessible and challenging, when pupils' prior knowledge is explored and valued and when teachers go beyond the labels assigned to pupils and expect more of them.

Part 4

Making history matter in schools

In this final section, we draw all the threads of the book together, seeking to develop a coherent, classroom-focused and compelling case for the successful teaching and learning of history. We try to link the underlying themes of the book – curriculum pedagogy and inclusion – through two analyses of the play of history in the contemporary curriculum. Chapter 11 is focused on pedagogy. We ask whether the success of pupils' learning about the past depends on a specific historical pedagogy and build up a case for the 'deep pedagogy' of the subject, exploring its implications for teachers. Finally, in Chapter 12 we explore the relationship between school history and some of the major themes of the contemporary curriculum: relevance, diversity, democratic values and identity, posing questions about the way history relates to the world young people must negotiate.

11

Is there a history pedagogy?

Throughout Part 3 of this book, we have explored the 'building blocks' of history pedagogy: evidence and enquiry, the second order concepts of change, continuity, causation, empathy and significance as well as strategies for communicating history. In Part 1 of the book we explored the processes by which the historical past becomes a classroom curriculum and the relationships between the historical past, the discipline of history, the popular representation of the past and the work which goes on in the classroom. The question we want to explore here is whether these building blocks make up a distinctive history pedagogy.

Understanding pedagogy

Pedagogy is a challenging term. Some thirty years ago, the educational historian Brian Simon wrote a critique of educational practice in England under the apparently strident title 'Why no pedagogy in England?' Simon described pedagogy as the 'science of teaching' and argued that 'no such science exists in England'. He described 'the educational tradition of the Continent, [where] the term 'pedagogy' has an honoured place… The concept of teaching as a science has strong roots in this tradition' (Simon 1981, reproduced 1985: 77). In England, by contrast, Simon argued that thinking about teaching and learning was highly 'eclectic', confusing aims and methods, and with no clear philosophical or conceptual underpinning for what was done in the classroom.

An enormous amount has changed in classroom practices since 1981, and a great deal more attention has focused on the way teachers teach in classrooms both in national policy and in research. In the later 1990s, the Conservative government established the National Literacy and National Numeracy projects which set out firm guidance on teaching primary literacy and numeracy based on research into best practice; the projects were subsequently taken up and expanded as the National Literacy and Numeracy Strategies by the incoming Labour government in 1997, and formed the basis of a massive investment in in-service training for primary teachers, defining a clear national approach to teaching in primary schools. In the first years of the twenty-first century, the principles of the primary strategies formed the basis for the Secondary National Strategy, extending the national programme of 'best practice'-informed professional development to secondary schools (DfES 2004). There was a concurrent interest in teaching and learning in research: the Teaching and Learning Research Programme (TLRP) was the most lavishly funded programme of educational research ever undertaken in the United Kingdom, with a series of research and dissemination projects developed to explore, research and develop teaching and learning in schools. Nonetheless, in 2004, Robin Alexander argued that there was 'still no pedagogy in England' (Alexander 2004: 19). Defining pedagogy as 'both the act of teaching and its attendant discourse', framed by 'ideas, values and evidence' (Alexander 2004: 19), Alexander argued that national policy remained ignorant about the underpinnings of pedagogy, and was under-informed on 'evidence and debate about children, learning, teaching, curriculum and culture' (Alexander 2004: 26). Given the enormous pressure exerted by policy on practice – not least through the programmes of briefing and training for teachers – Alexander argued that classroom practice was therefore as eclectic and pragmatic in 2004 as it had been twenty-five years earlier.

'Pedagogy', then, is a difficult concept in the culture and practice of many English schools. Already in this chapter we have hinted at two definitions – Simon, drawing on the *Oxford English Dictionary* definition, described pedagogy as 'the science of teaching'. For Alexander, drawing on extensive acquaintance with international education practices, it had both a more specific meaning, 'the act of teaching', and a wider conceptual hinterland – 'ideas, values and evidence' about 'children, learning, teaching, curriculum and culture'. In continental Europe, 'pedagogy' is a term which refers to more than the practice and techniques of teaching in the classroom; it refers also to the theories – of children, of learning – which underpin these practices, and it remains the case that in some European countries these are relatively formally taught to novice teachers before they work in classrooms. In this chapter, we pitch our discussion between these two poles – exploring the nature of classroom teaching in history but setting that in a slightly wider context to consider issues of learning, teaching and culture to explore the nature of pedagogy in history.

Pedagogic practices in history classrooms

It is sensible to begin with some pedagogic vignettes of history teaching. A teacher develops an extended dialogue with her pupils about the causes of the English Civil War, using her own extensive substantive knowledge and her pupils' prior knowledge to extend their higher order thinking skills and to explore complex questions of morality. A different teacher leads pupils through a careful discussion of an extensive extract from the Treaty of Versailles to set the Treaty in the wider context of twentieth-century history, the legacy of World War I and the question of whether the Treaty of Versailles laid the basis for World War II. A third teacher uses the web-based presentation created for Down House in Kent to explore the ways in which Charles Darwin's work carried significance in his own time and for us. Another teacher invites in elderly local residents as part of an oral history project in which pupils explore with the residents patterns of change and continuity in the local community. Elsewhere, pupils sort cards which describe, briefly, the causes of the Great Fire of London in 1666, into patterns which enable them to explore the short, medium and long-term causes of the fire. A different group of pupils sort descriptions of Nazi action against Jews in the 1930s to understand the dimensions of anti-semitism and the background to the Holocaust. Yet a further class of pupils use Post-It stickers on a laminated portrait of Queen Elizabeth I to pose questions about different features of the painting as part of a lesson which introduces them to Tudor propaganda. In a different classroom, pupils are given a writing frame which provides the bare bones of a structure for an essay they will develop over a series of lessons explaining the causes of the Industrial Revolution. A further class of pupils are asked to prepare fictional estate agents' property details for the 'sale' of the Roman villa at Lullingstone in the middle of the fourth century in order to develop their understandings of Romano-British culture. Finally, in another lesson, pupils use the Uffizi website to answer a series of questions about Renaissance painting as part of a lesson sequence on the nature of the classical 'rebirth' in the fifteenth century.

Each of these lessons is deploying a specific pedagogic technique which plays its part in developing pupils' **historical understanding**. The activities described here are not the principal purpose of the lesson, but a means to an end. To some extent, the activities described above could be interchangeable: the classroom discussion used to explore the causes of the English Civil War could have been used to explore the nature of Romano-British culture, or the Treaty of Versailles. The writing frame used to explore the causes of the Industrial Revolution could have been used to explore the execution of Charles I or the Italian Renaissance. The Post-It exercise could have been used on an archaeological reconstruction of a Roman villa or a picture of the Great Fire of London. Change and continuity in the local community could be explored through a series of maps, documents or photographs as well as through visits from local residents. Obviously there are limits to the interchangeability, but the point is that the activities are not defined, in many cases, by the topic. In each case, the classroom teacher made a series of decisions about **how to teach** the material and planned pupil activities in ways which enabled them to access the substantive historical content. The evidence we have is that, in making these decisions, teachers draw on a range of reflections – the decision-making process is relatively complex. In some cases, the decision will be based around the availability of a particularly useful local resource – perhaps the quality of contacts with the local community influencing the decision to bring in local residents – and in others it will be directly related to the challenges and opportunities presented by the class to be taught: in some cases, decisions to manage large, open-ended class discussions are not possible because of behaviour management issues in a particular class. In other cases, there are other factors: the time available, the demands of the curriculum or assessment. However, in many cases these decisions are underpinned by a teacher's own aims and aspirations for the lesson, the unit of work and the subject and, beyond this, by their deeper philosophies of education. The evidence we have (Husbands *et al*. 2003) is that teachers make extremely sophisticated decisions about the ways in which they plan to teach particular topics, drawing on a host of simultaneous considerations. There is very little evidence that teachers 'work through the textbook'; indeed, many are actively resistant to teaching through someone else's ideas. The process of pedagogic decision making is active and sensitive to context.

Furthermore, as we discussed in Chapter 9, few history teachers base their pedagogic decision making on a single aim (Husbands *et al*. 2003: 64). The lesson on

Charles I had as a primary objective the development of pupils' understanding of the execution of the king, but a secondary objective of the development of an argument based on historical evidence and a third purpose of developing pupils' listening and oral skills. The sequence of lessons focused around the writing frame for a lesson on the causes of the Industrial Revolution had as a primary historical objective the development of pupils' understanding of causation in relation to the Industrial Revolution, but it had a clear further objective in developing their literacy skills in constructing an essay: a later sequence of lessons in the year would offer a less structured writing frame. These pedagogic practices are, then, multi-layered. They serve a purpose in the development of pupils' historical understanding as well as other purposes in relation to cognitive or social skills. One of the difficulties of objectives-based lesson planning for experienced teachers is that there are always multiple objectives in play.

This observation about pedagogic practices in history prompts a further set of observations: taken as activities, none of the lessons we described above are distinctive to history. Pupils engage in extended debate and discussion in English and science; they sort cards in geography; they use writing frames in English and geography; they extract and analyse information from websites in information technology lessons, and so on. The activities themselves, although deployed in the context of learning about the past, are not in themselves indicative of a history pedagogy. They are generic activities, deployed in the services of historical understanding but effectively customizable across the curriculum and carrying with them a set of purposes beyond teaching and learning about the past. In itself, this may be the basis of effective cross-curricular or inter-disciplinary work, but it prompts the question about whether there is a pedagogy distinctive to history teaching.

Is there a history pedagogy?

The argument so far might suggest that there is no distinctive history pedagogy, but simply the exploration of the historical past through a series of often engaging activities designed to develop pupils' broader educational competences. Indeed, the language of competences and skills, of activities and resources, and the separation of content from each of them has become an increasingly insistent feature of contemporary educational debate. The Royal Society of Arts has developed a competency-based lower secondary curriculum called 'Opening Minds' which is focused on providing young people with life skills or 'competencies' covering citizenship, learning, managing information, relating to people and managing situations (http://www.openingminds. org.uk). In 'Opening Minds' the focus is explicitly on developing learning activities which develop these competencies, with subjects simply serving as repositories of exemplar material. Many of the lessons we described at the beginning of this chapter could have been taught in an 'Opening Minds' curriculum. At the other extreme, some approaches to curriculum separate content from activities and broader competencies by stressing the simple primacy of subject content. The Conservative secretary of state for education, Michael Gove, told *The Times* newspaper in 2010:

> I'm an unashamed traditionalist when it comes to the curriculum...Most parents would rather their children had a traditional education, with children sitting in

rows, learning the kings and queens of England, the great works of literature, proper mental arithmetic... That's the best training of the mind and that's how children will be able to compete.

(*The Times*, 6 March 2010)

Ironically, some of the activities in the lessons we described above could equally well conform to the requirements of this sort of curriculum specification too. Divergent though these views of the curriculum are, they share some similar starting points – separating curriculum content, learning activities and wider educational competences and then relating them in almost arbitrary ways.

A resolution to this issue, which clarifies some of the issues at stake, lies in digging a little deeper into the lessons described earlier in terms of Alexander's concern for 'ideas, values and evidence' (Alexander 2004). Although many of the activities in the lessons are not always themselves distinctive, there are some important distinctive features. In the first place, the underlying aims are specific to the teaching of history, as aims would be for any subject, and it is these which shape the ways in which decisions about how to teach are made. Although the activities may be in principle transportable across the curriculum, their underlying educational logic – and ultimately their power as pedagogic devices – derives from the purpose they serve in the history curriculum. As Chapter 9 suggested, the underlying purposes of the history curriculum are articulated through the longer term planning which teachers need to undertake. The lesson on the Civil War, or the lesson on Elizabeth I, or the sequence of lessons on the Industrial Revolution, for all their strengths as imaginatively conceived and expertly implemented teaching occasions, have relatively limited power on their own. They derive their importance from their place in a history curriculum developed to explore some overarching ideas in a coherent and connected sequence organized around underlying aims. Understanding the causes of the Civil War or Industrial Revolution are staging posts in the learning journey which is geared around understanding the past in relation to the present and the nature of what it means to think historically. History as an academic discipline has a distinctive set of aims emerging from its distinctive characteristics as a discipline. There is a body of (substantive) knowledge, as in any subject, but this knowledge is highly problematic. In consequence, the teacher has to juggle many aims at once – to communicate and foster knowledge and understanding of substantive knowledge while also helping pupils to understand why that knowledge is contestable and to make patterns with the knowledge which build understandings of the past and our own place in relation to it.

There is a further feature of the lessons we have already discussed, and one not immediately obvious. In the vignettes which introduced this discussion, we described pupils engaging in 'enquiry', using 'evidence' and producing written 'texts', and then observed that pupils engage in 'enquiry', use 'evidence' and produce written 'texts' in other curricular areas too. So much is true, but what is not clear is whether 'enquiry' means the same thing in history as it does in science, English, art or music, or whether 'evidence' is used in the same way in history as in these other subject areas. Both competency-based and 'traditional' knowledge-based views of the curriculum would suggest that there is an affirmative answer to this: in the case of the former because 'discussion', and 'evidence' are simply vehicles for the development of generic competencies, and the latter because they are simply the means through which knowledge is generated. Closer examination, and extensive research and curriculum development, suggests that this is not the case. Two examples will make the point. Like history teachers, science teachers use 'evidence' as the raw material for their lessons. However, 'evidence' is used in science lessons in quite different ways from the way it is used in history lessons. In science lessons, evidence is used to test theories, and to develop understandings of scientific processes (Mortimer and Scott 2003). In history, 'evidence' is tested and interrogated to produce usable information on which accounts of historical events or processes can be built. 'Enquiry' has a central place in geography classrooms just as in history classrooms (Roberts 2003), but the processes are different. Geographical enquiry involves the development of skills involved in the collection, analysis, interpretation and evaluation of information from a wide variety of sources to make their own sense of physical and human processes. Historical enquiry is perhaps less wide-ranging: it is disciplined by the pre-existent range of historical interpretations and limited by the range of evidence. In geographical enquiry, pupils generate evidence through their own observation and measurement; in historical enquiry they use already existing evidence.

These may appear somewhat fine distinctions but they translate into different assumptions and practices in the classroom about what – in these examples – counts as 'evidence' and what shapes an 'enquiry'. What shapes history in the classroom is different from what shapes geography, or science, or English, or mathematics, just as they too are distinctive. The result is, of course, demanding for teachers, if frustrating for curriculum policy makers. Teachers need to work hard at their classroom practice not simply because the classroom is a demanding situation in which to work but because the cognitive and intellectual agenda is demanding. Teachers need to help pupils build substantive knowledge, to help them develop conceptual lenses to make meaning from this knowledge and to help them understand that the knowledge is provisional and refracted through the evidence we have available and the assumptions and biases we bring to this. This is a demanding, 'deep' pedagogy.

Making sense of history in the curriculum

This idea of 'deep pedagogy' goes a long way to conceptualize what is distinctive about the practice of history teaching, and to frame the challenge for history teachers in terms of their professional expertise in responding to the challenges they face. The distinctiveness of history pedagogy lies not in the observed practices of history teachers – that surface 'eclectic' and pragmatic pedagogy which Brian Simon (1985) describes but in the underlying – deep – connections between, on the one hand, teaching and learning practices and on the other, the values, purposes and aims of the history curriculum. The interplay between these is at the core of successful history teaching. As Caroline Coffin argues, the relationships between individual and collective identity which are explored through historical discourse play a central part in the place of history in society (Coffin 2006: 8). This may seem an abstract argument, at some distance from the realities of the classroom and, in particular, from the challenges of teaching lower attaining pupils who struggle with many of the ideas, concepts and expectations of the history classroom. However, paradoxically, the principles of 'deep pedagogy' we have outlined here may be more important in preparing for work with pupils for whom learning is a challenge. These learners are those most likely to be confused by the ways in which teachers use apparently similar ideas differently, use language in relation to classroom work differently. More able, and older, learners may be better attuned to the different emphases placed on ideas like 'enquiry', 'evidence' 'discussion', 'change' or 'continuity'. Being clearer about the relationship between activities and their purposes, content and concepts may not make the most challenging pupils easy to teach, but it may remove some of the hidden barriers to their participation and engagement. Without an articulation of this 'deep pedagogy', it is unlikely that history will either secure its place in the school curriculum, or achieve the ambitious aims and purposes to which it aspires.

12

Making history matter:
relevance, diversity, heritage and morality

Much has been written ... about the place of history in schools and the related questions concerning how it should be taught. It is unfortunate that much of the impetus for this has come less from the consideration of history as a form of knowledge than from a slightly desperate attempt to provide a defence for its place in the curriculum.

(Rogers 1987: 3–4)

In this chapter, we broaden our focus to consider the contribution history makes to the curriculum and why this matters. We do so by exploring the four organizing themes of the book: the place of history in the contemporary school curriculum, issues of inclusion, the nature of pedagogy and the significance of professionalism. By way of introducing the discussion, we consider the different ways in which history matters to different stakeholders and the implications of this for practice in classrooms and schools. We then consider dimensions of the way history matters to pupils, examining the 'relevance' of history, the part history plays in issues of identity in a diverse society, and what it means for adolescents to learn to 'think historically'. Finally, we return to the place of history education in society, considering questions of morality, values and democracy through the lens of the history classroom,

Who does history matter to?

The educational world is crowded with stakeholders, with often strident, frequently conflicting views about what matters in education and why and how it should be taught. In Chapter 2 of this book, we saw that most societies require their young people to study history as part of compulsory schooling, and that they identify lofty aims for the place of history in the school curriculum: as a way of exploring issues of identity and inherited cultures, as a way of understanding the present, as a way of developing the knowledge and skills essential to functioning as an educated citizen of a complex society. One way of reframing this preoccupation is that the successful learning of history matters to *society*. History is a component in what it takes to make an educated society. Such a society would exhibit high levels of literacy, numeracy, scientific understanding and aesthetic appreciation but it would also be aware of its history, comfortable with its diversity and confident of its relationship with its past, as unafraid to confront darker corners as to celebrate triumph and heroism. What is captured here is both a knowledge base and an attitude of mind. History in schools can, but need not necessarily, provide understanding of the past in the light of the present, explore the lineage of contemporary problems and demonstrate to young people that society has not always been organized as it is today. History can, but does not necessarily, develop skills of evaluating evidence, constructing an argument and communicating it success-fully. As John Slater put it, history

> not only helps us to understand the identity of our communities, cultures and nations, by knowing something of our past, but also enables our loyalties to them to be moderated by informed and responsible scepticism. But we cannot expect too much. It cannot guarantee tolerance, though it can give it some intellectual weapons. It cannot keep open closed minds, although it may sometimes leave a nagging grain of doubt in them. Historical thinking is primarily mind-opening, not socializing.
>
> (Slater 1989: 16)

History, then, matters to society. It has been described as a form of citizenship educa-tion which sets citizenship into context (Arthur *et al.* 2001). The difficulty with this line of argument, however, lies in the difficulty societies have in articulating assumptions about education. Societies are complex; people disagree. Political debate about the his-tory curriculum too often presents a grotesque caricature of what the discipline might be in schools. Politicians make themselves spokespeople for society's needs, and in doing so polarize and simplify. Political debate about the place of history teaching rap-idly becomes crude, partly because of its distance from the classroom, but also because school history becomes a cipher for more profound disagreements. Ideas which are complementary, such as the interdependence of knowledge and understanding, the development of concepts across a range of different contexts, the provisional nature of evidence, are presented as competing. In political debate, 'knowledge of the past' becomes opposed to 'historical skills'. Nuances in understanding, say the inheritance of Empire, become choices about whether to celebrate or to condemn. The needs of some learners are assumed to be in opposition to the needs of others.

To insist that successful history education matters profoundly to society is not to argue that it serves the needs of sectional interests (Barton and Levstik 2004). What is clear is that history matters in different ways to different stakeholder groups. A number of examples will make this clearer. Universities have an obvious interest in history in schools: schools provide the supply of undergraduate and, eventually, academic historians on which universities depend and, less directly, provide a reading public which will 'consume' the work historians do. Historically, universities exercised influence over the content of school examinations through their examination boards and, although their influence has waned very considerably, academics in universities continue to express their views on the teaching of subjects in schools (Starkey 2005; Matthews 2009). As we saw in Chapter 1, however, history as an academic discipline in universities differs from history in schools, and this influences the debate. While universities have a legitimate concern about the school curriculum – in terms of stand-ards of entry to university, and the expectations they have of those coming to read particular subjects – Booth and Nicholls found 'ignorance among lecturers about what is being done in schools and...apparently little willingness to engage with [it]', while suggesting that 'greater attention needed to be paid to the progression of teaching methods to ensure effective long-term development in learning in the subject' (Booth and Nicholls 2005: 8). Even so, it is important to remember that universities' legitimate concern with progression right through to undergraduate history is a restricted one, potentially in tension with a concern for history for all learners: very few school pupils go on to read history at university, and the orientation of a history curriculum for all learners is potentially very different from one for those who may progress to history degrees.

In English schools, head teachers have extensive freedom, effectively as 'chief executives' of their school, over matters of finance, staffing, school organization and, increasingly, curriculum. The pressures on them are acute. They want to secure high levels of pupil achievement in ways which enable their pupils to become successful members of society, but the pressure of examination 'league tables' focuses this aspiration in acute ways. It is important not to stereotype the views of head teachers; many lead creative and imaginative schools, and are aware of the shifting nature of education and learning in the twenty-first century. Head teachers are frequently found referring to tensions they experience between the need to secure excellent examination results for each year group and the pressures to prepare young people for life beyond school, whether for employment or for adult life more generally. History 'matters' to head teachers in a number of ways: at the most instrumental of levels, history departments often deliver excellent examination results for pupils who take the subject. What is more challenging for head teachers is to articulate a place for history in the curriculum entitlement for all learners given the pressures on schools. Despite the considerable importance laid by politicians and others on history as a discipline, almost no schools have placed history in the core curriculum for 14- to 16-year-olds. The Historical Association survey and Ofsted surveys (Ofsted 2007; Historical Association 2010b) find evidence that history is squeezed in the 11–14 curriculum both because of the pressures on head teachers to gear learning around preparation for examination at 16 and because of demands on curriculum time.

Politicians and head teachers are just two, admittedly influential, groups of stakeholders who frame debate on the history curriculum. Because history matters in different ways to stakeholders, debate about its place in the school curriculum will always prove difficult to resolve. Indeed, for history teachers, debate about the nature of the discipline in schools is perhaps akin to steering a dinghy, sometimes running before a strong wind, sometimes tacking to make progress against the wind, only occasionally becalmed. In all of this noisy, sometimes ill-informed, debate, school history must matter above all to pupils themselves. Their voice and their needs matter the most but, as we saw in Chapter 4, they are often the least heard. A minority of young people may assume that history matters to them; more generally, adolescents are unpersuaded that the past is important. From a school viewpoint, it is often easy to see pupils as relatively passive 'consumers' of the curriculum. Recent research suggests that this is wrong. Keith Barton and Linda Levstik have explored some of the 'alternative' histories which pupils create about the past if they feel they are excluded from the dominant narrative in the classroom. As we have seen, Alan McCully's work in Northern Ireland has shown how pupils can pick and choose from the history they are taught in school to support existing viewpoints (McCully and Pilgrim 2004). As noted earlier, there is very little research on how gender and class affect pupils' response to school history, and some limited work on race and ethnicity; these areas are ripe for further study. However, what we do know is that pupils are active participants in their own creation of meaning. If teachers want history to matter – to have some impact – they need to think hard about young people's preconceptions and the ways in which history may or may not connect with their lives. While we have explored in this book – and, as professionals, applaud – examples of excellent practice to be found in many schools, we also believe that history is not always made to matter sufficiently to learners. The combination of complex subject matter, high literacy demands and unimaginative curriculum and examination specifications often make the subject remote and inaccessible for many learners. In the rest of this chapter, we explore some of the ways in which history can matter in pupils' education, but ultimately it is the teacher in the classroom who makes history 'matter' by finding an entry point into a largely unfamiliar world that offers pupils some connections between their own lives and the experiences of the past. It is to these connections that we now turn.

How does history matter to pupils?

History and relevance

One of the charges frequently levelled against history in the school curriculum – by employers, and indeed, by pupils – is that it 'lacks relevance', although it is a charge also levelled against often more obviously 'useful' subjects including mathematics (Sealey and Noyes 2010). 'Relevance' is a challenging educational concept. Attempts to make history 'relevant' have normally fallen into two major groups: those which focus on content and those which emphasize skills developed through history teaching. Content-based strategies themselves take a number of forms. Some emphasize the teaching of contemporary history. In his discussion of the curriculum, John White made a connection between 'relevance' and *contemporary* history, arguing that

> many of the overall [curriculum] aims are about pupils' roles as national and global citizens in rapidly changing cultural, political, economic, technological and social conditions. Yet the history curriculum contains very little work on the twentieth century.
>
> (White 2004:12)

Others see 'relevance' secured by tailoring the curriculum to pupils' backgrounds, either through local history projects or by exploring histories which reflect the migration histories of pupils in the schools. Jamie Byrom described this as 'resonance' rather than relevance, looking for instances when the study of the past somehow connects with the pupils for whatever reason. This has an obvious place in the history curriculum; it can be opportunistic – using a local event as a stimulus for a unit of work, or taking advantage of a nearby archaeological dig. Arguments for history based on 'skills' have some currency; in some schools, for example, history departments have secured a place for history in vocational courses on leisure and tourism through units of work on heritage. However, for all the talk of historical skills, history appears to have a relatively weak place in any skills-led curriculum; many of the generic skills developed in history lessons are also developed in other areas of the curriculum, and areas which may have a stronger claim on 'relevance' through their content.

What is relevant to one person is not relevant to another. Personal relevance can be transitory: no less than adults, young people change their minds about their interests and enthusiasms. "Relevance" is a slippery word dependent on the aims and values that underpin the rationale for teaching history. In some settings, it may be sensible to articulate the basis for a history curriculum in terms of particular skills, or around particular content emphases, but equally there are dangers. As Claire Fox warned (Historical Association 2009), if history teachers shackle themselves to trends then they may be vulnerable when particular trends lose their currency. There are other approaches to the demands of 'relevance' which are more firmly grounded in the 'deep pedagogy' outlined in Chapter 11. A starting point is that a grasp of history is vital to understanding the world around us and our place in it. An understanding of the past can illuminate the present because history provides us with 'a historical frame of reference' (Dickinson *et al.* 1984). This is largely because history is the study of people – their behaviours, strengths and achievements, weaknesses and failures. Sam Wineburg cites the much-quoted line from Cicero about human beings' natural desire to know what came before (Wineburg 2007: 6). In this sense, any history is potentially relevant because it is about those who have come before and who have developed solutions to problems, some familiar, some less so. The argument for relevance which follows from this starting point is not geared around particular skills or content, pressing though some of these may be, but in the part which an understanding of the past offers to all pupils. Articluating this 'relevance' is demanding of teachers. It depends on connecting overall aims, the selection of content, the choice of teaching approaches and the needs of learners in the setting in which they are taught. Put differently, it is a professional obligation of history teachers to make history matter. A clear sense of why they are teaching history, why some content has been preferred and why some teaching methods have been selected is an important dimension of this. History can be made 'relevant' in different ways and not only by drawing very direct links to the present. John Tosh comments that 'history teaching in schools is designed to accommodate as many different demands on content as possible, at the expense of conveying what historical perspective means, and how it might usefully be applied to current issues' (Tosh 2008).

Knowledge, narrative and big pictures

The evolution of the so-called 'new history' in the 1970s, with its focus on the nature of history and its evidential base, led to criticisms, often in the press, about the decline of knowledge in public examination arrangements. Pupil achievement in history, as measured in public examinations and in the national curriculum Attainment Targets, it was asserted, focused primarily on conceptual understanding and historical skills rather than on the accumulations of factual knowledge. In fact, as we saw in Chapter 5, the quality of historical thinking is profoundly influenced by pupils' grasp of substantive knowledge. Nevertheless, credit has not usually been awarded explicitly for the amount that a pupil knows but rather how they organize, analyse and interpret what they know, and this remains the case. Knowledge has always been central to teaching and learning history regardless of what political and media commentators might have argued. What the 'new history' did, perhaps, encourage was a view that *any* knowledge was appropriate because the knowledge was important only insofar as it provided the necessary vehicle for the development of particular ways of thinking, or to foster pupils' enjoyment. This view was bolstered by suspicions among some teachers that any fixed notion of 'what' to teach was dangerous and open to political manipulation (Husbands *et al.* 2003) and that it was healthier in a democracy for teachers to have as much choice as possible. More recently there has been renewed interest in the selection of content in history and more confident assertions of the importance of getting this selection 'right', though definitions of this rarely coincide. What the arguments generally have in common, however, is desire for pupils to be able to see bigger pictures in history so that their knowledge is less fragmented. This is not a new argument: in 1902 a report lamented the narrowness of pupils' historical knowledge and a tendency for teachers to focus too much on examination syllabuses (Keating and Sheldon 2011). However, the extent to which school history develops an understanding of these 'bigger pictures' remains a moot point.

Howson argued in 2007 that 'History is a major cultural achievement worth defending', not because it offers easy lessons to be learned but because an ordered understanding of the past is a *usable* past: one that equips pupils with the knowledge and understanding to place themselves in a context and to appreciate where they have come from and where they might be going (Howson 2007: 47). In the absence of explicit attempts to develop big picture understanding of the past, pupils will construct their own, even if it is hopelessly ill-informed, confused and even dangerous (Rogers 1987). The historian Kitson Clark captured this well when he wrote about 'a haphazard mass of misty knowledge, scraps of information, fiction in fancy dress and hardly conscious historical memories' from which some kind of version of the past is constructed and in which 'words are converted into spells, symbols are endowed with emotional force and stereotypes emerge which pretend to describe whole groups of people'. He went on to suggest that this could be of use to those who 'wish to invoke irrational loyalties' and 'direct the emotion of hatred' (Kitson Clark 1967: 7). This provides a powerful argument for the importance of substantive knowledge and its careful selection. Not knowing about certain aspects of the past is not only socially and culturally disadvantageous; it prevents people from being able to challenge 'dogmatic statements and sweeping generalizations' (MacMillan 2009: 167).

Given that teachers must select what to teach, they need to be sure that the selection is useful. These decisions will always be subject to change, for what may be defined as 'useful' knowledge for one generation may be very different for another: some historical topics wane in importance as contemporary preoccupations and perceptions change. Beyond individual topics, knowledge needs to be organized into some kind of framework to help pupils to see the past in a broader perspective. To privilege one part of the past over another – Henry VIII over Edward V, or World War I over the Boer War, for example – teachers need some kind of underpinning rationale which commands attention *now*. For some this rationale may be the role of history in communicating a sense of Britain's culture and heritage. For others, it may be about why the West, in the ascendancy for the past five hundred years, may now be losing that ascendancy (Ferguson 2004). For others, the ambition may be still greater: to create some sense of the history of humanity (Shemilt 2009). In each case, the outcome for pupils would be an enhanced understanding of the world or an aspect of it today and a greater appreciation of its roots. It is easier, perhaps, to be critical of some of the frameworks used in the past, such as the Whig interpretation of history (Butterfield 1965), the Marxist progression from feudalism to capitalism to socialism (Cohen 1979), or our 'island story' (Marshall 1905), than it is to articulate a coherent 'big picture' for the early twenty-first century, but this is a pressing obligation for teachers. As one teacher put it to us, pupils 'live in a temporary world – they have no sense of value as to what people have done and achieved'. Teaching and learning history, it could be argued, can change the way pupils see the world by providing a wider frame of reference than the present. It can potentially influence attitudes, values and even behaviours, though there is debate about the extent to which such outcomes should be deliberately planned for, which could compromise history's integrity, or left to emerge naturally in the normal course of teaching and learning (Lee and Shemilt 2007).

How does history matter to society?

The justification for the place of history on the school curriculum has for a long time focused on its moral and civic functions. As early as 1927, the Board of Education described history in schools as 'pre-eminently an instrument of moral training' (Haydn 2004b: 89). History still has a tremendous amount to contribute to developing questioning and self-aware individuals. This is a tall order and there is a strong case for restraint in the ambition of aims associated with history in schools. Nevertheless, a world without historical perspective and critical thinking is a world few would relish. In a complex world characterized by high levels of diversity, looming conflict over diminishing resources and accelerating global inequalities, there is a powerful argument for what Barton and Levstik call 'teaching history for the common good' (Barton and Levstik 2004). There are arguments, the polarization of which is often exaggerated, about whether history should be a 'carrier' for citizenship or a 'complement' to it (Lee and Shemilt 2007), which echoes the debate over the 'intrinsic' and 'extrinsic' aims of history (see, for example, Husbands *et al.* 2003). Whatever their academic success, whatever their ultimate vocational destination, pupils do need to develop understandings which equip them to participate fully in democratic society. Obviously, it would be possible to distort history as a subject if this goal were exclusive but good history curricula need to be informed by multiple aims, of which this is one. There are perhaps three ways in which history contributes to the 'common good'. First, in the kind of thinking it encourages; second, in the ways it helps pupils to explore identity and third, in helping pupils to think about values and attitudes, and all three intertwine. Underpinning these claims is an assumption that *what* society and teachers choose to teach does matter as well as how it is taught. As HMI noted in 1985: 'Skills are unlikely to be acquired, let alone effectively applied, unless they are related to content that has some inherent interest and appears to relate to the lives of the pupils' (quoted in Haydn 2004b: 91).

Thinking historically

We have already explored what it means to think historically. Here, the argument developed is how historical thinking is helpful to society and the common good and we therefore focus on three aspects: history's relationship with evidence, the way history illuminates complexity in human behaviour and relationships and the perspective history brings to current issues. Thinking historically partly means thinking about the status of what is known. Once pupils move beyond a belief that the history they read is somehow a copy of the past and develop an appreciation that it is based on incomplete evidence drawn from various sources, they begin to understand that historical claims are provisional and therefore subject to change. To think historically in this way is also to think in disciplined ways (Cooper and Chapman 2009): it is not possible to make warranted historical claims which are not supported by sufficient weight of evidence, or which depend on evidence which is deeply flawed, or which are countered by other evidence. To accept this premise is to understand something important about life in general: do not believe everything you read or hear and demand the evidence which supports claims that are made, whether it be by politicians, your bank or the advertising agency marketing the latest shampoo. Postman and Weingartner call history a 'crap-detecting' subject (*Observer*, 22 February 1998) for good reason: it is preoccupied with the status of claims. Unfortunately, there is little empirical evidence that pupils routinely transfer learning in history to their everyday lives, though we have each observed lessons where teachers make this transference relatively explicit, and such practices make it *possible* that pupils will, at a later date, be able to make these connections.

Secondly, thinking historically is about recognizing and understanding complexity, especially in human behaviour and relationships. Christine Counsell writes that a key aspect of history [teaching] is the

> diversity and complexity of past society. A good historical education will challenge stereotypes, avoid homogenization of nations or groups and help pupils to understand that not all people in the past thought and acted in the same way.
>
> (Counsell 2004a)

This is an essential component of historical thinking and one of its most fundamental contributions to the common good. To understand that the term 'Jew' in pre-war Europe meant many things, to understand that the move from Catholicism to Protestantism was far from uniform and smooth in England and to understand that the statement 'women had no rights before the twentieth century' is an oversimplification is also to open the possibility of understanding that not all Muslims today are Islamic fundamentalists, that not all women have equality with men and that claims by politicians that Britain is a tolerant society need some interrogation. Perhaps this is an ambitious claim: again, there is little empirical evidence that such a transfer of knowledge and attitudes take place. But if pupils have a disposition to challenge generalizations, and awareness that the labels assigned to people, necessary though some may be, can be misleading and even dangerous, this is at least an important starting point.

Finally, history lends perspectives to current issues. It is obviously fallacious to suppose that society can somehow avoid the mistakes of the past as if the situations that lie ahead are likely to be exact copies of those encountered previously. The past teaches no such easy lessons. Nonetheless, John Tosh's observation that drawing on appropriate historical experiences to inform our understanding of current issues can only be helpful, and could minimize difficulties that would otherwise escalate, is an apposite one. Tosh's example is instructive: he argues that throughout the later twentieth century politicians used the public memory of 'appeasement' in the 1930s to provide an apparently irrefutable analogy justifying particular courses of action. Memories of appeasement in the 1930s were drawn upon by Truman to justify American intervention in Korea in 1950, by Johnson in defending his policy in Vietnam in the 1960s and by Tony Blair in his stance on Iraq in 2003. However, as Tosh argues, 'the problem with the appeasement analogy is that it tends to be given privileged status over any other precedent'; in the case of Iraq, a different – and perhaps strong – precedent would have been provided by the dismal experiences of the British mandate in Iraq in 1920 (Tosh 2006: 23–4). Reflecting on our work in schools for this book, we felt that there were some opportunities missed in lessons to explore links with the recent past or the present and we were sometimes taken aback by the apparent lack of knowledge of some young people about current issues. For example in a history lesson on the Vietnam War, pupils in a lower set appeared not to know that British troops were currently fighting a war in Iraq. In our conversations with pupils, they struggled to relate the school history either to the world around them or to the 'world pictures' and 'stories' that they were developing beyond the classroom. Perhaps this is not surprising as, compared to many countries, pupils in the UK learn little about the recent history of their own country (Haydn 2004b). The Modern World Study, a compulsory element of the Schools History Project GCSE courses in which a modern world 'problem' was analysed and explained with reference to its historical roots, was abandoned in the revision of GCSE in 2009. Despite this, good practices persist. In a London school, for example, the Head of History sought to relate the past to the present as often as possible, partly through the use of good analogies, which can, if sloppy, over-simplify or distort, such as a comparison of the Obama–McCain election compared to Roosevelt.

Our place in the world: diversity, identity, heritage

Attempts to define our place in the world are complex and integral to our identity. We are defined by where we live, locally and nationally, who our parents are, what jobs we do, by our colour, our religion and by our class. Making sense of our world is a long process and one in which understandings of the past loom large. Questions about how we came to be here, why our local area looks the way it does, why Britain has its particular set of global relationships, why colour, class and religion define us in particular ways all depend to greater or lesser extents on our knowledge of the past. In recent years, a television programme in which notable individuals trace their family origins has become popular and the series title – *Who do you think you are?* – is well and tellingly chosen.

One aspect of this – the question of what constitutes 'Britishness' – has gathered pace during the first decade of the twenty-first century for a variety of reasons ranging from devolution and the strength of the European Union to the rise of the BNP and acts of terrorism carried out by British citizens. In a conference about Britishness convened by the Fabian Society in 2006, Gordon Brown, then Labour Chancellor, referred to the need to wrest the Union Jack away from the BNP and to use it as a 'symbol of unity' emphasizing values of fairness, liberty and responsibility 'which run like a "golden thread" through Britain's past' (Brown 2006). David Cameron subsequently used a speech at the Greatest Briton of 2005 award ceremony to outline his own views on the subject, claiming that Britishness is not about flags, but rather that 'reserve is an intrinsic part of being British'. Both saw a key role for history lessons in shaping a collective identity. Even the singer Billy Bragg, long associated with the radical left, warned at the Fabian conference that 'if we flinch from a discussion of our history, we leave it to the BNP and UKIP – it's a nettle we must grasp'. Although this debate was not new in 2006, it was conducted with a new urgency in the wake of the July bombings in 2005 (Kitson 2006). The issues at stake are fraught with uncertainty, not least because there is no consensus around the values associated with being British. In contrast to Brown and Cameron above, the newspaper columnist Yasmin Alibhai-Brown regards the concept of universally good British values as 'absurd' and sees the challenge as the creation of 'a new British identity which has evolved from historical meanings but is not bound by history' (Alibhai-Brown 2006). In other words, Britishness is an identity which reflects the realities of the present rather than being dependent on past actions and values. The historian Linda Colley argued that the very concept of 'Britons', and the emergence of a national collective identity, was a largely political creation of the eighteenth century: 'an invented nation, superimposed onto much older alignments and loyalties' (Colley 1992: 5).

Teachers are often suspicious of using history to promote any sense of British identity, not least because of the way British history was taught in the earlier part the twentieth century when the British Empire was only celebrated and the 'Great' in Great Britain was taken literally. One teacher said that he would 'hate to be teaching a subject which is about Britain's greatness...there are lots of things we should be proud of but also things we shouldn't' (Kitson 2006: 89). Nevertheless, teachers have been teaching mainly British – indeed, English – history at Key Stage 3 for much of the twentieth century and, when pushed to identify those topics which all pupils should learn about, cite mainly events and people drawn from Britain's past (Husbands *et al.* 2003). There seems to be a consensus that pupils ought to learn about British history, but there is room for considerable debate about how much of their history curriculum should be made up of British history and about the way this history is presented, and nuanced. Teachers need to be outward as well as inward looking in the ways they teach Britain's past. One of the defining features of Britain lies in its relationship to the rest of the world, from its earliest origins in the waves of invasion and settlement to the expansion of the Empire and its collapse. Its fortunes and relationships with other countries today are shaped by long historical experiences including Britain's geographical position between mainland Europe and North America, its adoption of Protestantism in the sixteenth century and its eighteenth- and nineteenth-century mastery of the seas. In this sense, to learn about Britain's past is to learn about much of the world, albeit through a British lens. In one East Anglian school we visited, the history department deliberately focuses primarily on British history where possible, using the locality of the school as a backbone. Far from making the history insular, the approach enables global connections to be made by examining the waves of immigration into Norwich in the Middle Ages, when, for example, one-third of the city's population spoke Dutch.

Keith Ajegbo, who led a review of citizenship and diversity for the government in 2005, argued that history is a component of citizenship education because of its role in exploring identity and diversity in the UK. History, he argued, can bring 'rigour to the debate' (Ajegbo 2007) while retaining its integrity as an academic component of the curriculum. There is some evidence about the way pupils connect identity and history. In Northern Ireland, where the historical roots of conflicting identities are especially resonant, teachers have traditionally shied away from tackling issues of identity, or indeed anything controversial, too overtly. The most recent research suggests that, consequently, pupils take what they want from the past to justify their preconceptions, whether that be from history classrooms or from elsewhere (McCully and Pilgrim 2004). Although there can often be understandable reasons for some teachers' tendency to 'play safe' in the classroom, the research, far from claiming that history can have no role to play in helping pupils understand fraught issues, points to a potentially positive correlation. In other words history can help pupils to explore challenging issues of conflict and identity, whereas when history teachers avoid tackling controversial issues pupils are likely to draw on 'street' knowledge which reinforces stereotypes. Nowhere is history teaching more profoundly intertwined with issues of national identity than in the teaching of the Holocaust in German schools. There, the principal objective of teaching about the Holocaust is not limited to the historical record, although the Holocaust is set squarely within the context of the Nazi rise to power. Instead, the purpose of teaching German pupils about the Holocaust is explicitly to make them appreciate the values and institutions that protect freedom and democracy (Holocaust Education Task Force 2009). At the same time, if history is to play a part in education for diversity and interdependence, much of the traditional content of school history needs careful consideration. British history may provide a window on the history of the world, but a history curriculum which takes only a British view is unlikely to prepare young people for understanding a world of global interdependence.

'Heritage' is a concept which is often seen as distinct from global interdependence: while learning for global interdependence – or 'global learning' as it has become known – appears to be associated with outward-looking perspectives, 'heritage' is often associated with introspective and 'backward-looking concerns' based on 'shar[ing] what we inherit among colleagues and communities, nations and faiths' (Lowenthal 1998: xiii, 55). History is not heritage and both historians and history teachers have often been critical of relating history to heritage; this has either been a relatively mild concern about the ways in which heritage reflects an uncritical nostalgia for an imagined, soft-focus past (Tosh 2006: 17) or deeper concerns about the ways in which heritage can be manipulated for quasi-political ends to shape perceptions about what 'the nation' might be (Wright 2009). In multicultural and diverse Britain, 'heritage' can often be seen as a way of celebrating an impossibly pretty past of thatched cottages, castles and, as the Conservative Prime Minister John Major put it, 'long shadows on cricket grounds, warm beer, invincible green suburbs, dog lovers and pools fillers and, as George Orwell said, "Old maids bicycling to holy communion through the morning mist"' (Major 1993). On the other hand, we all have a heritage: the heritage of family, communities in which our families have lived, shared and contested cultural frames of reference which go to make up the ways we think and feel. The difficulty is not with the idea of 'heritage' so much as the way it may be used selectively to approach the way we think about the past. 'Heritage' is the heritage of those who came to this country as refugees and immigrants as much as the heritage of those who owned the country-side, and of those who were disadvantaged as well as those who exercised power. As Raphael Samuel put it, heritage can be a way of advancing 'notions of ancestry and posterity...without embarrassment or bad faith' (Samuel 1995: 292). In this sense, one of the ways in which history in school matters to society is in the space it offers in which to explore what 'heritages' we share and over what heritages we differ. Heritage sites are, in practice, a staple of the history curriculum: Tracy Borman points out that there are some three million educational visits to such sites each year (Borman 2005). Heritage sites provide a basis for exploring competing notions of heritage within the context of a history curriculum – what Borman calls 'education by stealth'. Heritage matters to history when heritage sites are used historically, not when history lessons are used to explore particular presentations of the past.

Attitudes, values and dispositions

It is in the area of attitudes, values and dispositions where contemporary history teachers frequently start to feel uneasy. The root issue is the extent to which teaching aims to equip pupils with knowledge that will help them understand the world and navigate their way through it, or to change their beliefs and behaviour. The latter aspiration can appear hopelessly optimistic given the limited extent to which schools influence young people, quite apart from the limited possibilities open to a single school subject. Writing in 1985, HMI commented wryly that in relation to multicultural education, history syllabi were decked with often extravagant claims (HMI 1985). It is also quite contrary to the integrity of a subject which deals in provisionality and claims about the past based in evidence, not moral tenets by which to live one's life, to suppose that it can offer simple prescriptions for changing behaviour. On the other hand, schools teach about the Holocaust so that it helps to shape values and attitudes in positive ways just as they teach about slavery as a 'bad thing'. As John Slater wrote, schools are not even-handed in the way they teach everything, and it is not desirable that they should be: teachers do not start lessons with 'today, pupils, the case for the Holocaust'. In other words, teachers' attitudes, values and dispositions infuse their teaching in ways that are unavoidable and it is reasonable to expect that some of these may rub off on pupils. Of course, this can be problematic – teachers need to pay heed to the different values of the past and to understand that slavery was believed to be less abhorrent then than it is now – but teachers cannot shrug off their own values in doing so. On the whole, it is right to be sceptical of claims that, by learning certain things, pupils change their values and behaviour and it would be naive to assume that this is a necessary consequence of learning. There is, indeed, precious little evidence to suppose that the consequence of teaching individual topics is that pupils change their views.

Nevertheless, pupils' values, attitudes and behaviours are likely to emerge from a complex mixture of influences of which history, taught well, is likely to be one part, however small. Schools themselves do set out to influence pupils' attitudes and beliefs (Haydon 2007), and the argument we are advancing here is that the specific contribution of history to the school curriculum lies as much in its scope to develop certain attitudes and to develop a disposition to certain values as in the scope to extend pupils' knowledge and understanding. The past is not a source of moral instruction; as E.P. Thompson insisted,

> Our vote will change nothing. Yet in another sense, it may change everything. For we are saying that these values, and not those other values, are the ones which make this history meaningful to us, and that these are the values which we intend to enlarge and sustain in our own present.
>
> (Thompson 1978: 234)

History teachers – perhaps unlike professional historians – do work in institutions which are deeply concerned with moral as well as merely academic education, with personal development as well as intellectual or vocational training. Values are central to the teaching of history in schools. This sense of the centrality of values is captured in a scene from Alan Bennett's *The History Boys*. The play focuses on a group of boys in a northern grammar school. A new teacher, Irwin, is brought in to train the boys for 'Oxbridge' entrance. Irwin's advice is to be controversial, to turn an argument on its head, to not necessarily seek the 'truth', to grab the examiner's attention, because, he says, 'History nowadays is not a matter of conviction. It's a performance. It's entertainment. And if it isn't, make it so.' Irwin and Hector, the boys' previous, rather eccentric teacher, share a lesson in which the Holocaust is discussed as a possible topic in the forthcoming examination. One of the eight boys, Posner, is Jewish:

Hector: But how can you teach the Holocaust?

Irwin: That would do as a question. Can you...should you...teach the Holocaust?

Akthar: It has origins. It has consequences. It's a subject like any other.

Scripps: Not like any other, surely. Not like any other at all.

Hector: They go on school trips nowadays don't they? Auschwitz, Dachau. What has always concerned me is where they eat their sandwiches, drink their coke.

Crowther: The visitors' centre. It's like anywhere else.

Hector: Do they take pictures of one another there? Are they smiling? Do they hold hands? Nothing is appropriate. Just as questions on an examination paper are inappropriate. How can the boys scribble down an answer, however well put, that doesn't demean the suffering involved? And putting it well demeans it as much as putting it badly.

Irwin: It's a question of tone, surely. Tact.

Hector: Not tact, decorum.

[...]

Timms: You told us once…it was to do with the trenches, Sir…that one person's death tells you more than a thousand. When people are dying like flies, you said, that is what they are dying like.

Posner: Except that these weren't just dying. They were being processed. What is different is the process.

Irwin: Good.

Hector: No, not good. Posner is not making a *point*. He is speaking from the heart.

(Bennett 2004: 71–2)

Conclusion: learning history in a democratic society

Schools face profound challenges and we expect a great deal of them. We expect them to play a leading role in preparing young people for a technologically intensive, high-skill labour market by continuously raising standards of literacy and numeracy. We expect them to lay the foundations for lifelong learning by introducing young people to the skills and dispositions they will need to continue to engage with learning as the world changes around them. We expect them to introduce young people to the high-lights of the western cultural canon while making learners aware of the energy and dis-tinctiveness of other cultural traditions. We expect them to combat intolerance, racism and stereotyping. We expect them to reflect and celebrate cultural diversity whether their pupil populations are diverse or monocultural. We expect them to do these things with young people irrespective of their attainment, cultural heritage, family circum-stances. Their principal resource in meeting these challenges remains the curriculum, and here, too, society's expectations are daunting. We expect the curriculum – con-strained by resources, time, competing demands – to prepare young people for the future. We expect it to introduce cultural and social inheritances, to provide young people with knowledge and to extend their skills across an increasingly demanding range of technologies, to meet the demands of the most academically successful and those who struggle most with learning.

Within this curriculum, this book has explored the multilayered demands of his-tory teaching. The time available to teaching history is frequently limited, and there are multiple demands both on the curriculum as a whole and its individual components. Politicians in particular are notorious for demanding that more be taught without ever confronting what should be dropped. In respect of history teaching there are loud demands that it should reflect a clear narrative of a complex national history, introduce young people to the historical origins of contemporary challenges, develop their lit-eracy and their capacity to use evidence and argument, and prepare them successfully for external examinations.

Our expectations of young people are high too. We expect them to confront the vast extent of human history and to make some order out of it: to understand a sequence and to construct a meaningful narrative because without this the past is merely Arnold Toynbee's 'one damned thing after another'. We expect them to be able to use and evaluate historical evidence, because without this the substan-tive knowledge which is built up is indistinguishable from fiction. We expect them to develop mature emotional reactions to historical experiences of individuals and societies as a part of their social education. We expect them to develop the communicative abilities to convey all this for the purposes of assessment and to refine their own understandings.

This book has explored the part that the 'major cultural achievement' which is history plays in schooling. We have done so by exploring the ways in which curricula are developed in school and the way content and teaching methods are selected. We have considered the views of young people themselves, and the knowledge, techniques and approaches at the disposal of teachers. In this final section we have considered the part which learning about the past plays in schools and society. We are not naive about history education. It faces – and therefore history teachers face – profound challenges. The position of history in the curriculum is often weak. The subject has acquired the reputation of being 'difficult' and 'inaccessible' despite the energetic efforts of history teachers. However, we have outlined a vision of the discipline as vital in the learning of all young people. It is this, rather than frequently abstruse debates about curriculum content or form, which we regard as the essential curriculum debate.

Learning history is hard. It involves learning about the past, the processes by which the past is accessed, and the relationship between these two elements – between upper case History and lower case history. It drives a powerful pedagogy, potentially able to equip young people with tools and knowledge to negotiate their identity and the world into which they are growing. Arguments for the importance of history as an academic discipline matter less than the arguments for history as a critical – in every sense of the word – component in the *general education* of the young. Society needs young people to learn about the past because not knowing about the past and not understanding the provisionality of knowledge about the past are too painful to contemplate. Society needs young people to learn history because without it they cannot hope to make sense of their lives and their world. None of this is to say that teaching young people history is easy. It is – as we have explored in this book – demanding, intellectually and pedagogically. In the face of such a challenge it can be tempting for schools, and for history teachers, to assume that some young people do not 'need' history and cannot understand it. We have tried to show that this is not true. If, as we have argued, history matters to young people and to society, if it matters to their identity and cognitive development, if it lays the foundations for their capacity to participate as members of an open, diverse, unequal, complex society, then it must matter to all young people, because all our young people will live in the same society. Throughout this book, we have located the debates around history teaching in the voices of both young people who learn and those whom they study. There is a precious thread which connects Elizabeth Marsh, traversing the eighteenth-century world, and the Year 8 pupils with whose voices we end: that it is an enduring task for each of us to understand who we are, where we have come from, and what we might be.

Box 12.1 Year 8 pupils think about the purpose of history

These three boys and three girls are all from a low-attaining set in a rural school with an almost exclusively white intake.

Interviewer: Someone said that they like finding out about the past. Do you think there is stuff in the past to help you work out what is going on at the moment?

Boy 1: You'd be better off just learning about what's in the 'fore-world' like Afghanistan and that...

Boy 2: But how are you going to know the future?

Boy 1: No, what's happening now, like Afghan and that.

Girl 1: Yes, like the war...

Boy 1: ...and the Taleban and stuff.

Girl 2: But in history we do learn about wars and how they tried to make peace but they're still doing it now.

Interviewer: Don't you think we can learn stuff from the past though?

Boy 1: ...like the Twin Towers.

Girl 2: But we've never actually done anything about that.

Boy 3: I've watched it...

Boy 1: Cos it's history.

Interviewer: It's pretty recent history though isn't it? And because it's quite recent it's quite worrying because it could happen again.

Boy 1: But they're not afraid to die are they? They would do anything for their country. The people who went into the Twin Towers they just went into it – they didn't care if they died did they?

Girl 1: It's not for a country – it's for their religion.

Interviewer: So can history help us understand that?

Boy 2: I reckon it can but it's also religious.

Girl 2: In some ways I think [history] can help in life.

Int: How do you find out about what's happening in the world? Like politics and stuff?

Boy 1: People watch the news.

Int: So is it important to know what's going on?

All: Yes

Int: When do you get to vote?

All: 18 or over.

Int: How do you think you'll learn about how to vote? Do you think you'll want to vote?

Girl 2: It all depends...

Boy 1: I won't vote. Because I won't know who to vote for. I'm not that sort of person.

Int: So is it important to vote? Because it seems you're saying you could change...

Boy 2: ...the world!

References

Adey, K. and M. Biddulph (2001) The influence of pupil perceptions on subject choice at 14+ in geography and history, *Educational Studies*, 27(4): 439–50.

Ajegbo, K. (2007) *Curriculum Review: Diversity and Citizenship.* Report Number: 00045-2007DOM-EN. London: Department for Education and Skills.

Alexander, R. (2004) Still no pedagogy? Principle, pragmatism and compliance in primary education, *Cambridge Journal of Education*, 34(1): 7–33.

Alexander, R. J. (2000) *Culture and Pedagogy: International Comparisons in Primary Education.* Oxford: Blackwell.

Alexander, R. J. (2006) *Towards Dialogic Teaching: Rethinking Classroom Talk.* York: Dialogos.

Alexander, R. J. (2009) *Children, their World, their Education.* Final report and recommendations of the Cambridge Primary Review. London: Routledge.

Alibhai-Brown, Y. (2006) Who are we and what do we want to be? *Guardian.* http://www.guardian.co.uk/politics/2006/jan/13/thinktanks.uk, accessed 23 February 2011.

Allsop, S. (2010) Using 1980s popular music to explore historical significance, *Teaching History*, 137: 52–9.

Andrews, R. (1995) *Teaching and Learning Argument.* London: Cassell.

Arthur, J., Davies, I., Wrenn, A., Haydn, T. and Kerr, D. (2001) *Citizenship through Secondary History.* London: RoutledgeFalmer.

Ashby, R. (2005) Students' approaches to validating historical claims, in R. Ashby, P. Gordon and P. Lee (eds) *Understanding History: Recent Research in History Education (International Review of History Education Vol. 4).* London: RoutledgeFalmer.

Ashby, R. and Lee, P. (1987) Children's concepts of empathy and understanding in history, in C. Portal (ed.) *The History Curriculum for Teachers.* London: Falmer Press.

Bage, G. (1999) *Narrative Matters: Teaching History through Story.* London: Falmer Press.

Bage, G. (2000) *Thinking History 4–14: Teaching, Learning, Curricula and Communities.* London: RoutledgeFalmer.

Banham, D. (1998) Getting ready for the Grand Prix: learning how to build a substantiated argument in Year 7, *Teaching History*, 92: 6–15.

Banham, D. (2000) The return of King John: using depth to strengthen overview in the teaching of political change, *Teaching History*, 99: 22–31.

Banham, D. and Culpin, C. (2002) Ensuring progression continues into GCSE: let's not do for our pupils with our plan of attack, *Teaching History*, 109: 16–22.

Banham, D. and Hall, R. (2003) JFK: the medium, the message and the myth, *Teaching History*, 113: 6–12.

Barber, M. and Mourshed, M. (2007) *How the World's Best-performing School Systems Come out on Top*. New York: McKinsey and Company.

Barnes, D. (1976) *From Communication to Curriculum*. Harmondsworth: Penguin Education.

Barnes, S. (2002) Revealing the big picture: patterns, shapes and images at Key Stage 3, *Teaching History*, 107: 6–12.

Barton, K. (2005) Primary sources in history: breaking through the myths, *Phi Delta Kappan*, 86(10): 745–53.

Barton, K. (2008), A sociocultural perspective on children's understanding of historical change: comparative findings from Northern Ireland and the United States, in L. S. Levstik and K. C. Barton (eds) *Researching History Education: Theory, Method, and Context*. New York: Routledge.

Barton, K. and Levstik, L. (2004) *Teaching History for the Common Good*. Mahwah, NJ: Lawrence Erlbaum Associates.

Barton, K. C. (2009) The denial of desire: how to make history education meaningless, in L. Symcox and A. Wilschut (eds) *National History Standards: The Problem of the Canon and the Future of Teaching History*. Charlotte, NC: Information Age Publishing.

Barton, K. C. and McCully, A. (2005) History, identity and the school curriculum in Northern Ireland: an empirical study of secondary students' ideas and perspectives, *Journal of Curriculum Studies*, 37(1): 85–116.

Barzun, J. and Graff, H. F. (1970) *The Modern Researcher*. New York: Harcourt Brace.

Bennett, A. (2004) *The History Boys*. London: Faber and Faber.

Biddulph, M. and K. Adey (2004) Pupil perceptions of effective teaching and subject relevance in history and geography at Key Stage 3, *Research in Education*, 71(1): 1–8.

Black, P. and Wiliam, D. (1998) Assessment and classroom learning, *Assessment in Education*, 5(1): 7–71.

Black, P., Harrison, C., Lee, C., Marshall, B. and Wiliam, D. (2002) *Working Inside the Black Box: Assessment for Learning in the Classroom*. London: Kings College.

Black, P., Harrison, C., Lee, C., Marshall, B. and Wiliam, D. (2003) *Assessment for Learning: Putting it into Practice*. Maidenhead: Open University Press McGraw-Hill Education.

Bloom, B. S. (1956) *Taxonomy of Educational Objectives: The classification of Educational Goals*. New York: Longmans, Green.

Boaler, J. (2002) *Experiencing School Mathematics: Traditional and Reform Approaches to Teaching and their Impact on Student Learning*. London: Routledge.

Booth, A. and Nicholls, D. (2005) History Teaching in Higher Education: Breaking Down the Barriers to Progression and Dialogue. *Working Paper*. Coventry: University of Warwick HEA Subject Centre for History.

Booth, M. (1978) Inductive thinking in history: the 14–16 age group, in G. Jones and L. Ward (eds) *New History, Old Problems: Studies in History Teaching*. Swansea: University College of Swansea, Faculty of Education.

Borman, T. (2005) *Bringing History to Life: The Role of Heritage in Education*. London: Institute for Historical Research.

Bourdieu, P. (1984) *Distinction. A Social Critique of the Judgement of Taste*. Cambridge, MA: Harvard University Press.

Bradshaw, M. (2009) Drilling down: how one history department is working towards progression in pupils' thinking about diversity across years 7, 8 and 9, *Teaching History*, 135: 4–12.

Braudel, F. and Matthews, S. (1980) *On History*. Chicago, IL: University of Chicago Press.

Brendon, P. (2008) *The Decline and Fall of the British Empire*. London: Vintage.

Britton, J. (1970) *Language and Learning*. London: Penguin Books.

Brooker, E. (2009) Telling tales. Developing students' own thematic and synoptic understandings at Key Stage 3, *Teaching History*, 136: 45–52.

Brown, G. (2006). The Future of Britishness. Keynote speech given at Fabian Society Conference, Who Do We Want to Be? London, 14 January. http://www.fabians.org.uk/events/speeches/the-future-of-britishness, accessed 22 February 2011.

Brown, G. and Woodcock, J. (2009) Relevant, rigorous and revisited: using local history to make meaning of historical significance, *Teaching History*, 134: 4–11.

Brown, G. and Wrenn, A. (2005) 'It's like they've gone up a year!' Gauging the impact of a history transition unit on teachers of primary and secondary history, *Teaching History*, 121: 5–13.

Bruner, J. S. (1960) *The Process of Education*. Cambridge, MA: Harvard University Press.

Bruner, J. S. (1972) *The Relevance of Education*. London: Allen and Unwin.

Bruner, J. S. (1996) *The Culture of Education*. Cambridge, MA: Harvard University Press.

Burnham, S. (2007) Getting Year 7 to set their own questions about the Islamic Empire, 600–1600, *Teaching History*, 128.

Burnham, S. (2009) Making pupils want to explain: using Movie Maker to foster thoroughness and self-monitoring, *Teaching History*, 133: 39–44.

Burnham, S. and Brown, G. (2004) Assessment without level descriptions, *Teaching History*, 115: 5–15.

Burrow, J. (2007) *A History of Histories: Epics, Chronicles, Romances and Inquiries from Herodotus and Thucydides to the Twentieth Century*. London: Allen Lane.

Butler, A. C., Zaromb, F. M. Lyle, K. B. and Roediger III, H. L. (2009) Using popular films to enhance classroom learning: the good, the bad, and the interesting, *Psychological Science*, 20(9): 1161–8.

Butler, S. (2003) 'What's that stuff you're listening to Sir?' Rock and pop music as a rich source for historical enquiry, *Teaching History*, 111: 20–5.

Butterfield, H. (1965) *The Whig Interpretation of History*. New York, London: W.W. Norton and Company.

Byrom, J. (1998) Working with sources: scepticism or cynicism? Putting the story back together again, *Teaching History*, 91: 32–5.

Byrom, J. (2000) Why go on a pilgrimage? Using a concluding enquiry to reinforce and assess earlier learning, *Teaching History*, 99: 32–5.

Byrom, J. (2003) Continuity and progression, in *Past Forward: A Vision for School History 2002–2012* London: Historical Association.

Card, J. (2004) Seeing double: how one period visualises another, *Teaching History*, 117: 6–11.

Carr, E.H. (1961) *What is History?* London: Macmillan.

Chakravarty, G. (2005) *The Indian Mutiny and the British Imagination*. Cambridge Studies in Nineteenth-Century Literature and Culture. Cambridge: Cambridge University Press.

Chancellor, V. (1970) *History for their Masters: Opinion in the English History Textbook, 1800–1914*. Bath: Adams and Dart.

Chapman, A. (2003) Camels, diamonds and counter-factuals: a model for teaching causal reasoning, *Teaching History*, 112: 46–53.

Chapman, A. (2006) Asses, archers and assumptions: strategies for improving thinking skills in history in Years 9 to 13, *Teaching History*, 123: 6–13.

Chapman, A. (2007) Relics rock: constructing stonehenge, *Teaching History*, 127: 20–1.

Chapman, A. (2008) 'Cause and Consequence' in *A Guide to the New Key Stage 3 Programme*, available at http://www.history.org.uk/secondaryguide121554.html, accessed 2 May 2011.

Chapman, A. (2009) Review essay. Making claims you can sustain: the importance of historical argument, *Teaching History*, 135: 58–9.

Chapman, A. (2010) Historical interpretations, in I. Davies (ed.) *Debates in History Teaching*. London: Routledge.

Chapman, A. and Facey, J. (2004) Placing history: territory, story, identity and historical consciousness, *Teaching History*, 116: 36–41.

Chisholm, L. (2004) The history curriculum in the (revised) National Curriculum Statement: an introduction, in S. Jeppie (ed.) *Towards 'New' Histories for South Africa: On the Place of the Past in our Present*. Cape Town: University of Cape Town Press.

Clark, V. (2001) Illuminating the shadow: making progress happen in casual thinking through speaking and listening, *Teaching History*, 105: 26–33.

Claxton, G. (1999) *Wise Up: Learning to Live the Learning Life*. London: Bloomsbury Publishing.

Coffield, F., Moseley, D., Hall, E. and Ecclestone, K. (2004) *Learning Styles and Pedagogy in Post-16 Learning. A Systematic and Critical Review*. London: Learning and Skills Research Centre.

Coffin, C. (2006) *Historical Discourse: The Language of Time, Cause and Evaluation*. London: Continuum.

Cohen, G. A. (1979) *Karl Marx's Theory of History: A Defence*. Oxford: Oxford University Press.

Colley, L. (1992) Britishness and otherness: an argument, *Journal of British Studies*, 31: 309–29.

Colley, L. (2007) *The Ordeal of Elizabeth Marsh: A Woman in World History*. Harmondsworth: Penguin Books.

Conway, D. (2005) Why history remains the best form of citizenship education, *Civitas Review*, 2.

Cooper, H. (2005) *Exploring Time and Place Through Play: Foundation Stage – Key Stage 1*. London: David Fulton Publishers.

Cooper, H. and Chapman, A. (2009) *Constructing History 11–19*. London: Sage Publications.

Counsell, C. (1997) *Analytic and Discursive Writing at Key Stage 3*. Historical Association. http://www.history.org.uk/resources/secondary_resource_1948.html, accessed 22 February 2011.

Counsell, C. (2000a) Historical knowledge and historical skills: a distracting dichotomy, in J. Arthur and R. Phillips (eds) *Issues in History Teaching*. London: Routledge.

Counsell, C. (2000b) 'Didn't we do that in Year 7?' Planning for progress in evidential understanding, *Teaching History*, 99: 36–41.

Counsell, C. (2003a) Editorial, *Teaching History*, 111.

Counsell, C. (2003b) *History for all in Past Forward: A Vision for School History 2002–2012*. London: Historical Association.

Counsell, C. (2004a) Looking through a Josephine Butler-shaped window: focusing pupils' thinking on historical significance, *Teaching History*, 114: 30–6.

Counsell, C. (2004b) *History and Literacy in Year 7*. London: John Murray.

Counsell, C. (2009) Editorial, *Teaching History*, 135: 3.

Counsell, C. (2010a) The place of diversity within the changing requirements of the history curriculum in M. Riley and J. Byrom (eds) *Dimensions of Diversity: How Do We Improve our Teaching of Social Complexity in History?* London: Historical Association. http://www.history.org.uk/resources/secondary_resource_1326,1328_11.html, accessed 23 February 2011.

Counsell, C. (2010b) What do we want students to *do* with historical change and continuity? in I. Davies (ed.) *Debates in History Teaching*. London: Routledge.

Counsell, C. and the Historical Association Secondary Education Committee (1997) *The Twentieth Century World: Planning Study Unit 4 of the National Curriculum for History*. London: Historical Association.

Crawford, K. and Foster, S. (2008) *War, Nation, Memory: International Perspectives on World War II in School History Textbooks*. Greenwich, CT: Information Age.

Culpin, C., Dawson, I., Banham, D., Edwards, B. and Burnham, S. (2009) *History: Pupil's Book Year 8*. London: Hodder Education.

Cunnah, W. (2000) History teaching, literacy and special educational needs, in J. Arthur and R. Phillips (eds) *Issues in History Teaching*. London: Routledge.

Cunningham, D. L. (2004) Empathy without illusion, *Teaching History*, 114: 24–9.

Cunningham, R. (2001) Teaching pupils how history works, *Teaching History*, 102: 14–19.

Dawn, T., Harkin, J. and Turner, G. (2000). *Teaching Young Adults. A Handbook for Teachers in Post-compulsory Education*. London: Routledge Falmer.

Dawson, I. (2003) *What is History? Year 7 Starter Unit for Key Stage 3*. London: Hodder Education.

Dawson, I. (2004) Time for chronology? Ideas for developing chronological understanding, *Teaching History*, 117: 14–24.

Dawson, I. (2008) Thinking across time: planning and teaching the story of power and democracy at Key Stage 3, *Teaching History*, 130: 14–21.

DES (Department of Education and Science) (1985) *History in the Primary and Secondary Years: An HMI View*. London: HMSO.

DES (1989) National Curriculum History Working Group: Interim Report. London: HMSO.

DfES (Department for Education and Skills) (2003) *Every Child Matters* (Green Paper). Norwich: The Stationery Office.

DfES (2004) *Pedagogy and Practice: Teaching and Learning in Secondary Schools*. London: DfES.

Dickinson, A., Gordon, P. and Lee, P. (2001) *International Review of History Education: Raising Standards in History Education, Volume 3*. London: Woburn Press.

Dickinson, A., Lee, P. and Rogers, P. J. (1984) *Learning History*. London: Heinemann Educational Books.

Dickinson, A. K. and Lee, P. J. (1978) *History Teaching and Historical Understanding*. London: Heinemann Educational Publishers.

Dixon, J. (2003) The hidden crisis in GCSE History, *Teaching History*, 110: 41–3.

Donaldson, M. (1978) *Children's Minds*. London: Fontana.

Donaldson, M. (1986) *Children's Explanations. A Psycholinguistic Study*. Cambridge: Cambridge University Press.

Donovan, M. S. and Bransford, J. D. (2005) *How Students Learn: History, Mathematics and Science in the Classroom*. Washington, D C: The National Academies Press.

Edexcel (2009) Specification: GCE History: 236 http://www.edexcel.com/migrationdocuments/ GCE%20New%20GCE/UA024847%20GCE%20in%20History%20Iss%202%20 210510.pdf, accessed 29 April 2011.

Edwards, A. D. and Furlong, V. J. (1978) *The Language of Education*. Oxford: Heinemann Educational Publishers.

Edwards, C. (2006) Putting life into history: how pupils can use oral history to become critical historians, *Teaching History*, 123: 21–5.

Epstein, T. (2009). *Interpreting National History: Race, Identity, and Pedagogy in Classrooms*. New York: Abingdon, Routledge, Taylor and Francis.

Evans, R. J. (1997) *In Defence of History*. London: Granta.

Evans, S. and Pate, G. (2007) Does scaffolding make them fall? Reflecting on strategies for developing causal argument in Years 8 and 11, *Teaching History*, 128: 18–29.

Evans, S., Grier, C., Phillips, J. and Colton, S. (2004) 'Please send socks'. How much can Reg Wilkes tell us about the Great War? *Teaching History*, 114: 7–16.

Ferguson, N. (2004) *Colossus: The Rise and Fall of the American Empire*. London: Penguin.

Ferro, M. (1984) *The Use and Abuse of History: Or, How the Past is Taught to Children*. London: Routledge and Kegan Paul.

Fines, J. (1994) Evidence: the basis of the discipline, in H. Bourdillon (ed.) *Teaching History*. London: Routledge.

Flutter, J. (2002) Thinking and talking about learning, *Teaching Thinking*, Spring: 42–6.

Flutter, J. and Rudduck, J. (2004) *Consulting Pupils: What's In It for Schools?* London: RoutledgeFalmer.

Foster, R. (2008) Speed cameras, dead ends, drivers and diversions: Year 9 use a 'road map' to problematise change and continuity, *Teaching History*, 131: 4–8.

Foster, S. and Crawford, K. (2006) *What Shall We Tell the Children? International Perspectives on School History Textbooks*. Greenwich, CT: Information Age.

Foster, S., Lee, P. and Ashby, R. (2008) Usable historical pasts: a study of students' frameworks of the past. Full Research Report, ESRC End of Award Report. Swindon: ESRC.

Galton, M. and Williamson, J. (1992) *Group Work in the Primary Classroom*. London: Routledge.

Galton, M., Simon, B. and Croll, P. (1980) *Inside the Primary Classroom*. London: Routledge and Kegan Paul.

Galton, M., Steward, S., Hargreaves, L., Page, C. and Pell, T. (2009) *Motivating Your Secondary Class*. London: Sage Publications.

Gombrich, E.H. (2005) A *Little History of the World*. London: Yale University Press.

Gosden, P. H. J. H. and Sylvester, D. W. (1969) *History for the Average Child*. Oxford: Blackwell Publishers.

Gove, M. (2009) Failing schools need new leadership. Speech to Conservative Party Conference, 7 October 2009.

Hall, K. (2008) The Holy Grail? GCSE history that actually enhances historical understanding! *Teaching History*, 131: 9–16.

Hammond, K. (2002) Getting Year 10 to understand the value of precise factual knowledge, *Teaching History*, 109: 10–15.

Hanushek, E. and Welch, F. (2006). *Handbook of the Economics of Education: 1*. Amsterdam: North Holland.

Hargreaves, D. (2005) *About Learning*. Report of the Learning Working Group. London: Demos.

Harris, R. (2005) Does differentiation have to mean different? *Teaching History*, 118: 5–12.

Harris, R. and Burn, K. (2011) Curriculum theory, curriculum policy and the problem of ill-disciplined thinking, *Journal of Education Policy*, (26) 2: 243–59.

Harris, R. and Haydn, T. (2006) Pupils' enjoyment of history: what lessons can teachers learn from their pupils? *The Curriculum Journal*, 17(4): 315–33.

Harris, R. and Haydn, T. (2008) Children's ideas about school history and why they matter, *Teaching History*, 132: 40–8.

Harris, R. and Haydn, T. (2009) '30 per cent is not bad considering...' Factors influencing pupil take-up of history post-Key Stage 3: an exploratory enquiry, *Teaching History*, 134: 27–35.

Harris, R. and Luff, I. (2004) *Meeting Special Needs in History*. London: David Fulton Publishers.

Hart, B. and Risley, T. R. (1995) *Meaningful Differences in the Everyday Experience of Young American Children*. Baltimore, MD: Paul H. Brookes Publishing Co.

Hart, S., Dixon, A., Drummond, M.J. and McIntyre, D. (2004) *Learning Without Limits*. Maidenhead: Open University Press McGraw-Hill Education.

Hartley, J. P. (1953) *The Go-Between*. London: Hamish Hamilton.

Hastings, C. and Jones, B. (2005) Lottery-funded film under fire for anti-British bias. *Daily Telegraph*, 14 August.

Haydn, T. (2004a) What do they do with the information? Computers in the history classroom: some lessons from the United Kingdom. Proceedings of the 12th UNESCO/IITE International Conference on Information Technologies in Education, ITE-2002, Moscow, 1–8 November.

Haydn, T. (2004b) History, in J. White (ed.) *Rethinking the School Curriculum: Values, Aims and Purposes*. London: RoutledgeFalmer.

Haydn, T. (2005) Pupil perceptions of history at Key Stage 3. Final Report for QCA, October. London: Qualifications and Curriculum Authority.

Haydn, T., Arthur, J. and Hunt, M. (1997) *Learning to Teach History in the Secondary School*. London: Routledge.

Haydon, G. (2007) *Values in Education*. London: Continuum.

Hillyard, G. (2010) Dickens...Hardy...Jarvis?! A novel take on the Industrial Revolution, *Teaching History*, 140: 16–24.

Historical Association (online) http://www.history.org.uk/resources/secondary_resource_1215, 1296_59.html, accessed 9 March 2011.

Historical Association (2009) We assume an understanding of history is vital but is it? Round Table Debate. Podcast at the HA Annual Conference Sat 9 May. http://www.history.org.uk/resources/secondary_resource_2279.html, accessed 22 February 2011.

Historical Association (2010a) A Guide to the New Key Stage 3 programme. London, Historical Association. http://www.history.org.uk/resources/secondary_guide_1215,1703_54.html, accessed 22 February 2011.

Historical Association (2010b) *Survey of History in English Secondary Schools:* London: Historical Association.

HMI (Her Majesty's Inspectorate of Education) (1985) *History in the Primary and Secondary Years: An HMI View*. London: HMSO.

Hodge, R. and Kress, G. (1988) *Social Semiotics*. Cambridge: Polity Press in association with Basil Blackwell.

Holocaust Education Task Force (2009) http://www.holocausttaskforce.org/memberstates/member_germany.html, accessed 6 March 2011.

Holt, J. C. (1989) *Robin Hood*. London: Thames and Hudson.

Hoodless, P. (1996) *Time and Timelines in the Primary School*. London: Historical Association.

Hooper-Greenhill, E. (2007) *Museums and Education: Purpose, Pedagogy, Performance.* London: Routledge.

House of Commons Children, Schools and Families Committee (2010) *Transforming Education Outside the Classroom*. London: House of Commons.

Howells, G. (1998) Being ambitious with the causes of the First World War: interrogating inevitability, *Teaching History*, 92: 16–19.

Howells, G. (2005) Interpretations and history teaching: why Ronald Hutton's *Debates in Stuart History* matters, *Teaching History*, 121: 29–35.

Howson, J. (2007) 'Is it the Tuarts then the Studors or the other way round?' The importance of developing a usable big picture of the past, *Teaching History*, 127: 40–7.

Howson, J. (2009) Potential and pitfalls in teaching 'big pictures' of the past, *Teaching History*, 136: 24–33.

Hunt, M. (2000) Teaching historical significance, in J. Arthur and R. Phillips (eds) *Issues in History Teaching*. London: Routledge.

Husbands, C. (1996) *What is History Teaching? Language, Ideas and Learning About the Past*. Buckingham: Open University Press.

Husbands, C. (2010) What do history teachers (need to) know? A framework for understanding and developing practice, in I. Davies (ed.) *Debates in History Teaching*. London: Routledge.

Husbands, C. and Pendry, A. (2000) Thinking and feeling. Pupils' conceptions about the past and historical understanding, in J. Arthur and R. Phillips (eds) *Issues in History Teaching*. London: Routledge.

Husbands, C., Kitson, A. and Pendry, A. (2003) *Understanding History Teaching. Teaching and Learning About the Past in Secondary Schools*. Maidenhead: Open University Press McGraw-Hill Education.

Jenkins, K. (1997) *The Postmodern History Reader*. London: Routledge.

Jewitt, C. (2008) Teachers' pedagogic design of digital interactive whiteboard materials in the UK Secondary School, *Designs for Learning*, 1(1): 42–54.

Johansen, M. and Spafford, M. (2009) 'How our area used to be back then': an oral history project in an east London school, *Teaching History*, 134: 37–46.

Jones, H. (2009) Shaping macro-analysis from micro-history: developing a reflexive narrative of change in school history, *Teaching History*, 136: 13–21.

Keating, J. and Sheldon, N. (2011) History in education: trends and themes in history teaching 1900–2010, in I. Davies (ed.) *Debates in History Teaching*. London: Routledge.

Kelly, N., Rees, R. and Shuter, J. (1999) *Black People of the Americas (Living Through History)*. Oxford: Heinemann Library.

Kitson, A. (2003) Reading and enquiring in Years 12 and 13: a case Study on Women in the Third Reich, *Teaching History*, 111: 13–19.

Kitson, A. (2005) History teaching and reconciliation in Northern Ireland, in E. A. Cole (ed.) *Teaching The Violent Past*. Lanham, MD: Rowman and Littlefield.

Kitson, A. (2006) Who are we? *BBC History Magazine,* Vol 7, issue 3: 89.

Kitson, A. (2008) 'Using Evidence' in A *Guide to the New Key Stage 3 Programme*, available at http://www.history.org.uk/resources/secondaryresource1215,127259.html, accessed 2 May 2011.

Kitson Clark, G. (1967) *The Critical Historian*. London: Heinemann.

Klein, S. (2008) History, citizenship and Oliver Stone: classroom analysis of a key scene in Nixon, *Teaching History*, 132: 32–39.

Knight, P. (1996) *The National Curriculum is excellent: Secondary history teachers, teacher educators and the National Curriculum*, in *Current Change and Future Practice: Fresh Perspectives on History Teacher Education, History and History Teaching*. Leicester: University of Leicester School of Education/Standing Conference of History Teacher Educators.

Knight, S. (1999) Interviews in Sherwood. http://www.boldoutlaw.com/robint/knight1.html, accessed 29 August 2010.

Kress, G. and Van. Leeuwen, T. (1996) *Reading Images. The Grammar of Visual Design*. London, New York: Routledge.

Kress, G. and Van Leeuwen, T. (2001) *Multimodal Discourse: The Modes and Media of Contemporary Communication*. London: Arnold.

Kress, G., Jewitt, C., Ogborn, J. and Tsatsarelis, C. (2001) *Multimodal Teaching and Learning: The Rhetorics of the Science Classroom*. London: Continuum.

Kutnick, P., Hodgkinson, S., Sebba, J., Humphreys, S., Galton, M., Steward, S. *et al.* (2006) *Pupil Grouping Strategies and Practices at Key Stage 2 and 3: Case studies of 24 Schools in England. RR796*. London: Department for Education and Skills.

Kutnick, P., Sebba, J., Blatchford, P., Galton, M., Thorp, J., Ota, C. *et al.* (2005) An extended review of pupil grouping in schools. Research Report 688. London: Department for Education and Skills.

Laville, C. (2006) Historical consciousness and the historical education: what to expect from the first to the second, in P. Seixas (ed.) *Theorising Historical Consciousness*. Toronto: University of Toronto Press.

Lee, P. and Ashby, R. (2000) Progression in Historical Understanding among Students Ages 7–14, in P. N. Stearns, P. Seixas and S. Wineburg (eds) *Knowing, Teaching and Learning History: National and International Perspectives*. New York, London: New York University Press.

Lee, P. and Howson, J. (2009) 'Two out of five did not know that Henry VIII had six wives': history education, historical literacy, and historical consciousness, in L. Symcox and A. Wilschut (eds) *National History Standards: The Problem of the Canon and the Future of Teaching History*. Charlotte, NC: Information Age Publishing.

Lee, P. and Shemilt, D. (2003) A scaffold, not a cage: progression and progression models in history, *Teaching History*, 113: 13–23.

Lee, P. and Shemilt, D. (2004) 'I just wish we could go back in the past and find out what really happened': progression in understanding about historical accounts, *Teaching History*, 117: 25–31.

Lee, P. and Shemilt, D. (2007) New alchemy or fatal attraction? History and citizenship, *Teaching History*, 129: 14–19.

Lee, P. J. (2005) Putting principles into practice: understanding history, in J. B. M. S. Donovan (ed.) *How Students Learn History in the Classroom*. Washington, DC: National Academy of Sciences.

Lee, P. J. and Ashby, R. (1987) Discussing the evidence, *Teaching History*, 48: 13–17.

Lee, P. J., Dickinson, A. and Ashby, R. (1993) *Progression in Children's Ideas About History: Project CHATA (Concepts of History and Teaching Approaches: 7 to 14)*. Proceedings of the Annual Meeting of the British Educational Research Association, Liverpool, England, 5–8 September.

Lee, P. J., Dickinson, A. and Ashby, R. (1996) Project CHATA: concepts of history and teaching approaches at Key Stages 2 and 3: children's understanding of 'because' and the status of explanation in history, *Teaching History*, 82: 29–35.

Le Roy Ladurie, E. (1978) *Montaillou: Cathars and Catholics in a French Village*, London: Scolar Press.

Lewis, M. and D. Wray (1996) *Writing Frames*. Reading: National Centre for Language and Literacy, University of Reading.

Lively, P. (1987) *Moon Tiger*. London: Andre Deutsch.

Lo, J. T.-Y. (2000) Changes in Hong Kong's history curriculum: implications and complications, *New Horizons in Education (Journal of Education, Hong Kong Teachers' Association)*, 2: 50–7.

Lomas, T. (1990) Teaching and assessing historical understanding. London: Historical Association.

Lowenthal, D. (1998) *The Heritage Crusade and the Spoils of History*. Cambridge: Cambridge University Press.

Luff, I. (2000). 'I've been in the Reichstag': rethinking roleplay, *Teaching History*, 100: 8–17.

Luff, I. (2001) Beyond 'I speak, you listen boy!' Exploring diversity of attitudes and experiences through speaking and listening, *Teaching History*, 105: 10–18.

Luff, I. (2003) Stretching the straight jacket of assessment: use of role play and practical demonstration to enrich pupils' experience of history at GCSE and beyond, *Teaching History*, 113: 26–35.

McAleavy, T. (1993) Using Attainment targets in Key Stage 3: AT2 interpretations of history, *Teaching History*,

McAleavy, T. (1998) The use of sources in history, *Teaching History*, 91: 10–16.

MacBeath, J., Galton, M., Steward, S., Page, C. and Edwards, J. (2004) *A Life in Secondary Teaching: Finding Time for Learning*. Cambridge: University of Cambridge, Faculty of Education with the National Union of Teachers (NUT).

MacBeath, J., Myers, K. and Demetriou, H. (2001) Supporting teachers in consulting pupils about aspects of teaching and learning, and evaluating impact, *Forum*, 43(2): 78–82.

McCann, E. (1993) *War and an Irish Town*. London: Pluto Press.

McCully, A. and Pilgrim, N. (2004) 'They took Ireland away from us and we've got to fight to get it back'. Using fictional characters to explore the relationship between historical interpretation and contemporary attitudes, *Teaching History*, 114: 17–22.

McFahn, R., Herrity, S. *et al.* (2009) Riots, railways and a Hampshire hill fort: exploiting local history for rigorous evidential enquiry, *Teaching History*, 134: 16–23.

McIntyre, D., Pedder, D. and Rudduck, J. (2005) Pupil voice: comfortable and uncomfortable learnings for teachers, *Research Papers in Education* 20(2): 149–68.

MacMillan, M. (2009) *The Uses and Abuses of History*. London: Profile Books.

Major, J. (1993) *Speech to the Conservative Group for Europe*, London, 22 April.

Mars der, G. (2006) Teach history of empire in schools. Paper presented to Fabian Review conference, London, 14 January.

Marshall, H. E. ([1905] 2005) *Our Island Story*. Tenterden: Galore Park Publishing in association with Civitas.

Martin, M. and Brooke, B. (2002) Getting personal: making effective use of historical fiction in the history classroom, *Teaching History*, 108: 30–5.

Massachusetts Department of Education (2003) *Massachusetts History and Social Science Framework*. Malden, MA: Massachusetts Department of Education.

Mastin, S. J. (2002) 'Now listen to Source A' : music and history, *Teaching History*, 108: 49–54.

Mastin, S. J. and Wallace, P. (2006) Why don't the Chinese play cricket? Rethinking progression in historical interpretations through the British Empire, *Teaching History*, 122: 6–14.

Matthews, D. (2009) The strange death of history teaching (fully explained in seven easy-to-follow lessons) http://cf.ac.uk/carbs/faculty/Matthewsdr/history4.pdf, accessed 22 February 2011.

Mortimer, E. F. and Scott, P. H. (2003) *Meaning Making in Secondary Science Classrooms*. Maidenhead: Open University Press.

Moss, G., Jewitt, C., Levacic, R., Armstrong, V., Cardini, A. and Castle, F. (2007) *Interactive Whiteboards, Pedagogy, and Pupil Performance: An Evaluation of the Schools Whiteboard Expansion Project* (London Challenge). London: Department for Children, Schools and Families.

Mulholland, M. (1998) The Evidence Sandwich, *Teaching History*, 91: 17–19.

Murray, M. (2002) 'Which was more important Sir, ordinary people getting electricity or the rise of Hitler?' Using Ethel and Ernest with Year 9, *Teaching History*, 107: 20–5.

Nagy-Zekmi, S. (2006) *Paradoxical Citizenship: Essays on Edward Said*. Lanham, MD: Lexington Books.

National Curriculum Board (2009) *Shape of the Australian Curriculum: History*. Barton, Act: Commonwealth of Australia: http://www.acara.edu.au/verve/_resources/Australian_Curriculum_-_History.pdf, accessed 29 April 2011.

New York City, Department of Education (2009) *New York City High School Scope and Sequence: Global History and Geography, American History, Economics, Participation in Government*. New York: New York City Administration.

Nicholls, J. (2006) *School History Textbooks across Cultures. International Debates and Perspectives*. Oxford: Symposium Books.

Oates, T. (2010) *Could Do Better: Using International Comparisons to Refine the National Curriculum in England*. Cambridge: Cambridge Assessment.

Ofsted (2007) *History in the Balance: History in English Schools 2003–07*. London: Ofsted.

Partington, G. and Roux, W. L. (1980) *The Idea of an Historical Education*. London: Routledge.

Pell, T. (2009) Is there a crisis in the lower secondary school? in M. Galton, S. Steward, L. Hargreaves, C. Page and T. Pell *Motivating your Secondary Class*. London: Sage Publications.

Pell, T., Galton, M. Steward, S. Page, C. and Hargreaves, L. (2007) Promoting group work at Key Stage 3: solving an attitudinal crisis among young adolescents? *Research Papers in Education*, 22(3): 309–32.

Phillips, I. (2002) Historical significance: the forgotten 'key element'?, *Teaching History*, 106: 14–19.

Phillips, I. (2008) *Teaching History*, London: Sage Publications.

Phillips, R. (1998) Contesting the past, constructing the future: history, identity and politics in schools, *British Journal of Educational Studies*, 46(1): 40–53.

Phillips, R. (2001) Making history curious: using Initial Stimulus Material [ISM] to promote enquiry, thinking and literacy, *Teaching History*, 105: 19–25.

Phillips, R. (2002) *Reflective Teaching of History 11–18*. London: Continuum.

Philpott, J. (2009) *Captivating Your Class: Effective Teaching Skills*. London: Continuum.

Pickles, E. (2010) How can students' use of historical evidence be enhanced? A research study of the role of knowledge in Year 8 to Year 13 students' interpretations of historical sources, *Teaching History*, 139: 41–51.

Pollard, A. (2010) *Professionalism and Pedagogy: A Contemporary Opportunity. A Commentary by the Teaching and Learning Research Programme and the General Teaching Council for England*. London: TLRP.

Pring, R. (2003) Nuffield Review of 14–19 *Education and Training Working Paper 2. Aims and Purposes: Philosophical Issues*. The Nuffield Review of 14–19 Education. London: Nuffield Foundation.

Pring, R., Hayward, G., Hodgson, A., Johnson, J., Keep, E., Oancea, A. *et al.* (2009) *Education for All. The Future of Education and Training for 14–19 year olds*. London and New York: Routledge, Taylor and Francis.

QCA (1998) *Education for Citizenship and the Teaching of Democracy in Schools* (Crick Report). London: QCA.

QCA (2005) *History 2004/5 Annual Report on Curriculum and Assessment*. London: QCA.

QCA (Qualifications and Curriculum Authority) (2007a) *National Curriculum. Primary Curriculum Key Stage1 and Key Stage 2: History*. Coventry: QCA.

QCA (2007b) *History: Programme of Study for Key Stage 3 and Attainment Target*. Coventry: QCA.

QCA (2007c) *Assessment of History*. http://curriculum.qcda.gov.uk/key-stages-1-and-2/assessment/assessmentofsubjects/assessmentinhistory/index.aspx, accessed 6 March 2011.

Rayner, L. (1999) Weighing a century with a website: teaching Year 9 to be critical, *Teaching History*, 96: 13–22.

Richards, J. (1977) *Swordsmen of the Screen: From Douglas Fairbanks to Michael York*. London: Routledge and Kegan Paul.

Riley, M. (1997) Big stories and big pictures: making outlines and overviews interesting, *Teaching History*, 88: 20–2

Riley, M. (2000) Into the Key Stage 3 history garden: choosing and planting your enquiry questions, *Teaching History*, 99: 8–13.

Roberts, M. (2003) *Learning Through Enquiry: Making Sense of Geography in the Key Stage 3 Classroom*. Sheffield: Geographical Association.

Rogers, P. (1987) History: The Past as a Frame of Reference, in C. Portal (ed.) *The History Curriculum for Teachers*. London: The Falmer Press.

Rogers, R. (2009) Raising the bar: developing meaningful historical consciousness at Key Stage 3, *Teaching History*, 133: 24–30.

Rose, J. (2009) *Independent Review of the Primary Curriculum: Final Report*. London: DCSF.

Rowbotham, S. (1975) *Hidden from History: 300 Years of Women's Oppression and the Fight Against it*. London: Pluto Press.

RSA (Royal Society of Arts) *Opening Minds*. London: RSA. http://www.openingminds.org.uk.

Rubie-Davies, C., Hattie, J. and Hamilton, R. (2006) Expecting the best for students: teacher expectations and academic outcomes, *British Journal of Educational Psychology*, 76:429–44.

Rudduck, J. (2005) Pupil voice is here to stay. Project Paper. QCA Futures project paper

Rudduck, J. and McIntyre, D. (2007) *Improving Learning Through Consulting Pupils*. Abingdon: Routledge.

Rudham, R. (2001) A noisy classroom is a thinking classroom: Speaking and Listening in Year 7 history, *Teaching History*, 105: 35–41.

Samuel, R. (1995) *Theatres of Memory: Past and Present in Contemporary Culture*. London: Verso Books.

Sanders, W. L. and Rivers, J. C. (1996) Cumulative and residual effects of teachers on future student academic achievement. University of Tennessee Value-Added Research and Assessment Center, Knoxville, Tennessee.

Schama, S. (2005) *Rough Crossings: Britain, the Slaves and the American Revolution*. London: BBC Books.

Schools Council (1973) *A New Look at History*. Edinburgh: Holmes McDougall.

Sealey, P. and Noyes, A. (2010) On the relevance of the mathematics curriculum to young people, *Curriculum Journal*, 21(3): 239–53.

Sebba, J., Brown, N., Steward, S., Galton, M. and James, M. (2007) *An Investigation of Personalised Learning Approaches used by Schools. RR843*. Nottingham: DfES Publications.

Seixas, P. (1993) Historical Understanding among Adolescents in a Multicultural Setting, *Curriculum Inquiry*, 23(3): 301–27.

Seixas, P. (1994) A discipline adrift in an integrated curriculum: history in British Columbia schools, *Canadian Journal of Education* 19(1): 99–107.

Sheldrake, R. and Banham, D. (2007) Seeing a different picture: exploring migration through the lens of history, *Teaching History* 129: 39–47.

Shemilt, D. (1980) *History 13–16 Evaluation Study*. Edinburgh: Holmes McDougall.

Shemilt, D. (1987) Adolescent ideas about evidence and methodology in history, in C. Portal (ed.) *The History Curriculum for Teachers*. London: Falmer Press.

Shemilt, D. (2000) The caliph's coin, in P. N. Stearns, P. Seixas and S. S. Wineburg (eds) *Knowing Teaching and Learning History: National and International Perspectives*. New York and London: New York University Press.

Shemilt, D. (2009) Drinking an ocean and pissing a cupful: how adolescents make sense of history, in L. Symcox and A. Wilschut (eds) *National History Standards: The Problem of the Canon and the Future of Teaching History*. Charlotte, NC: Information Age Publishing.

Shoham, E. and Shiloah, N. (2003) Meeting the historian through the text: students discover different perspectives on Baron Rothchild's 'guardianship system', *Teaching History*, 111: 32–6.

Shulman, L. (1986) Those who understand: knowledge growth in teaching, *Educational Researcher* 15(2): 4–14.

Simon, B. (1985) Why no pedagogy in England?, in B. Simon (ed.) *Does Education Matter?* London: Lawrence & Wishart.

Slater, J. (1989) *The Politics of History Teaching: A Humanity Dehumanized?* London: Institute of Education, University of London.

Smart, D. (2010) Going to the pictures: learning to see the life histories of minorities within majority narratives, in A. Bathmaker and P. Harnett (eds) *Exploring Learning, Identity and Power through Life History and Narrative Research*. London: Taylor and Francis.

Soo Hoo, S. (1993) Students as partners in research and restructuring schools, *The Educational Forum*, 57: 386–93.

Starkey, D. (2005) *What history should we be teaching in Britain in the 21st century*? Paper presented to Institute of Historical Research, Conference, University of London History in British Education, 14–15 February. http://www.history.ac.uk/resources/history-in-british-education/first-conference/starkey-paper, accessed 29 April 2011.

Stearns, P. N., Seixas, P. and Wineburg, S. (2000) *Knowing Teaching and Learning History: National and International Perspectives*. New York: New York University Press.

Stevens, R., Wineburg, S., Herrenkohl, L. R. and Bell, P. (2005) Comparative understanding of school subjects: past, present, and future, *Review of Educational Research*, 75(2): 125–57.

Sweerts, E. and Grice, J. (2002) Hitting the right note: how useful is the music of African-Americans to historians?, *Teaching History*, 108: 36–41.

Sword, F. (1994) Points of contact, *Journal of Education in Museums*, 15: 7–9.

Sylvester, D. (1994) Change and continuity in history teaching 1900–93, in H. Bourdillan (ed.) *Teaching History: A Reader*. London: Routledge in association with the Open University.

Taylor, L. (2009) *GTIP Think Piece – Concepts in Geography*, available at www.geography.org.uk/gtip/thitkpieces/concepts/#5817, accessed 2 May 2011.

Thatcher, M. (1995) *The Downing Street Years*. London: HarperCollins.

Thompson, E. P. (1978) *The Poverty of Theory*. London: Merlin.

Tosh, J. (2006) *The Pursuit of History: Aims, Methods and New Directions in the Study of Modern History*. Harlow: Pearson Longman.

Tosh, J. (2008) *Why History Matters*. Basingstoke: Palgrave Macmillan.

Traille, K. (2007) 'You should be proud about your history. They make you feel ashamed': teaching history hurts, *Teaching History*, 127: 31–7.

Turner-Bisset, R. (1999) The knowledge bases of the expert teacher, *British Educational Research Journal*, 25(1): 39–55.

Tyrer, G. (2010) *Learning to Lead: Using Leadership Skills to Motivate Students*. London: Continuum.

Vygotsky, L. S. (1962) *Thought and Language*. Cambridge, MA: MIT Press.

Vygotsky, L. S. (1963) Learning and mental development at school age, in B. Simon and J. Simon (eds) *Educational Psychology in the USSR*. London: Routledge and Kegan Paul.

Vygotsky, L. S. (1978) *Mind in Society*. Cambridge, MA: Harvard University Press.

Walsh, B. (1998) Review of 'Homebeats' Struggles for Racial Justice CD-ROM, *Teaching History*, 93: 47–8.

Walsh, B. (2008) Stories and their sources: the need for historical thinking in an information age, *Teaching History*, 133: 4–9.

Waterhouse, P. (1983) *Managing the Learning Process*. London: McGraw-Hill.

Wenger, E. (1998) *Communities of Practice: Learning, Meaning and Identity*. Cambridge: Cambridge University Press.

White, J. (2004) *Rethinking the School Curriculum: Values, Aims and Purposes*. London: RoutledgeFalmer.

Whitty, G. (2008) Twenty years of progress? English education policy 1988 to the present, *Educational Management, Administration and Leadership*, 36(2): 165–84.

Wilschut, A. (2009) Canonical standards or orientational frames of reference? The cultural and the educational approach to the debate about standards in history teaching, in L. Symcox and A. Wilschut (eds) *National History Standards: The Problem of the Canon and the Future of Teaching History*. Charlotte, NC: Information Age Publishing.

Wilson, M. D. (1985) *History for Pupils with Learning Difficulties*. London: Hodder and Stoughton.

Wilson, S. and Wineburg, S. S. (1988) Peering at history through different lenses: the role of disciplinary perspectives in teaching history, *Teachers College Record*, 89(4): 525–39.

Wineburg, S. (2000) Making historical sense, in P. N. Stearns, P. Seixas and S. Wineburg (eds) *Knowing, Teaching and Learning History: National and International Perspectives*. New York and London: New York University Press.

Wineburg, S. (2001) *Historical Thinking and Other Unnatural Acts: Charting the Future of Teaching the Past*. Philadelphia, PA: Temple University Press.

Wineburg, S. (2007) Unnatural and essential: the nature of historical thinking, *Teaching History*, 129: 6–12.

Wood, D. (1988) *How Children Think and Learn: The Social Contexts of Cognitive Development*. Oxford: Blackwell Publishing.

Woodcock, J. (2005) Does the linguistic release the conceptual? Helping Year 10 to improve their casual reasoning, *Teaching History*, 119: 5–14.

Woolley, M. (2003) 'Really weird and freaky': using a Thomas Hardy short story as a source of evidence in the Year 8 classroom, *Teaching History*, 111: 6–11.

Woolnough, G. (2006) Tough on crime, tough on the causes of crime: using external support, local history and a group project to challenge the most able, *Teaching History*, 124: 37–45.

Wrenn, A. (1999) Substantial sculptures or sad little plaques? Making 'interpretations' matter to Year 9, *Teaching History*, 97: 21–8.

Wright, P. (2009) *On Living in an Old Country: The National Past in Contemporary Britain*. London: Verso.

Index